Digital Humanities

IN THE LIBRARY:

Challenges and Opportunities for Subject Specialists

Editors

Arianne Hartsell-Gundy,
Laura Braunstein,
Liorah Golomb

Published in collaboration with
the ACRL Literatures in English Section

The paper used in this publication meets the minimum requirements of American National Standard for Information Sciences–Permanence of Paper for Printed Library Materials, ANSI Z39.48-1992. ∞

Library of Congress Cataloging-in-Publication Data

Digital humanities in the library : challenges and opportunities for subject specialists / edited by Arianne Hartsell-Gundy, Laura Braunstein, and Liorah Golomb.
    pages cm
  Includes bibliographical references and index.
  ISBN 978-0-8389-8767-4 (pbk. : alk. paper) -- ISBN 978-0-8389-8769-8 (epub) -- ISBN 978-0-8389-8768-1 (pdf) -- ISBN 978-0-8389-8770-4 (kindle)
  1. Humanities libraries--United States. 2. Humanities--Electronic information resources. 3. Humanities--Research--Data processing. 4. Humanities--Study and teaching (Higher)--United States. 5. Academic libraries--Relations with faculty and curriculum--United States. 6. Academic librarians--Effect of technological innovations on. 7. Reference libraries--Effect of technological innovations on. I. Hartsell-Gundy, Arianne, editor. II. Braunstein, Laura, editor. III. Golomb, Liorah, editor.
  Z675.H86D54 2015
  025.06'0013--dc23

                              2015006339

The authors dedicate this book to the members of the ACRL Literatures in English Section, whose knowledge, experience, and support make us all better librarians.

Laura Braunstein dedicates this book to her non-digital humans — Andy, Isaac, and Naomi.

Arianne Hartsell-Gundy dedicates this book to her husband Jeff, who always knows when to provide encouragement, hugs, and chocolate.

Contents

Part 1
Why Digital Humanities? Reasons for Subject Specialists to Acquire DH Skills

Part 2
Getting Involved in Digital Humanities

Part 3
Collaboration, Spaces, and Instruction

Part 4
Projects in Focus: From Conception to Completion and Beyond

Foreword

Joan K. Lippincott
Associate Executive Director, Coalition for Networked Information

MANY ACADEMIC libraries today have developed or are considering starting a program to support digital humanities scholarship. This book, with its variety of approaches and emphases, can be used in a strategic planning process to inform the many choices that can be made when a library supports digital humanities. While the focus is on the role of subject specialist librarians in the realm of digital humanities, this book provides an overview of the wide array of librarians and others who may be involved in digital humanities projects and the range of activities that are involved in such projects. Digital humanities projects involve content (often a combination of analog, digitized, and born digital), software tools, and technology infrastructure; they are impacted by policy issues such as intellectual property as well as institutional policies in such areas as promotion and tenure, and they often have a connection with both the research and teaching and learning programs of their institutions.

While a digital humanities program in the library can start on a small scale, it is important from the outset to have some established goals along with strategies to achieve them and mechanisms for evaluating the program at regular intervals. As a first step, librarians should talk with a variety of faculty on campus, including those who are already practicing digital humanities scholarship, others who might have some interest in incorporating some digital methods into their scholarship, some who have an interest in engaging their students in new types of digital work through course assignments, and also to graduate students who may not have an advisor who is conversant with digital humanities but who wish to develop a digital project. Understanding the needs at the institutional level and where the library can provide some resources and expertise is a critical first step.

Digital humanities methodologies and products have been around for decades, both with and without librarians as partners or collaborators with their faculty creators. In recent years, more libraries are recognizing that they may want to invest resources, including staff expertise and time, technology infrastructure such as repositories, and physical spaces such as digital scholarship centers or labs, to make a more formal commitment by the library to this type of scholarship. While some of the faculty who have spearheaded large digital humanities initiatives may have had minimal interaction with libraries in the past, they sometimes realize, when they reach a point where they must migrate their project to a new platform or when they don't have the capability to provide for data curation or preservation of their initiatives, that it may be useful to reach out to libraries for certain types of expertise. In addition, there is a new set of constituencies for librarians who have some expertise in digital humanities, particularly faculty, graduate students, and undergraduate students who do not have the knowledge and/or technologies to begin to develop projects but who have the interest.

While librarians have the capabilities to educate audiences about digital humanities and promote projects as scholarly and classroom resources, it is the faculty who, in most cases, initiate large-scale, multi-year digital projects, along with collaborators, perhaps with the exception of some text encoding initiatives. One of the key elements that subject librarians bring to the ability of libraries to work as partners on digital scholarship is their relationship with academic departments. Subject librarians should serve as the library's eyes and ears, getting to know which faculty are working on digital projects or are considering moving into that arena. It is encouraging to see examples in some of this book's chapters, of subject librarians who had no particular expertise with specialized technologies used in digital humanities projects, begin to educate themselves or embed themselves in teams with the specific intention of not only learning about technologies but learning to use those technologies. Their descriptions point out that having had direct participation in developing digital projects, they can much better advise faculty and students about a variety of project management decisions and issues. On the other hand, there is no requirement for subject librarians to have direct experience with various technologies in order to play a role in library or campus digital humanities initiatives.

It is likely that we will see growth in small-scale digital humanities projects as more individuals get involved in this type of work. As several chapters describe, one of the most fruitful ways for librarians to become involved in digital humanities is through work with graduate students. Humanities graduate students may wish to learn more about digital scholarship either because of intrinsic interest in new methodologies that can address new types of research questions, and/or because they realize that experience with digital humanities project creation may increase their marketability when they are seeking a position in their field. Many of those graduate students do not have faculty mentors with the necessary skills to guide them in creating digital work nor access to expensive software and facilities in which to work. Libraries are increasingly providing this infrastructure, and some are intentionally fostering a community of digital scholars who share expertise.

One of the aspects of digital humanities work that has the most opportunity for subject librarian involvement is the interest in incorporating digital projects into student class assignments. In this book, examples from several libraries demonstrate the deep engagement that many students develop with their topic when they are given assignments to create new digital content as part of a course. Subject librarians can reach out to faculty to discuss the potential of these kinds of assignments and work closely with them to develop mechanisms for working with students.

As many of the chapters in this book point out, digital humanities projects are, by their nature, collaborative. Subject librarians involved in digital humanities will want to collaborate both internally in the library with experts in digital technologies, instruction librarians, special collections librarians, archivists, and others. In addition, many subject librarians are working on digital humanities teams with members from many institutional units, including faculty, information technologists, and staff from a teaching and learning center. Some projects, both in the small college environment as well as in large universities, involve cross-institutional and even international collaborations.

It is disappointing to read in a few of the examples in this book, of libraries where administrators or colleagues do not understand or support the work of librarians collaborating with faculty and students on digital humanities projects. If librarians are partnering with faculty in new ways, they must often invest considerable time in the digital humanities work in which they engage. They face resistance by some librarians who see this as time away from librarians' core responsibilities. And yet, despite obstacles in some libraries, the librarians who authored these chapters persisted and produced achievements that increased the visibility of the library in their institutions, strengthened their role in the teaching and/or research programs of their colleges, and deepened faculty members' and students' understanding of their expertise. Working in such partnership relationships, becoming embedded in the mission-critical aspects of higher education—research, teaching, and learning—and infusing librarians' particular expertise, collections, and values into new types of research, is, in fact, a core responsibility of 21st century librarians and libraries.

Introduction

Laura R. Braunstein, Liorah Golomb, and Arianne Hartsell-Gundy

THIS COLLECTION began, like many book projects, because people wanted to read something like it. Members of the Literatures in English Section of the Association of College and Research Libraries, a division of the American Library Association, found themselves facing new challenges with the emergence of the community of practice we call the digital humanities. Though there were several excellent books that could help subject librarians gain an understanding of digital humanities in general, such as *Digital Humanities in Practice* and *Debates in the Digital Humanities*,[1] there were few publications aimed specifically at subject librarians. This book is intended to help subject librarians understand the possibilities of digital humanities and to help them navigate relationships among faculty, students, digital humanities librarians, and themselves.

Traditionally, subject specialists at academic libraries (sometimes called liaisons or bibliographers, depending on the philosophies of individual libraries and the different responsibilities required) are responsible for working with different disciplines, such as English or philosophy. Generally the work requires outreach to departments, reference and research help in a variety of formats, library instruction, and collection management. New developments, such as publishing trends, budget challenges, and the changing nature of many academic departments, are increasingly requiring subject specialists to take on new duties and roles. In some cases, a subject specialist might become more involved with open-access efforts on campus or assist faculty with data management plans. These new directions can require learning new skills and redefining position descriptions. Those subject specialists who work with humanities fields are also finding themselves with new duties and roles as a result of new interest in the digital humanities.

Digital humanities—what used to be called "humanities computing"—is an emerging, collaborative field in which digital tools and technologies are applied to the traditional objects and methods of the humanities. For academic subject librarians, digital humanities has the potential to lead to new partnerships with faculty to support their research, teaching, and scholarship. Some institutions and libraries are still determining how best to support digital humanities initiatives. The recent OCLC report *Does Every Research Library Need a Digital Humanities Center?* lays out both the importance of libraries engaging with digital humanities and the potential of different models of support.[2] The report makes it clear that while some institutions may benefit from a specialized digital humanities center with digital humanities librarians, other libraries and librarians can play meaningful roles in different ways. We believe that humanities subject specialists can play an important role in these discussions and projects, but they need proper training and knowledge. As the OCLC report states, "A respected subject librarian can work with an academic department to supplement support already provided to faculty members."[3] This book provides valuable discussions around the role of subject specialists in digital humanities, gives practical advice regarding support of and collaboration with digital humanities projects, and describes real-world examples to inspire subject specialists to increase their own knowledge and expertise.

While this collection was produced in collaboration with the ACRL Literatures in English Section and originated in conversations among its members, our contributors come from across the scholarly community. Chapter collaborators include digital humanities librarians, special collections librarians, social science librarians, archivists, professional editors, teaching faculty, graduate students, and colleagues from a center for faculty engagement.

This book is organized into four parts: "Why Digital Humanities? Reasons for Subject Specialists to Acquire DH Skills," "Getting Involved in Digital Humanities," "Collaboration, Spaces, and Instruction," and "Projects in Focus: From Conception to Completion and Beyond." We have designed the book to have a natural progression, moving from an introduction to digital humanities, to advice on establishing a digital humanities presence, to examples of successful digital humanities initiatives, and, finally, individual case studies, though of course readers should dip into whatever sections are most helpful for them.

Part 1, "Why Digital Humanities? Reasons for Subject Specialists to Acquire DH Skills," consists of four chapters that illuminate the complicated definitions, theories, and relationships involved in digital humanities. In chapter 1, "Traversing the Gap: Subject Specialists Connecting Humanities Researchers and Digital Scholarship Centers," Katie Gibson, Marcus Ladd, and Jenny Presnell (Miami University of Ohio) begin by introducing us to the relationship of subject specialists to researchers and digital humanities centers. They identify the needs and skills of both researchers and digital centers and suggest a variety of roles that subject specialists can play in the development of a digital project. Chapter 2, "Moderating a Meaningful DH Conversation for Graduate Students in the Humanities," by Kathleen A. Langan and Ilse Schweitzer VanDonkelaar (Western Michigan University), introduces us to the possibilities of using digital humanities to work with graduate students. It is a case study of subject librarians helping to train graduate students in digital humanities, thus increasing both librarians' and students' professional skills. In chapter 3, "Construction and Disruption: Building Communities of Practice, Queering Subject Liaisons," Caro Pinto (Mount Holyoke College) examines the possibilities of organizational change and the roles that liaisons, archivists, and metadata specialists play. Pinto describes a symposium hosted by the Five Colleges Consortium on the changing landscape of scholarship with regard to the digital humanities and how it led to subject liaisons participating in a DH-focused community of practice culminating in the creation of an online exhibit.

This section is rounded out by explanations of relevant literary theories: in chapter 4, "Distant Reading, Computational Stylistics, and Corpus Linguistics: The Critical Theory of Digital Humanities for Literature Subject Librarians," David D. Oberhelman (Oklahoma State University) addresses the need for subject librarians to understand the theoretical implications of DH. In order to work effectively with (and as) DH-focused researchers, librarians must understand how DH both revitalizes and challenges the field of literary study.

Part 2, "Getting Involved in Digital Humanities," is designed to help the reader understand ways in which subject specialists can join the DH community of practice at their institutions. In chapter 5, "Digital Humanities Curriculum Support inside the Library," Zoe Borovsky and Elizabeth McAulay (UCLA) present a case study of librarians collaborating with a professor to implement a DH project in an archaeology course. They describe how librarians participated in creating assignments and group projects that fostered student engagement in the research process. Chapter 6, "A Checklist for Digital Humanities Scholarship," from Elizabeth Lorang and Kathleen A. Johnson, provides practical advice on beginning a project. It describes librarian participation in University of Nebraska–Lincoln's Center for Digital Research in the Humanities and includes valuable practical points to consider throughout a project's life cycle. Chapter 7, "In Practice and Pedagogy: Digital Humanities in a Small College Environment," looks at some of the unique challenges of establishing digital humanities at liberal arts institutions. Christina Bell (Bates College) discusses the roles subject librarians can play in incorporating digital humanities into an existing environment and without the resources available to many large research institutions.

Part 3, "Collaboration, Spaces, and Instruction," provides examples of successful library initiatives that involve subject specialists. In chapter 8, "Digital Humanities for the Rest of Us," Judy Walker gives concrete examples of collaborations among librarians in different departments and across the university. She discusses how library subject specialists, special collections librarians, and the staff of the University of North Carolina at Charlotte's Digital Scholarship Lab partnered with campus computing services and other university centers to provide DH training and support for faculty and students. Chapter 9, "Collaboration and CoTeaching: Librarians Teaching Digital Humanities in the Classroom," focuses on how librarians can become involved in digital humanities instruction on several different levels. The authors, Brian Rosenblum, Fran Devlin, Tami Albin, and Wade Garrison (University of Kansas), describe efforts by librarians with subject, instruction, and digital scholarship expertise to provide instruction and training in DH to graduate students and faculty. In chapter 10, "Spaces, Skills, and Synthesis," Anu Vedantham and Dot Porter (University of Pennsylvania) discuss how the creation of library spaces can facilitate collaboration in digital humanities. The authors describe the evolution of support for DH work at Penn through the library's adaptation of spaces, facilities, technical support, and faculty advising.

Part 4, "Projects in Focus: From Conception to Completion and Beyond," provides case studies of individual projects that involve subject librarians, including both the successes and failures of these projects. Chapter 11, "A Digital Adventure: From Theory to Practice," from Valla McLean and Sean Atkins (MacEwan University), shows how a general inquiry about digital storytelling led to a successful project. The chapter offers both pedagogical theory and practical applications related to digital humanities. In chapter 12, "'And There Was a Large Number of People': The Occom Circle Project at the Dartmouth College Library," Laura R. Braunstein, Peter Carini, and Hazel-Dawn Dumpert discuss the project management process for digitizing an important collection of primary documents. The project provides a case study in organizational change and an example of how subject specialists can work within their libraries' existing cultures to develop new skills and connections to support and foster the digital humanities. Chapter 13, "Dipping a Toe into the DH Waters: A Librarian's Experience," from Liorah Golomb (University of Oklahoma) outlines the author's efforts to teach herself more about the tools involved in creating digital humanities projects. Golomb documents her experience text-mining dialogue from the CW Network television show *Supernatural*, including preparing transcripts for mining; locating, testing, and selecting tools; the challenges of examining text in a visual medium; and suggestions for further research. In chapter 14, "Second Time Around; or, The Long Life of the Victorian Women Writers Project: Sustainability through Outreach," Angela Courtney and Michael Courtney (Indiana University) provide a brief history of the Victorian Women Writers Project and discuss preservation and maintenance in the digital environment. The chapter explores the potential roles of subject librarians working to maintain a project as a freely available online resource.

We hope that these chapters will help readers as they become involved with digital humanities projects and initiatives, both large and small. There are many opportunities for subject specialists to collaborate with faculty, students, and colleagues; to use their skills and knowledge to envision and lead projects; and to help shape the direction of the digital humanities as long as we are willing to take risks in the face of new challenges.

Notes

1. Claire Warwick, Melissa Terras, and Julianne Nyhan, eds., *Digital Humanities in Practice* (London: Facet Publishing, 2012); Matthew K. Gold, ed., *Debates in the Digital Humanities* (Minneapolis: University of Minnesota Press, 2012).
2. Jennifer Schaffner and Ricky Erway, *Does Every Research Library Need a Digital Humanities Center?* (Dublin, OH: OCLC Research, 2014).
3. Ibid., 11.

Bibliography

Gold, Matthew K., ed. *Debates in the Digital Humanities.* Minneapolis: University of Minnesota Press, 2012.

Schaffner, Jennifer, and Ricky Erway. *Does Every Research Library Need a Digital Humanities Center?* Dublin, OH: OCLC Research, 2014.

Warwick, Claire, Melissa Terras, and Julianne Nyhan, eds. *Digital Humanities in Practice.* London: Facet Publishing, 2012.

Digital *Humanities*

IN THE LIBRARY:

PART 1

Why Digital Humanities?
Reasons for Subject
Specialists to Acquire
DH Skills

CHAPTER ONE

Traversing the Gap
Subject Specialists Connecting Humanities Researchers and Digital Scholarship Centers

Katie Gibson, Marcus Ladd, and Jenny Presnell

Introduction

Subject specialist librarians have a central role to play in the development of digital humanities projects and in the activities and community of digital scholarship centers. Many different parties come together to create digital projects. Subject librarians can provide the bridge between research scholars and technology librarians in the creation of various types of digital projects and various models of collaboration and throughout all stages of project development. This chapter will explore those relationships, models, and stages of project development and highlight the role of the subject librarian.

For the purposes of this chapter, digital humanities projects fall into two distinct categories, projects of first-order content and those containing second-order content.[1] First-order content projects are a digital re-creation of already existing materials such as digitized collections of letters. Little or no analysis of the materials is included. Second-order content projects take digital materials and enhance them, using any of a variety of digital tools and techniques to more fully understand a research question: for example, mapping where a letter in a collection of correspondences was written to better understand the geographical context in which it was written, or correlating literacy rates with the locations of libraries and bookstores.[2] In some cases the end product of such research is a traditional journal article or monograph that analyzes the primary source material in ways that would have been impossible in the pre-digital age. In other cases, the final result of the project is a digital object, a collection, an online presentation of scholarship, or some combination of these, even though articles and other publications might be written about the project and process. A digital humanities project may involve some first-order content creation but must include the insight gained by using one or more digital tools to interpret data or some additional layer of scholarship.

Unlike traditional humanities research, digital humanities scholarship is not a solitary affair. Generally, no single person has all the skills, materials, and knowledge to create a research project. By nature, the digital humanities project, big or small, requires a collaborative team approach with roles for scholars, "technologists," and librarians.[3]

Scholars

Scholarship is the center of any digital humanities project and the scholar—a faculty member, a postdoctoral student, or an independent researcher—is commonly the person who brings a research question to the project group. The scholar might already bring his or her own data and be requesting support in learning the appropriate tool to explore the research project,[4] or the scholar might have a question but need support in finding or creating data. In larger collaborative projects, the scholar is a major player in the development of second-order content from primary source collections, such as annotated collected works of famous figures or documents, definitive editions of literary works, or collections of historical data. Scholars know how to structure a question and have a depth of knowledge in the content area. However, they might lack knowledge of end-user behavior and information architecture.

Technologists

Technologists know the tools and technology used to create and sustain a large digital collection or to analyze a set of data. They are up-to-date on appropriate software, provide the metadata and bibliographic control, create the user interfaces, maintain server space, and work with issues of access and preservation.[5] While the subject librarians, as part of their liaison duties, are called upon to keep abreast of the most current technologies available to aid in research in their field, technologists are experts in the creation process rather than the content.

Compared to the librarians and scholars, the project's technologists are likely to come from a wider variety of sources. In many cases, they may be information technology staff from the university IT department, making them attuned to the overall university information management system but less familiar with humanities research and librarianship. Alternatively, assistance might be sought outside the university entirely, contracting support from professional information management companies. These companies often feature large-scale operations, capable of serving multiple clients simultaneously. However, they will be more removed from academic culture (particularly that of a specific university), and the project will most likely be to them one of many disparate tasks. The technology support may also come from within the library or a related department. So-called "digital librarians" are a hybrid of technologist and librarian, with a specific proficiency in developing online collections and other repositories.

Another common solution to the demand for humanities research–focused technologists has been the development of digital scholarship centers. While these centers focus on the software and other tools used by technologists, they are culturally and physically closer to the scholars and librarians; indeed, many of these centers are housed within university libraries. Miami University is a midwestern public university of approximately 16,000 students. Although it is primarily an undergraduate residential campus, there are some graduate programs and one doctorate program in the humanities. In spring 2013, the Center for Digital Scholarship opened at Miami and occupies space within King Library, the main campus library and a focal point for student gatherings. By being physically located in the same building as the humanities librarians (as well as the humanities materials and special collections), the Center for Digital Scholarship is able to foster more direct and personal connections to the humanities subject librarians. The Center for Digital Scholarship began as the Digital Initiatives department under Technical Services but split off to become an autonomous department within the library system. This sort of evolution, with a digital scholarship center growing out of a preexisting department or group within a library, has also occurred at the University of Oregon. These digital scholarship centers possess direct, strong ties to the librarians at the university due to their origins and staff but are more likely to need to work to develop connections with faculty.

In contrast to evolving from a preexisting department, other digital scholarship centers—such as the one found at the University of Notre Dame—are entirely new creations. Still others might be born of library initiatives but be staffed more by people from scholarly—rather than librarian—backgrounds. Centers like these, such as the Scholars' Lab at the University of Virginia, possess many more direct connections to other scholars, although not all their staff may be as immediately familiar with library culture. But whatever their origin or composition, all these centers for digital scholarship possess the same goals of collaboration and innovation in research.

Humanities Subject Librarians

Beyond the standard repertoire of librarian skills, subject librarians possess advanced knowledge (and often an advanced degree) in their particular areas. They are responsible for curating a library collection and are closely familiar with its unique strengths. But, beyond collections, a subject librarian is also a liaison who has built working relationships with departments and understands the research interests and instructional needs of their faculty, staff, and students. As with all areas of the library, the position of subject librarian has evolved over recent decades and will continue to do so. The role of "subject bibliographer" has given way to a model that "encompass[es] the broadening scope of scholarship, especially involving digital archival and special collections, digital tools and progressive service models."[6] Librarians were seen at one time as keepers of warehouses and repositories. However, they are now collection builders and managers, instructors, and evaluators of information. They have become adept at adapting to a changing information environment and to shifts in scholarly production. Because of this adaptability, subject librarians have the ability to keep up with changes in technology and patterns of scholarship.

Scholars, technologists, and humanities subject librarians each bring a unique approach: the scholar, content knowledge; the technologist, the necessary technological skills; and the subject librarian, the overarching understanding of digital humanities research. While they are often trying to communicate with different languages, understandings, and approaches, all want to work together toward common goals: ensuring broad access to resources of cultural heritage and information, finding new and valuable ways to manipulate data, improving communication—both in teaching and in learning—and, most important, finding a way to make a significant impact on the greater public. With subject knowledge and a holistic view of technology tools, the subject librarian is in a unique position to mediate between all participants.

Subject Librarian Roles in Digital Humanities

Digital humanities projects are created in a diverse array of local arrangements and combinations of team members, but most often involve libraries. The Ithaka report *Sustaining the Digital Humanities: Host Institution Support beyond the Startup Phase* outlines three common models found at institutions with established digital humanities programs.[7] In the service model, whether it be a university IT department, a library, or an instructional technology service, "the service unit seeks to meet the demand expressed by faculty, often with a strong focus on meeting an individual's research needs."[8] In libraries, this takes the form of making existing structures and services, such as metadata and repositories, available to scholars. The library acts in a supportive capacity, but it is not necessarily an active participant in the research. Rather, "the service model primarily aims to help the faculty on campus learn about DH methods, foster campus-wide discussion on the topic, encourage discussions and roundtables and build" projects.[9] A common observation about the service model is that librarians "see their work not as supporting research, but as research, period, and they view the relationships they have with faculty as being most productive when they are partnerships of equals."[10]

In a lab model, the organization functions more like a biology lab, representing "a robust cycle of support, fueled by innovative projects and the grant funding they attract."[11] Teams in the lab model form to address needs as they arise and can grow to bring in additional people as grant funding and need allow. Because this model is flexible and brings together people in a project-centered collaboration, there is great variety in lab model collaborations.

Finally, the network model is a more organic connection of services and resources on a campus, a connection that grows to meet other needs, but all the services have resources to contribute to the success of a digital humanities project. Miami University's digital humanities efforts generally fall into this model, with support coming from the libraries' Center for Digital Scholarship, the Humanities Center, the office of Advanced Learning Technologies, and university IT services. Each has resources available to support different aspects of a digital humanities project.

No matter the local arrangement, the subject librarian has a role to play. Skills such as selection, acquisitions, cataloging, access, preservation, online systems development, and digitization, "often found in the backrooms of our libraries,"[12] are crucial to the success of digital humanities projects. Libraries have been identified as resources where faculty can learn from librarians the skills necessary to complete digital humanities projects, such as text encoding, metadata creation, and preservation and long-term sustainability.[13] But, while there is a clear role for libraries, previous research makes little distinction between types of librarians and the contributions each might make. Even though the role of a subject librarian will certainly be defined by the needs of a project and local political and technological circumstances, there are several essential ways a subject librarian might support a digital humanities project throughout the process of its creation and dissemination. Many of these potential roles draw on the skills subject librarians have developed throughout their careers as liaisons, instructors, collectors, and information providers.

Recruitment and Gathering Interest

It is imperative that librarians seek out opportunities and collaborators, rather than waiting for them to seek out the library. Many libraries participate in digital humanities projects, but often only in response to a researcher request.[14] As liaisons to departments and persons knowledgeable in their fields, subject librarians have an already-developed network of connections for this purpose. Subject liaisons should work to identify which of their faculty members are already involved in digital humanities work—or would likely show an interest in it. While it may be with the best intentions, fearing to bother faculty or take on a leadership role in a scholarly project is a hindrance to developing the subject librarian's full potential as part of a digital humanities collaboration by relegating the librarian to a support position rather than that of a peer.

The subject librarian's participation at this stage of the process is essential in institutions that have no or little interest in digital humanities projects. The subject librarian has a crucial role to play in working with technologists to educate faculty on shifts in patterns of scholarship. Subject librarians can work with the faculty in their liaison departments to provide information on the expanded opportunities to use digital tools to ask new questions and to take new approaches to scholarship. They may also use background knowledge to create digital projects of their own. One of many benefits of this would be giving an example of digital scholarship to faculty who may have had little exposure to such approaches. At Miami University Libraries, for example, the subject librarian for Spanish began a text-encoding project with the English librarian with letters between Mexican playwright Rodolfo Usigli and George Bernard Shaw, letters that were contained in a manuscript collection held in Special Collections. Awareness of this project, due to conversations between the Spanish subject librarian and the faculty in the department of Spanish and Portuguese, has led to an interest in creating additional digital projects using other materials in the manuscript collection. The university libraries and the department of Spanish and Portuguese have begun a collaboration with the aim of connecting with other campus departments and Mexican cultural institutions to find support for a large-scale digital humanities project.

Efforts to create a digital humanities community at Miami University illustrate these potential roles for subject librarians in the early stages of developing projects on campus. In 2012, a university-wide working group of subject librarians, technologists, and the Miami University Humanities Center formed to investigate faculty interests in the digital humanities. The working group distributed a survey to humanities faculty in an effort to gauge interest on campus. The survey asked respondents to identify their status in the university and their division; whether they had a strong sense of the work being done in the digital humanities and, if so, if they could identify particularly powerful or helpful work in DH; whether they had done or planned to do any DH projects; and what kind of resources they would need in order to do work in DH. Results were surprisingly indicative of a need for basic information and education about digital approaches and methodologies in humanities research.

To introduce the campus community to the breadth of digital humanities, technologists and subject librarians worked with the university's Humanities Center to plan and host a Digital Humanities Symposium. The symposium was well received by faculty and graduate students in the humanities. Subsequently the campus-wide Digital Humanities Working Group provided support to bring in a consultant to examine the digital humanities environment. The consultant's final report provided suggestions for improvement in service models and communication strategies for all the potential partners in digital humanities work. Currently the libraries' digital humanities advisory committee (made up of subject librarians and technologist librarians) is working with the Humanities Center on creating a faculty institute to provide structured support to faculty as they develop and create digital projects.

As with all of our suggested roles for subject librarians, participation in the project-planning process can be adapted to the digital humanities model at a particular institution. In a service model, recruitment and gathering interest meets the need of educating scholars about the services provided. A subject librarian operating in a lab model might work to identify projects that would benefit from his or her expertise and offer to be part of a project team. Those at institutions with a network model might draw on their already strong network of faculty and campus resources to identify pools of resources from which a scholar might draw support.[15] These roles are flexible and should be adapted as needed to fit local situations.

In the Project-Planning Stages

While developing a faculty base for humanities projects, it is useful to identify library participants and think about the project-planning process and how to engage the scholar. In the preliminary planning stages of a project, a subject librarian's contributions can shape its trajectory and long-term success. The subject librarian's participation begins with the very first point of selecting topic, scope, and content. Trained to ask questions about the value that an item can bring to the collection as a whole, librarians have long been familiar with the task of selection. The librarian/scholar partnership in selection leads to a better project because a scholar can bring intellectual rigor to selection, and a librarian, a more targeted approach.[16] By being slightly removed from the object of study, a subject librarian is able to make decisions based on collection strength or institutional and preservation needs or ability to answer the original research question, rather than solely on the personal interest brought by a faculty scholar.[17] The subject librarian might also help balance the perspective of the technologists on the project, expanding the selection criteria beyond technical considerations, such as the ease of digitization and coding. This same perspective can also work in reverse. A subject librarian's knowledge of technical considerations can help limit a project's scope to the items most able to benefit the collection while also making the best use of a technologist's time and resources.

Also essential in early planning is establishing access and organization. Metadata librarians and other technologists, with expertise in information architecture, are less likely to have a broad knowledge of a given subject area as well as the necessary selection skills. Likewise, scholars are not likely to have a deep understanding of the need to build a consistent and rigorous system of organization of the information they are creating. Whether or not subject librarians catalog, they have some knowledge of organizing information, metadata, and subject hierarchies. Subject librarians can play a role in the selection and organization of controlled vocabulary and of information-access points. Subject librarians take the scholar's deep knowledge of a subject area, translate it through their knowledge of information organization, and convey it in terms that can facilitate the work of a metadata librarian.

Just as selection and organization are square in a librarian's skill set, so too are a knowledge of issues related to digital preservation and long-term access. Here again, the subject librarian can play an intermediary role between the technologists' interest in maintaining the existing infrastructure, preferred file formats, and digital preservation conventions, and the scholar's immediate concerns, such as scope, material selection, and organization.[18] The subject librarian must balance a scholar's interests and ideas for the project with the scope of the project, the needs of a collection, and the technical considerations of a long-term preservation plan.

During Implementation

Perhaps the subject librarian's greatest contribution to digital humanities projects during implementation is to connect faculty to resources in support of digital scholarship available in their university.[19] If subject librarians develop knowledge of the technological tools available, they can contribute an understanding of how one might be used to answer a question from the scholar's disciplinary approach. A technologist might know that a tool like Voyant can analyze a text for word use and proximity, but the subject librarian can help a scholar to meaningfully interpret the results.

Subject librarians can contribute their knowledge of information-seeking habits and end-user behavior when interacting with digital information sources. As Harkema and Nelson note, "liaison librarians are responsible for assessing the needs of their community of scholars and students and providing them with the best, most relevant resources available."[20] A librarian's experiences on the reference desk and in the classroom provide concrete examples of the different levels of expectations of users new to digital scholarship. For example, a digital collection of historical student newspapers has many potential uses. An alumnus searching a collection of digital student newspapers would likely be interested in browsing for an article from his time as a student without any specific need. A student with an assignment would be more interested in efficient and targeted searching capabilities to help her find articles on a particular event or activity. A subject librarian understands that any project has various levels of potential use and that access points to the information need to be created. Often the end users interact with a collection in ways not originally imagined by its creators, and anticipating this contributes to the overall usability of a project.

Upon Completion

Subject librarians can continue to contribute to a project long after its completion. Their participation in deciding what to include in a digital collection "will increase the odds that valuable scholarship in digital form will not be lost. In fact, [the librarian's] goal should be to help make this scholarship easily found, readily used, and permanently preserved."[21] The subject librarian can assist in keeping the collection current and relevant by playing a role in the promotion of and access to the completed project through reference interactions, instruction, and internal and external promotion. No project is ever truly finished and will need to be revisited and updated in response to developing user behavior. Through their interaction with end users, subject librarians can bring functional and usability issues to the technologist's attention.

Subject librarians work with faculty to evaluate the impact of their scholarship. Especially important is the liaison's role in working with departments to understand the value of digital scholarship in the tenure process. In the digital environment, they can work with faculty to identify the most appropriate metrics to demonstrate a project's impact in the scholar's field. For example, another project may replicate methodology or data originally generated in a project, much as one scholar might cite another's journal article. The subject librarian's perspective can anticipate future reuse of data and methodology, facilitating its use by future scholars, potentially leading to greater long-term impact.

Practical Suggestions for Subject Librarians

A subject librarian must have an active role in each stage of a project's life cycle. In this active participation, a librarian acts as a translator between the technical and metadata librarians and the scholars working on digital humanities projects. A subject librarian's knowledge allows him or her to translate technology to the scholar and the scholarship to the technologist. Having a basic understanding of available content management systems, the skills and local resources technologists provide, and the ways all of these can be leveraged to answer a faculty member's research question will lead to more successful collaborations. Just like a language interpreter, those with success are able to understand and navigate the richness of a local culture while connecting to and understanding the perspective and needs of the visitor to that culture.

To build this understanding, subject librarians must see the imperative to evolve along with shifts and changes in patterns of scholarship. Table 1.1 includes some practical suggestions to help subject librarians develop and promote successful digital humanities research at their institutions.

Table 1.1

Suggestions for subject librarians to help develop and promote successful digital humanities research at their institutions.

Level of commitment	Possible activities
Low commitment	• Connect with graduate students in humanities programs, especially those who have not yet begun the thesis or dissertation process. • Learn the basics of your institution's technological infrastructure and environment. • Learn about preservation formats and standards. • Learn about alt-metrics and alternative ways to measure the impact of digital scholarship. • Explore successful digital humanities projects.
Moderate commitment	• Host a symposium on digital humanities and invite external participants (including faculty on campus, faculty already engaged digital humanities scholarship, technologists, and librarians). • Work with faculty and undergraduate classes to design an assignment using a digital humanities tool. • Provide workshops for faculty on digital humanities tools or developments in scholarship. • Provide training for technologists in subject background for projects. • Seek free training on digital humanities tools provided by developers. • Work with technologists or online tools such as Scratch, Code School, or Code.org to learn the basics of coding (PHP, MySQL, and Apache, for example).
Intensive commitment	• Initiate a new digital humanities project using the librarian's unique subject collections.

Librarians need to be perceived as integral players on a team because they can offer both technical and intellectual skills. Although historically librarians have described themselves using the concept of library service, Trevor Muñoz argues that focusing a librarian's role in a digital humanities project in this way diminishes the role the librarian plays.[22] By nature, no matter the size, the digital humanities project is a collaborative team approach, and "the need for multiple skills is undeniable, and underscores the need for scholars, librarians, and programmers to work together."[23] Nowviskie also makes this argument, using a corporate team model for digital humanities projects in academia.[24] Support for digital humanities is not just another service for libraries to offer patrons, but rather an opportunity for subject librarians to be full partners when it comes to scholarship production.

Notes

1. Chris Alen Sula, "Digital Humanities and Libraries: A Conceptual Model," *Journal of Library Administration* 53, no. 1 (January 2013): 10–26, doi:10.1080/01930826.2013.7 56680.
2. See Fiona Black, Bertrum H. MacDonald, and J. Malcolm W. Black, "Geographic Information Systems: A New Research Method for Book History," *Book History* 1 (1998): 11–31, www.jstor.org/stable/30227281.
3. Bethany Nowviskie, "Skunks in the Library: A Path to Production for Scholarly R&D," *Journal of Library Administration* 53, no. 1 (January 2013): 53–66, doi:10.108 0/01930826.2013.756698.
4. Ibid.
5. Ibid.
6. Micah Vandegrift and Stewart Varner, "Evolving in Common: Creating Mutually Supportive Relationships between Libraries and the Digital Humanities," *Journal of Library Administration* 53, no. 1 (January 2013): 68, 10.1080/01930826.2013.756699.
7. Nancy Maron and Sarah Pickle, *Sustaining the Digital Humanities: Host Institution Support beyond the Start-up Phase* (New York: Ithaka S&R, June 18, 2014), www.sr.ithaka.org/sites/default/files/SR_Supporting_Digital_Humanities_20140618f.pdf.
8. Ibid., 23.
9. Ibid., 31.
10. Ibid., 24.
11. Ibid.
12. Mary M. Case, "Partners in Knowledge Creation: An Expanded Role for Research Libraries in the Digital Future," *Journal of Library Administration* 48, no. 2 (2008): 142, doi:10.1080/01930820802231336.
13. Harriett E. Green, "Facilitating Communities of Practice in Digital Humanities: Librarian Collaborations for Research and Training in Text Encoding," *Library Quarterly* 84, no. 2 (April 1, 2014): 219–34, doi:10.1086/675332; Craig Harkema and Brent Nelson, "Scholar-Librarian Collaboration in the Publication of Scholarly Materials," *Collaborative Librarianship* 5, no. 3 (July 2013): 197–207, http://collaborativelibrarianship.org/index.php/jocl/article/view/243/206; Sula, "Digital Humanities and Libraries."
14. Vandegrift and Varner, "Evolving in Common."
15. Maron and Pickle, *Sustaining the Digital Humanities*, 34.

16. Harkema and Nelson, "Scholar-Librarian Collaboration," 201.
17. Miranda Remnek, "Adding Value to Slavic Electronic Texts: Approaches for Scholars and Librarians," *Slavic and East European Information Resources* 6, no. 2–3 (2005): 151–67, doi:10.1300/J167v06n02_10.
18. Sula, "Digital Humanities and Libraries."
19. Green, "Facilitating Communities of Practice."
20. Harkema and Nelson, "Scholar-Librarian Collaboration," 203.
21. Case, "Partners in Knowledge Creation," 145.
22. Trevor Muñoz, "In Service? A Further Provocation on Digital Humanities Research in Libraries," *dh + lib* (blog), June 19, 2013, http://acrl.ala.org/dh/2013/06/19/in-service-a-further-provocation-on-digital-humanities-research-in-libraries.
23. Remnek, "Adding Value to Slavic Electronic Texts," 161.
24. Nowviskie, "Skunks in the Library."

Bibliography

Black, Fiona, Bertrum H. MacDonald, and J. Malcolm W. Black. "Geographic Information Systems: A New Research Method for Book History." *Book History* 1 (1998): 11–31. www.jstor.org/stable/30227281.

Case, Mary M. "Partners in Knowledge Creation: An Expanded Role for Research Libraries in the Digital Future." *Journal of Library Administration* 48, no. 2 (2008): 141–56. doi:10.1080/01930820802231336.

Green, Harriett E. "Facilitating Communities of Practice in Digital Humanities: Librarian Collaborations for Research and Training in Text Encoding." *Library Quarterly* 84, no. 2 (April 1, 2014): 219–34. doi:10.1086/675332.

Harkema, Craig, and Brent Nelson. "Scholar-Librarian Collaboration in the Publication of Scholarly Materials." *Collaborative Librarianship* 5, no. 3 (July 2013): 197–207. http://collaborativelibrarianship.org/index.php/jocl/article/view/243/206.

Maron, Nancy, and Sarah Pickle. *Sustaining the Digital Humanities: Host Institution Support beyond the Start-up Phase.* New York: Ithaka S&R, June 18, 2014. www.sr.ithaka.org/sites/default/files/SR_Supporting_Digital_Humanities_20140618f.pdf.

Muñoz, Trevor. "In Service? A Further Provocation on Digital Humanities Research in Libraries." *dh + lib* (blog), June 19, 2013. http://acrl.ala.org/dh/2013/06/19/in-service-a-further-provocation-on-digital-humanities-research-in-libraries.

Nowviskie, Bethany. "Skunks in the Library: A Path to Production for Scholarly R&D." *Journal of Library Administration* 53, no. 1 (January 2013): 53–66. doi:10.1080/01930826.2013.756698.

Remnek, Miranda. "Adding Value to Slavic Electronic Texts: Approaches for Scholars and Librarians." *Slavic and East European Information Resources* 6, no. 2–3 (2005): 151–67. doi:10.1300/J167v06n02_10.

Sula, Chris Alen. "Digital Humanities and Libraries: A Conceptual Model." *Journal of Library Administration* 53, no. 1 (January 2013): 10–26. doi:10.1080/01930826.2013.756680.

Vandegrift, Micah, and Stewart Varner. "Evolving in Common: Creating Mutually Supportive Relationships between Libraries and the Digital Humanities." *Journal of Library Administration* 53, no. 1 (January 2013): 67–78. doi:10.1080/01930826.2013.756699.

Moderating a Meaningful DH Conversation for Graduate Students in the Humanities

Kathleen A. Langan and Ilse Schweitzer VanDonkelaar

Introduction

The nature of academic librarianship traditionally calls for librarians to serve as subject liaisons. To fulfill such a role, it is common for academic librarians to hold an additional higher degree beyond the MLS. According to a recent study, "13% are doctoral degree holders; 47% have a second masters' degree."[1] This educational background allows librarians to be professionally ambidextrous to institutions of higher education (IOHE) in ways that one does not expect from other faculty on campus. Academic librarians work fluidly across fields, departments, and units as specialists to support the academic community in a variety of capacities, such as providing research consultation, teaching research methodology, and assisting in course development. The ability to navigate between these academic spheres proves an invaluable advantage when accommodating an inherently interdisciplinary field of study like the digital humanities (DH), which relies heavily on cross-campus cooperation. Not only do subject librarians have the necessary content knowledge, they also have an additional kick of technical aptitude that positions them to mediate a DH conversation and to facilitate collaboration in otherwise disparate DH efforts across campus.

Because of its nebulous nature, DH is a nonhierarchical, integrative discipline. It is often hard to identify who might be best suited as campus liaison to a DH initiative. Some institutions are fortunate to have an appointed DH lead or team. For those institutions that do not have a formally identified point person—as is the case at Western Michigan University (WMU)—the responsibility often falls to a librarian who acts as liaison for humanities-related subjects. As a result, these librarians are charged with teaching DH skills, pedagogy, and methodology, not only to faculty but also, and arguably more important, to graduate students. This chapter presents the importance of the subject librarian's role in developing a purposeful DH initiative devoted to the professional preparation of graduate students. It describes a case study at WMU, where momentum for a centralized DH initiative found its source and purpose in a cohort of vocal graduate students who turned to subject librarians for guidance. This unexpected collaboration culminated in much needed and realistic DH learning opportunities for graduate students, developed by subject librarians.

Situating the Conversation

WMU is a mid-sized, midwestern, doctorate-granting public university with a full-time enrollment of approximately 21,000 undergraduate and 5,000 graduate students. WMU is a tier 1 research institute with over 900 full-time board-appointed faculty. Even though individual faculty members are involved with DH projects, there is no current centralized digital humanities initiative, nor is there any formal DH curriculum.

Unlikely Initiators of the DH Conversation at WMU

In the spring of 2013, doctoral students from WMU's English department approached subject librarians to learn more about digital humanities with the strong concern that they lacked any formal exposure to or training in

DH. They worried that the apparent gap in formal DH training or applied knowledge would hinder their success when applying and interviewing for academic faculty positions. DH was fast becoming a prominent skill set found in a high percentage of the faculty job descriptions posted on the Modern Language Association (MLA) Job Information List (JIL). In turning to subject librarians, they sought answers to questions such as these. How could they become more conversant in the broader academic discussion regarding DH? How could they become aware of technical, philosophical, and pedagogical issues or identify key players involved in DH initiatives? While these concerns were immediate and personal for the students involved, their questions set in motion a broader collaboration that extended across disciplinary lines at WMU and resulted in a plan to formalize the teaching of DH at the graduate level. The question about the unstable job market also opens up the discussion of time to degree, incurred debt, and, ultimately, attrition rates. What ethical responsibility does the institution hold for these students? If students feel they are at a disadvantage when entering the job market, how do they justify pursuing a higher degree? How can different parts of IOHE help?

The National Conversation on the State of Graduate Studies in the Humanities

The concerns of WMU's graduate students are realistic, validated by the national conversation regarding the current state of graduate education in the humanities, a conversation that is happening among various constituents such as the MLA and the American Historical Association (AHA), which are framing the current state of graduate education around the future of their fields and professions. For the better part of the 2000s, potential jobs in the humanities greatly outnumbered degrees earned. In the 2008–09 cycle, however, the ratio reversed, with a significant decrease in jobs offered, a trend that continues today.[2] In the 2012–13 cycle, the number of tenure-track positions advertised in the MLA JIL fell by roughly 5 percent.[3]

Not only is the field getting smaller, the nature of the field is changing, requiring more technological expertise, as evident in job descriptions for academic positions. In his essay "Digital Humanities and the 'Ugly Stepchildren' of American Higher Education," Luke Waltzer describes the downturn in the humanities job market and the concurrent flourishing of DH and alternative-academic (alt-ac) positions and initiatives in IOHE as well as in governmental and private funding bodies, such as the National Endowment for the Humanities' (NEH) Office of the Digital Humanities, HASTAC (Humanities, Arts, Science, and Technology Alliance and Collaboratory), Google, and the Andrew Mellon Foundation, to name a few.[4] This increase in industry support for technological approaches to humanities research and teaching is likewise reflected in academic job ads. According to the MLA Office of Research, "ads tagged with the index term 'technology and digital media' represented 19.0% of ads in the English edition (up from 7.7% in 2003–04, when this option first appeared) and 10.2% of ads in the foreign language edition (up from 5.9% in 2003–04)."[5] A simple job search on the 2013 MLA JIL with "digital humanities" in the description yielded 19 (of 259 total) results. Of these positions, several exclusively sought DH experts and included the following titles: digital humanities design consultant, director of digital studies center, assistant professor in DH, postdoc in DH, assistant professor in emerging media. Multiple other job descriptions seeking candidates for professorships in literature and the environment, Shakespeare studies, eighteenth-century and Victorian literature, and rhetoric and communication all listed DH as a desirable subspecialty. Academic jobs now require expertise in multiple areas, alongside teaching experience and an expectation that candidates will already be published in their fields. Concurrently, many graduate students are aware that the likelihood of securing a tenure-track position is low enough that they must also market themselves to the growing non-academic and alt-ac employers, which are recruiting students with hybrid expertise in technology and humanities.

The recent push to prepare students for alt-ac positions emerges in the midst of a conventional and pervasive academic elitism that devalues non-tenure-track faculty positions. Historically, the sentiment among academics has been that students compromise or settle for something less when they choose an alt-ac job, as these positions may be viewed as less than desirable and less prestigious than tenure-track positions. This is a demoralizing outcome for humanities graduates who find themselves without faculty positions and potentially disconnected from their departments and cohorts and who may carry feelings of being undervalued second-class citizens of academia if this prevailing mindset does not change.

By offering recommendations and best practices to universities and departments, professional associations such as the MLA and AHA proactively acknowledge the need to responsibly prepare graduate students with a meaningful and applicable education. In a 2012 interview, then MLA president Michael Bérubé is paraphrased as saying, "curriculums… should be redesigned to emphasize collaboration, but the question will be how it's valued by future employers, and by institutions themselves."[6] Bérubé is quoted as saying collaboration "runs up against the barriers of the institutional reward system," but also that "'interdisciplinarity' will play a crucial role in reforming graduate education in the humanities, in part because it will prepare graduates for a greater array of employment, both inside and outside academe."[7] Though DH is not explicitly mentioned as one of those collaborative initiatives, it is definitely understood. In fact, this collaborative, interdisciplinary approach could be seen as a clear training path toward equalizing alt-ac careers. According to Vimal Patel, Russell Berman, who led the MLA task force on higher education said, "Departments should be more clear with students from the start that tenure-track jobs are becoming harder to find… and should also explain to students what else they could do with a language or literature Ph.D. Career options off the tenure track."[8] Berman is also quoted as saying, "the subject matter may, in fact, be far from literature… but the rich professional formation acquired during the course of doctoral study can be put to good use."[9] Students won't necessarily need to look outside of their field if we or they broaden the definition of the field itself.

This trend is happening in other humanities-related disciplines where job offers are falling and attrition is high. In 2011, the president and the executive director of the AHA made similar pleas for change in graduate education. They stated that the AHA needs "to examine the training we offer, and work out how to preserve its best traditional qualities while adding new options. If we tell new students that a history PhD opens many doors, we need to broaden the curriculum to ensure that we're telling the truth…. There's the whole exploding realm of digital history and humanities, and the range of skills required to practice them."[10] Moreover, as Waltzer points out, redefining graduate education in the humanities to include training in digital tools and creation is specifically suited for and already being undertaken by students: "Graduate students and junior scholars are more confidently embracing what digital tools can mean for their work and are more likely than their predecessors to imagine a career path that revolves around their identities as digital humanists."[11]

The MLA has called for academic programs to embrace technology when envisioning a new graduate curriculum. In Flaherty's summary of the MLA report, she highlights that the report calls for "more technological training, and says students should be encouraged to test and develop new tools and techniques for the study of literature and languages."[12] The MLA executive council also recognizes the benefit in developing interdisciplinary connections with others on campus.

However, in a June 2014 response to the MLA report, ten humanities scholars pointed out that the new career training suggested by the report "places increased burdens on graduate program faculty (directors, in particular). The report somehow expects faculty to provide training for students in areas where faculty themselves may not be adequately trained" including, as the authors of this response point out, "significant training in new digital methodologies."[13] Library faculty, particularly those fluent in digital research methods, seem to be the ideal candidates to supplement traditional humanities training. In the article "Who Prepares Humanities Ph.D.'s for a Nonacademic Search?" Wood and Gurwitz enumerate several potential campus members to train doctoral humanities students, including advisors, the department itself, and campus career services.[14] Surprisingly, nonacademic unit services such as libraries were noticeably absent from the article, odd because academic librarians represent very successful role models for nontraditional academic career paths.

WMU's Annual Enrollment and Degrees Conferred

WMU offers three doctoral programs traditionally defined under the humanities: English, Spanish, and comparative religion, and one interdisciplinary doctoral program in history. Add to this the average head count in traditional humanities-focused master's programs in communication, English, Spanish, comparative religion, and philosophy and the numbers rise quickly. There are also two interdisciplinary master's programs in history and medieval studies.

There are, on average, 115 students annually completing a higher degree in a humanities-related program from WMU and entering the workforce. This number justifies the need for institutional responsibility to provide viable and relevant professional development to graduate students. Attrition is a real concern for departments, and students leave programs for many reasons. In 2013, a national survey of graduate students in history revealed that "students did not feel they had been adequately prepared for the nonacademic job market by either their departments or their universities."[15]

The Emerging DH Conversation at WMU

Turning to their own faculty in English, Spanish, or history to learn about DH would have seemed the obvious choice for WMU graduate students, but the students recognized that librarians have obvious technical advantages and an institutional familiarity and flexibility necessary to start a successful conversation. Subject librarians developed a series of events to educate graduate students broadly on DH and to bring together faculty members and students working at various levels of familiarity with DH. Each activity or event was born from the previous one; the initiative was very organic in nature. Response to and attendance at all events were overall positive and encouraging, validating a much needed conversation.

Event One

The first event was a one-shot session folded into a spring 2013 Graduate Student Research Fair, planned and sponsored by University Libraries, in which graduate students were introduced to the library's digital resources. This session was a small DH discussion group, organized by our Humanities Librarian and Head of Special Collections, envisioned as a "meat and potatoes" introduction to key terms in DH, as well as an exploratory talk to determine how much interest graduate students had in digital studies. From this initial plea, students expressed a need for more in-depth instruction.

Event Two

To answer this request, librarians put together a summer seminar series on DH. Not limited to graduate students, this summer series had a goal to garner exposure and publicity for extant DH projects and resources and to begin a broader conversation with faculty, students, staff, and administrators interested in DH. In the four-session series, invited speakers included faculty and staff from subject departments and technical units, such as the libraries' digitization center, and covered technical aspects of DH or content-driven projects. In the course of this summer series, it became apparent that each of the faculty presenters had worked independently and with relatively little institutional support to develop his or her DH project. Attendees, including the Director of the University Center for the Humanities, suggested that we should continue this conversation in a more public venue to raise awareness of our faculty's current work in DH as well as to determine how the university might better support interdepartmental DH ventures.

Event Three

Interest in DH emerged from across campus, and a third wave of events was held the following semester for administrators, faculty, and students in the form of a working group sponsored by the WMU Center for the Humanities. For this interdisciplinary working group, the goal was to identify expertise and infrastructure to support a centralized DH initiative, keeping graduate students' needs central to the mission. More important, the subject librarian worked in close collaboration with a graduate student from the English department to plan each group meeting's agenda and to move this initiative forward.

The interdisciplinary working group in fall 2013 was funded by the WMU University Center for the Humanities and was open to the entire community with a guided conversation in hopes of answering one key question: Is there a need or a desire for a centralized DH initiative at WMU? Because the conversation was allowed to develop organically, the focus moved away from this initial question and toward "How can we best serve our students and faculty, given the resources we have?" Each of the four monthly meetings addressed a different topic of DH at WMU:

1. Identifying and showcasing extant projects and experts. Can we build a knowledge base from their experiences?

2. Navigating the digital diaspora. Identifying technical and financial resources and ways to collaborate.

3. Implications for graduate students. Institutional responsibility for professional development for future leaders in the field.

4. How do we use this new information? What projects or outcomes are feasible?

Over the course of this multi-month discussion, participants kept circling back to the same issues: a need to determine what resources for building and maintaining DH projects were already available to the WMU community and where these resources could be found. One participant in the first working group meeting noted that the very discussion demonstrated a need to have not only a central person who would deal with all DH-related requests on campus, but also a central process or a way of communicating so that faculty, staff, and students would know who's doing what and where and with whom (as relates to digital projects), and what resources they might need. At the conclusion of the first meeting, participants agreed to work together to create a Google document in which the working group could compose a mission statement for the digital humanities at WMU, using other centers and initiatives as exemplars. At the second meeting, "Navigating the Digital Diaspora," as the conversation increasingly turned to the idea of locating a DH center on campus, one administrator observed that there was too much concern about where our initiative would be housed, when the group should be focusing on getting people together and talking to each other. The key necessity at this point was to streamline the process of organizing DH projects and getting those projects underway, and the "center" would follow. Another participant suggested a new way to understand the concept of a "DH center"—that is, to regard the "center" as a point person (or people) and to establish an advisory board to lead and coordinate tutorials, workshops, and mentoring on DH projects. These points of conversation evolved into larger goals of constructing a workflow document that would streamline the process of locating support, funding, and resources at WMU for faculty pursuing DH research, as well as developing a means of surveying or assessing what kinds of independent digital projects were already underway on campus.

Attendance at each working group meeting varied depending on the topic, though there was a good representation of different constituencies (faculty, administrators, staff, and students) at all meetings. At the end of the semester, it was decided to continue to meet bimonthly with a core group of volunteers during the spring of 2014. Goals included completing projects suggested during fall meetings, including the workflow document, as well as planning a THATCamp (The Humanities and Technology Camp) for spring 2014, and a future graduate-level course in digital humanities.

Outcomes Born from the Conversation

There have been many tangible and intangible outcomes as a direct result of this year-long conversation, including short-, medium-, and long-term.

Short-term outcomes include developing a self-help digital workflow guide, available on WMU Libraries online research guides for faculty, staff, and students. Tracing the process of a typical humanities project from its genesis to publication, the workflow guide prompts the user to conceptualize the design and requirements of a DH project in terms of purpose, audience, sustainability, technical and financial requirements, upkeep and updating, copyright requirements, and necessary collaborators. After posing these questions, the workflow guide suggests resources available at

WMU and beyond to support the researcher as the project moves forward. It includes contact information and information regarding considerations to anticipate during the development and creating of a DH project. The document also connects people, offices, and resources for teaching with established DH projects. This is a living document and will require continuous updating as resources change.

Medium-term outcomes include the development and hosting of a THATCamp at WMU in May 2014. WMU is fortunate to be the host of the annual world-renowned International Congress on Medieval Studies (ICMS). Each year, thousands of medievalists (ranging from undergraduates to emeriti to independent scholars) from around the world descend on Kalamazoo, Michigan, from Wednesday through Sunday in early May to share research and to network. This year, the authors attached a THATCamp to the ICMS with the hope of continuing it annually. For this first venture, we invited a keynote speaker from WMU to discuss game theory in the context of teaching and researching in the humanities. The camp was advertised to the traditional ICMS clientele as well as WMU faculty, staff, and graduate students, using primarily social media outlets and university public relations venues. In total, there were about twenty campers, including a number of medievalists from around the country, several subject librarians among them. Half of its attendees were graduate students from various programs at WMU. Largely an experiment, this was regarded as an opportunity to host interested and curious parties from on and off campus to talk informally about different aspects of teaching humanities and technology.

Long-term goals include developing courses for a more formalized DH education, including introductory graduate seminars with a potential for more advanced courses in the future. Teaching is the natural conclusion to better preparing students for the job market, whether they pursue traditional faculty jobs or alt-ac careers. An ever-increasing number of individual DH-related courses and academic programs in DH are appearing across different institutions both nationally and internationally. However, it is difficult to get such efforts started, as some faculty would prefer to dedicate their time to their own research instead of teaching or developing new coursework, even though they recognize the importance of teaching.[16] With little support for their own DH research projects, it is not surprising that few faculty members are qualified or willing to guide graduate students through the new DH quagmire. With faculty perhaps too encumbered with the hassles of developing DH projects to commit to teaching introductory seminars in DH, subject librarians seem a more efficient choice to lead DH initiatives on campus, as they are not as ensconced in one discipline and constantly engage with organizational resources and technology-based infrastructure. The interdisciplinary nature of academic librarianship puts subject librarians in an ideal position to foster collaboration among key players on campus, including graduate students. Yet it may be hard to drum up support to pull librarians from traditional duties and allow them to teach a DH graduate course: Warwick calls it a "circular problem."[17] In paraphrasing Terras, Warwick agrees that "the lack of teaching programmes may be partially due to the fact that it has taken some time for digital humanities to be accepted as a legitimate discipline."[18]

Other broader long-term goals include the possibility of creating an undergraduate minor and a graduate certificate, programs that would take advantage of existing courses in the WMU catalog. We will also explore marketing DH courses and programs to students from non-humanities departments, such as graphic design, geographic information systems (GIS), and computer sciences.

Developing an Academic Presence at the Graduate Level

The most important development of this collaboration has been creating a long term-goal and formalizing graduate instruction in DH with the creation of a for-credit DH seminar for graduate students. Though developed for the immediate and practical benefit of students, this seminar will also (hopefully) bring visibility and relevance to the DH research being performed independently by WMU faculty; as Warwick has it, "teaching is important to digital humanities in many ways: it helps to train the next generation of digital humanities scholars and practitioners, of course, but it also gives the subject a sense of stability in institutional terms."[19] At WMU, graduate students were very vocal in their support of formal instruction.

In response, our intention is to offer this one seminar as a test run and then submit an application to the graduate curriculum faculty senate committee to add it to the course catalog. In the process of developing a digital humanities course, however, institutional administrative barriers due to accreditation, funding, and other factors hindered the creation of a truly interdisciplinary initiative despite broad interest across departments, units, and colleges. Before any content, syllabus, or pedagogical approach could be developed, several administrative necessities needed to be addressed.

The first issue in developing a graduate course in DH was finding a philosophically appropriate academic home. Since the libraries are not an academic unit, they are unable to house a course. A DH course attached to one particular academic department contradicted the interdisciplinary spirit of the field. It was decided that the WMU Graduate College, the overarching unit providing support and advocacy for graduate students (not to mention granting their degrees), would be the best academic home for this course. The next hurdle was finding an instructor of record who met the Graduate College's rigorous standards for instruction. For all the suitability and strengths of the subject librarian to serve as a DH point person on campus, administrative issues emerge when the librarian is called upon to teach. At WMU, for example, since University Libraries are not an academic unit, they cannot nominate someone to teach at the Graduate College; the nomination has to be from a doctoral-granting department. (The WMU English department was willing to nominate the librarian as the instructor of record.) Though this issue has been resolved, other issues emerge for the librarian who does not serve as instructor on a regular basis: Does the librarian receive release time and fold this course in with her other normal duties, or does she teach this course as an overload? Another unresolved issue is to decide between a face-to-face course, an online courses, or a hybrid course. Choosing e-learning, while eminently suitable to a course on digital tools, methods, and texts, brings on other sets of issues, as those courses are set up and paid for by a different nonacademic unit at WMU. Ultimately, answers to these questions will come largely from the college that ends up housing this course; the librarian as instructor must work with administrators to map out this new instructional territory.

Intangible Outcomes

If anything, being involved in the planning process proves to the graduate students that one does not need to be so leery of DH, that the field is neither impenetrable nor mysterious. Handing over responsibilities to the graduate students as initiators of a campus-wide conversation as well as directly involving them in organizing events that require pulling people in from all levels of the university—upper administration to faculty to students to staff—is invaluable. The exposure to the policies and procedures of these sorts of events have the unintended benefit of showing graduate students what will be expected of them for the service portion of the tenure process. So much emphasis is placed on teaching and scholarship, yet it is events like this that move universities forward, foster collaboration, and initiate change.

The graduate students who attended the aforementioned DH events were exposed to upper-level administrative discussions that revolved around campus planning, academic units, and how the greater academic entity functions. As part and parcel of this, graduate students (especially those who were involved from the beginning of this venture) were also exposed to the difficulties of mobilizing disparate offices and individuals across a university to move toward a common goal. Chief among these challenges was the issue of funding, as again and again we were told that, while offices and administrators were (in their own words), philosophically, intellectually, and spiritually supportive of our goals, the realities of an ever-shrinking university budget made establishing a "Center for DH" a near-impossibility. Additional challenges became obvious when faculty and librarians talked about difficulties they had experienced when trying to get all of their ducks in a row to apply for funding for DH projects. Finally, graduate students witnessed a certain level of cooperation fatigue when, after several meetings, attendance began to lag and the working group self-selected itself down to a core group of truly motivated members. With this reduction in participation, and with more responsibilities for planning, organizing, and developing content falling to the subject librarian and a graduate student from the English Department, it became apparent the degree to which these kinds of ventures require a constellation of elements to keep themselves afloat: dynamic and innovative leaders, continued funding, interested and involved stakeholders from across the campus, a clear vision for future work and goals, and members willing to volunteer time and effort to contribute to group projects.

As the year waned, the organizers saw a drop-off in a number of these elements (not to mention experiencing their own fatigue at having to manage this group and its projects on top of other full-time job requirements). The challenge of seeing the various short- and long-term goals through to completion at the end of the academic year made clear the requirement for both the energy (and job-search-related anxiety) of graduate students to push us forward, as well as the knowledge of how to navigate convoluted university systems and communications that comes with experience in faculty or library roles.

Recommendations

As we move forward with our plans for the graduate-level DH course and continue the discussion of the place of DH at WMU, we offer this advice to universities, librarians, and students who find themselves in positions similar to ours:

Think interdisciplinarily. If one unit, office, or department says no, look around you. There is a solution (or a home!) somewhere. As subject librarians, realize that institutional and administrative barriers may prevent you from developing or teaching a course. You may need to work closely with colleagues in other departments or units to plead your case.

Clarify professional duties. It is worth mentioning that there was institutional misunderstanding of the definition of information literacy. Administrators questioned why a subject librarian would want to teach a course in digital humanities because it is not true information literacy. Even though other teaching librarians understood the impact of teaching a semester-long graduate course on digital humanities, subject librarians may find that they need to justify themselves. In reality, teaching a semester-long graduate course in digital humanities to support graduate students in being better prepared is as important, if not more, than teaching one-shot information literacy to first-year writing students. It is truly demand-driven service. There are tangible outcomes that can be assessed to measure programmatic effectiveness. It could potentially attract more graduate students, thereby generating more revenue for departments or units. Finally, it increases the visibility of the university libraries as providing relevant academic support as well as the academic value of subject librarians.

Time. This process has thus far taken fifteen months, with another academic year projected to work through the various administrative hurdles to launch either new programs or courses. It took a lot of public events and discussions to identify what our unique institutional need actually was. Rather than going into the conversation with an already-made decision, it is recommended that you listen to all participants. It is surprising to see who emerges as the most organized in vision and motivation—in this case, the graduate students. The audience will, of course, vary from institution to institution.

The New Academic Model

The new reality for the humanities will likely see more complex models of collaboration; as Reid has it, "the default mode for humanities academic labor has been for a professor to work independently.... As the humanities shift into a digital assemblage, however, these practices are changing, and this is already apparent in digital humanities fields, where research indicates a growing amount of collaboration."[20] Reid is partly correct, yet this observation leaves out the librarians who work with faculty to produce this research. As the humanities take on more digital tools and forms, the scholar/subject librarian relationship, which previously produced isolated instances of collaboration for independent scholarship and research, will shift to more multiphasic, team-based initiatives, setting many other changes in motion: changes in job responsibilities, graduate education, and subject librarian responsibilities. As we add graduate students to this equation, more complex research projects provide moments when students can be trained collaboratively by subject librarians and subject faculty, working as part of a larger team with more diverse expertise. These collaborations also provide recruitment and mentorship opportunities for librarians as they work together with graduate students in a newly emerging academic model where technology, humanities, research, and teaching intersect. This intersection, DH librarianship, is fast becoming a hybrid discipline of its own, defusing the ac/alt-ac debate.

Adding a technological component to the study of the humanities has created a philosophical schism between the old and new guard; unfortunately, the "digital" *can* drive people, resources, and ideas apart. And yet, with this ideological change, job expectations are evolving to a point where new scholars and freshly minted PhDs are expected to be conversant in the new philosophies and methodologies of digital research, thus rectifying the schism and uniting old and new approaches to pedagogy and research. This is quite a lot to expect of graduate students, and certainly necessitates re-envisioning humanities graduate education. In fact, the new vision of graduate education modernizes and renews the role and function of the subject librarian in higher education, whose traditional role on campus is threatened, because of other reasons, by obsolescence. By taking on the responsibility of teaching DH, subject librarians are teaching to a new vision of information literacy, that of multiliteracy, which encompasses digital and media literacy, and serving as academic and professional mentors to graduate students who might not have previously seen them in that light.

IOHE hold an ethical responsibility to graduate students and their professional development. Following the examples set forth by the MLA and AHA, the Association of College and Research Libraries (ACRL) is well positioned to provide organizational support to subject librarians as integrative to graduate education in the humanities and for preparing graduate students to be viable in the field of digital academia. By developing DH-related seminars, working groups, and courses, subject librarians foster the otherwise orphaned academic discipline of DH and are pivotal in uniting disparate DH efforts scattered across departments, people, and pedagogies. At WMU, subject librarians provided more than just basic instruction on DH theories and applications for graduate students. They established a working coalition and institutionalized the teaching of DH, ensuring that the "digital" becomes a part of the WMU humanities legacy.

Notes

1. Shin Freedman, "Questions about Academic Librarians: Factors Influencing Our Academic Identity" (presentation, Charleston Conference: Issues in Book and Serial Acquisition, Charleston, SC, November 6–9, 2013), 320, doi:10.5703/1288284315280.

2. Modern Language Association Office of Research, *Report on the MLA* Job Information List, *2012–13* (New York: Modern Language Association, October 2013), www.mla.org/pdf/rptjil12_13web.pdf; David Laurence, "Our PhD Employment Problem, Part 1," figure 1, *The Trend* (blog), February 26, 2014, http://mlaresearch.commons.mla.org/2014/02/26/our-phd-employment-problem.

3. Luke Waltzer, "Digital Humanities and the 'Ugly Stepchildren' of American Higher Education," in *Debates in the Digital Humanities*, ed. Matthew K. Gold (Minneapolis: University of Minnesota Press, 2012), 335–37.

4. Ibid.

5. MLA Office of Research, *Report on the MLA* Job Information List, 3.

6. Michael Bérubé, paraphrased in Colleen Flaherty, "Fixing Humanities Grad Programs," *Inside Higher Ed*, December 7, 2012, para. 8, www.insidehighered.com/news/2012/12/07/mla-president-says-reforming-graduate-education-humanities-requires-hard-decisions#ixzz33E2CqU9B.

7. Ibid., para. 8, 11.

8. Russell Burman, quoted in Vimal Patel, "Ph.D. Programs Should Change but Not Shrink, MLA Says," *Chronicle of Higher Education*, May 28, 2014, para 7, http://chronicle.com/article/PhD-Programs-Should-Change/146809.

9. Ibid., para. 8.

10. Anthony T. Grafton and James Grossman, "No More Plan B: A Very Modest Proposal for Graduate Programs in History," *Perspectives on History: A News Magazine of the American Historical Association* 49, no. 7 (October 2011), para. 11, www.historians.org/publications-and-directories/perspectives-on-history/october-2011/no-more-plan-b.

11. Waltzer, "Digital Humanities and the 'Ugly Stepchildren,'" 339.

12. Colleen Flaherty, "5-Year Plan," *Inside Higher Ed*, May 28, 2014, www.insidehighered.com/news/2014/05/28/mla-report-calls-phd-program-reform-including-cutting-time-degree; see also Modern Language Association, *Report on the MLA Task Force on Doctoral Study in Modern Language and Literature* (New York: Modern Language Association, May 2014), www.mla.org/pdf/taskforcedocstudy2014.pdf.

13. 10 Humanities Scholars, "Don't Capitulate. Advocate," *Inside Higher Ed*, June 24, 2014, para. 8, www.insidehighered.com/views/2014/06/24/essay-critiques-mla-report-graduate-education#ixzz35flA96jv.

14. L. Maren Wood and Beatrice Gurwitz, "Who Prepares Humanities Ph.D.'s for a Nonacademic Search?" *Chronicle of Higher Education*, July 15, 2013, para. 9–20, http://chronicle.com/article/Who-Prepares-Humanities/140253.

15. Ibid., para. 8.

16. Claire Warwick, "Institutional Models for Digital Humanities," in *Digital Humanities in Practice*, ed. Claire Warwick, Melissa Terras, and Julianne Nyhan (London: Facet Publishing, 2012), 208–9.
17. Ibid., 208.
18. Ibid.; see also Melissa Terras, "Disciplined: Using Educational Studies to Analyse 'Humanities Computing,'" *Literary and Linguistic Computing* 21, no. 2 (2006): 229–246, doi:10.1093/llc/fql022.
19. Warwick, "Institutional Models," 209.
20. Alexander Reid, "Graduate Education and the Ethics of the Digital Humanities," in *Debates in the Digital Humanities*, ed. Mathew K. Gold (Minneapolis: University of Minnesota Press, 2012), 356.

Bibliography

Flaherty, Colleen. "5-Year Plan." *Inside Higher Ed*, May 28, 2014. www.insidehighered.com/news/2014/05/28/mla-report-calls-phd-program-reform-including-cutting-time-degree.

———. "Fixing Humanities Grad Programs." *Inside Higher Ed*, December 7, 2012. www.insidehighered.com/news/2012/12/07/mla-president-says-reforming-graduate-education-humanities-requires-hard-decisions#ixzz33E2CqU9B.

Freedman, Shin. "Questions about Academic Librarians: Factors Influencing Our Academic Identity." Presentation, Charleston Conference: Issues in Book and Serial Acquisition, Charleston, SC, November 6–9, 2013. doi:10.5703/1288284315280.

Grafton, Anthony T., and James Grossman. "No More Plan B: A Very Modest Proposal for Graduate Programs in History." *Perspectives on History: A News Magazine of the American Historical Association* 49, no. 7 (October 2011). www.historians.org/publications-and-directories/perspectives-on-history/october-2011/no-more-plan-b.

Laurence, David. "Our PhD Employment Problem, Part 1." *The Trend* (blog), February 26, 2014. http://mlaresearch.commons.mla.org/2014/02/26/our-phd-employment-problem.

Modern Language Association. *Report on the MLA Task Force on Doctoral Study in Modern Language and Literature.* New York: Modern Language Association, May 2014. www.mla.org/pdf/taskforcedocstudy2014.pdf.

Modern Language Association Office of Research. *Report on the MLA Job Information List, 2012–13.* New York: Modern Language Association, October 2013. www.mla.org/pdf/rptjil12_13web.pdf.

Patel, Vimal. "Ph.D. Programs Should Change but Not Shrink, MLA Says." *Chronicle of Higher Education,* May 28, 2014. http://chronicle.com/article/PhD-Programs-Should-Change/146809.

Reid, Alexander. "Graduate Education and the Ethics of the Digital Humanities." In *Debates in the Digital Humanities*, edited by Mathew K. Gold, 350–67. Minneapolis: University of Minnesota Press, 2012.

10 Humanities Scholars. "Don't Capitulate. Advocate." *Inside Higher Ed*, June 24, 2014. www.insidehighered.com/views/2014/06/24/essay-critiques-mla-report-graduate-education#ixzz35flA96jv.

Terras, Melissa. "Disciplined: Using Educational Studies to Analyse 'Humanities Computing.'" *Literary and Linguistic Computing* 21, no. 2 (2006): 229–246. doi:10.1093/llc/fql022.

Waltzer, Luke. "Digital Humanities and the 'Ugly Stepchildren' of American Higher Education." In *Debates in the Digital Humanities*, edited by Matthew K. Gold, 335–49. Minneapolis: University of Minnesota Press, 2012.

Warwick, Claire. "Institutional Models for Digital Humanities." In *Digital Humanities in Practice*, edited by Claire Warwick, Melissa Terras, and Julianne Nyhan, 193–216. London: Facet Publishing, 2012.

Wood, L. Maren, and Beatrice Gurwitz. "Who Prepares Humanities Ph.D.'s for a Nonacademic Search?" *Chronicle of Higher Education*, July 15, 2013. http://chronicle.com/article/Who-Prepares-Humanities/140253.

CHAPTER THREE

Construction and Disruption

Building Communities of Practice, Queering Subject Liaisons

Caro Pinto

In Germany today, not only does the monument vanish, but so too do the traditional notions of the monument's performance. How better to remember forever a vanished people than by the perpetually unfinished, ever-vanishing monument?

—James E. Young[1]

SOCIETIES BUILD monuments to remember. Monuments rise to mourn the dead, to commemorate victory in war, and to reflect on injustice. Monuments are meant to influence future behaviors: to wage peace or to bend societies toward justice. Libraries are also memorial environments: many are imposing, glorious brick structures that emulate cathedrals, holding history within their walls. Culturally, we read architectural elements like brick and paned glass as the physical manifestation of the library. At Mount

Holyoke, many students remark that our Reading Room *feels* like a library with its wood beams and bookshelves that invite them to contemplate and study.

While monuments were designed to facilitate collective memory, some enable collective forgetting, like the counter-monuments built in reaction to the bloody wars of the twentieth century.* Perhaps the library building's suggestive power has also run its course; libraries are being renovated to facilitate new types of inquiry and research, while notions of "virtual libraries" and "libraries without walls" dominate library design discourse.† Monuments and libraries are physical structures but also sets of ideas. Certainly, the work of digital humanities in libraries is not exactly parallel to how monuments instruct us to remember a vanished people or incidents of horrible violence, but memory studies holds lessons for digital humanists. "Doing digital humanities" is a process; it is a set of practices requiring deep engagement with computing, technology, and critical reflection in order to create strategies for positive library futures and engagement with teaching, learning, and scholarship on our campuses and in public discourse.

The Digital Will Not Save You

Literary scholar Murray Roston taught his students at UCLA "every generation faces a system of inherited assumptions and urgent concerns."[2] This generation of librarians faces a system of inherited concerns about the relevance of libraries in the digital era, as well as urgent calls for new training

---

*   James Young's 1992 article in *Critical Inquiry* defined counter-monuments as "brazen, painfully self conscious memorial spaces conceived to challenge the very premises of their being" (James E. Young, "The Counter-Monument: Memory against Itself in Germany Today," *Critical Inquiry* 18, no. 2 [January 1, 1992]: 271). Built to critique the traditional monuments built after World War I that failed to prevent the violence and mass murder of the Second World War, counter-monuments demand that memorial practices extend beyond the construction of a monument.

†   Hannah Bennett reflected on how perceptions of libraries have shifted from physical entities into ideas in *Art Documentation* in 2013 (Hannah Bennett, "The Psyche of the Library: Physical Space and the Research Paradigm," *Art Documentation* 32, no. 2 [Fall 2013]: 174–85, www.jstor.org/stable/10.1086/673511).

and preparation for a rapidly changing job market. How do we stay relevant in a shifting landscape that assumes that to hold steady is anathema to our profession? We celebrate change agents and push for disruption. *New Yorker* writer Jill Lepore reflected on the current embrace of "disruption" as the solution to a variety of challenges: "Everyone is either disrupting or being disrupted.... This fall, the University of Southern California is opening a new program: 'The degree is in disruption,' the university announced. "Disrupt or be disrupted," the venture capitalist Josh Linkner warns in a new book, '... mean[s] that the time has come to panic as you've never panicked before.'"[3]

Academic library discourse also incorporates the language of disruption. The newsletter *Keeping Up With...* , published by the Association of College and Research Libraries, echoes these concerns about relevance, covering topics such as big data, patron-driven acquisitions, and digital humanities.[‡] Indeed, creative destruction drives many of the changes seen in library hiring, retention, space planning, and collections. The tone of these changes ranges from gentle to corrosive.[4] The discourse of creative disruption sometimes suggests that librarians are toiling at empty reference desks in bookless libraries devoid of people. Such libraries are empty, meaningless monuments to knowledge.

The question of disruption and crisis extends to the future of the humanities. Who will save the humanities? "The humanities are in crisis again, or still. But there is one big exception: digital humanities, which is a growth industry," wrote Adam Kirsch in *The Atlantic*.[5] Are the digital humanities the disruptor-savior for traditional libraries? If so, how should librarians at smaller, teaching-oriented institutions develop digital humanities programs and services? At Mount Holyoke College, we took inspiration from

---

‡   The Association of College and Research Libraries describes the *Keeping Up With...* newsletter series as "an online current awareness publication from the Association of College and Research Libraries (ACRL) featuring concise briefs on trends in academic librarianship and higher education. Each edition focuses on a single issue including an introduction to the topic and summaries of key points, including implications for academic libraries" (ACRL, "Keeping Up With... ," accessed October 25, 2014, www.ala.org/acrl/publications/keeping_up_with). For more information, visit the website.

a symposium that started conversations about how to build digital humanities communities of practice. The event, held in May 2013, was organized under the auspices of the Five College Consortium, a network of institutions in western Massachusetts: Amherst College, Hampshire College, Mount Holyoke College, Smith College, and the University of Massachusetts Amherst.[6] The day taught us about the importance of flexibility and the value of archival materials, collaboration, and administrative support. While the symposium aimed to address these questions at a consortial level, individual institutional participants pondered how to enact local changes. Our cross-functional group at Mount Holyoke College, now called RAD (Research and Instructional Support, Archives and Special Collections, and Digital Assets and Preservation), coalesced organically outside of traditional organizational lines. RAD actively engages with projects that meet college learning goals and objectives, especially those that speak to the intersection of technology and the traditional liberal arts. We do not interact in compartmentalized spaces, but over coffee in the library atrium, in a classroom trying to boot a circa 2000 iMac, or in a windowless conference room nudging cascading style sheets toward their rightful place in a digital exhibition. Our community of practice at Mount Holyoke was not built from the top down; it is project-based and student-focused, blessed by our administration to support curricular engagement and to ensure that our graduates are ready for the disruption-happy world they are inheriting. In the words of Johanna Drucker, "the *next* university… is a fully integrated and distributed platform" evolved from "monastic centers" and laboratory cum industrial incubator.[7] Guerilla digital humanities groups, task forces, projects, and teams are crucial steps toward realizing the "*next* university."

It Takes a Village to Build a Digital Project

Many humanists worship at the altar of the individual creative genius, believing that their best work is completed without the assistance of anyone else. Indeed, as journalist Joshua Wolf Shenk argues, "the idea of the solitary creator is such a common feature of our cultural landscape (as with Newton and the falling apple) that we easily forget it's an idea in the first place."[8] Indeed, many humanities projects—particularly live or recorded music or theatrical productions—require the talents of many individuals. Digital humanities projects also shatter the myth of the solitary genius in that they depend upon the sustained collaboration of multiple people with diverse expertise. They are often the direct result of sustained collaborative vision, resource development, and time management. It takes a village to build a digital project. Projects like One Week | One Tool illustrate how digital projects are impossible to build without robust teams, support for those teams, and teamwork to collaborate effectively. Indeed, One Week | One Tool is a self-described barn raising.§ These communities organize themselves to construct the technical foundations, critical content, and public discourse that propels and sustains their projects. These dynamic communities of practice evolve to meet the demands of the present, disappearing and reappearing to meet new challenges.

The humanities may not have been originally imagined to be group endeavors, but the work of the digital demands a sum greater than one part. Faculty, librarians, archivists, and technologists must collaborate.[9] Libraries must also find ways to better facilitate cross-department, cross-functional organization in addition to forging new types of relationships with faculty. Some organizations are evolving to meet this challenge. Research universities like the University of Florida and Michigan State have reorganized themselves to better facilitate digital projects. As Laurie Taylor and Blake Landor note of Florida: "The Digital Humanities Library Group was created without a specific charge other than to address/discuss issues in digital humanities and to schedule training in support of the group's members. While the formation of the group was approved by Library Administration… it is very much a grassroots cohort of primarily Subject or Liaison Librarians brought together by a common interest."[10]

Thomas Padilla described the Michigan State University Digital Scholarship Collaborative, noting that "Direct ties to subject areas combined

---

§ The website of the One Week | One Tool project relates its mission to barn raisings: "For centuries rural communities throughout the United States have come together for 'barn raisings' when one of their number required the diverse set of skills and enormous effort required to build a barn—skills and effort no one member of the community alone could possess" (One Week | One Tool homepage, accessed October 25, 2014, http://oneweekonetool.org).

with appointments to other parts of the library strengthens our ability to be effective with respect to collection preparation to support computational analysis, communicating principles of data curation, and staying informed about needs of the campus community."[11] Indeed, these examples of cross-department, cross-functional organization are on the rise within libraries. They are working to meet evolving scholarly needs and to enlist many different library constituents to support digital humanities initiatives. This kind of nimble group structure engages digital technology to facilitate new directions in the humanities.

Digital humanities centers at research universities employ faculty and staff that can scale up to meet complex demands and have a population of graduate students to help with the challenging work of enacting these changes. What does digital humanities look like on a smaller scale at a teaching institution? How can smaller colleges do digital humanities? According to William Pannapacker of Hope College, these institutions hold special advantages: "Because of their teaching focus... faculty members are more likely to be able to experiment with projects that may not lead to traditional scholarly publications. Some liberal arts colleges even have a culture of faculty-student collaborative research, which translates perfectly into the project-building methods of the digital humanities."[12] Small liberal arts colleges may lack larger budgets, flashy centers, and an army of graduate students, but they do have agile pathways for incorporating digital humanities into their curricula and job descriptions. In many ways, liberal arts colleges are ripe for DH innovations in staffing, collaborations, and the primacy of student-directed work.

If You Fund It, They Will Come

The Andrew W. Mellon Foundation has funded several liberal arts college digital humanities initiatives, including the Tri-Co Digital Humanities Initiative (Tri-Co DH), Five Colleges, Incorporated (5CollDH), and Hamilton College. In the Five Colleges, Mellon's funding fosters new collaborations and encouragement for faculty to incorporate the digital into the curriculum. As the website states, "Five College Digital Humanities provides grants and training to, as well as encourages, faculty members within the consortium to incorporate digital technologies into humanities studies and student research. From 2011 to 2015, 5CollDH will fund faculty and staff through our collaborative grants program, and groups of students through our student fellowship program."[13] One of the central questions for librarians in the consortium has been this: How do we participate? How can librarians be change makers and active agents in these digital projects? In the Five Colleges, librarians wanted to make substantial contributions to this growing endeavor. To integrate the "digital" into the curriculum would require sustained collaboration between librarians, technologists, and faculty. Librarians wondered how to begin tackling this task across the campuses to transform the digital humanities from an abstraction into an actionable set of practices.

The libraries in the Five College Consortium are autonomous, but collaborate in meaningful ways with a shared integrated library system, a shared depository, and reciprocal lending among all five campuses. The libraries also collaborate administratively with committees, task forces, and working groups. One such committee was the Digital Environment Development and Coordinating Committee (DEDCC), which scanned the horizon to help librarians understand future challenges and opportunities. During the 2012–13 school year, DEDCC engaged in exploratory conversations about how to collaborate with faculty and students to "do" digital humanities in the Five Colleges. The group decided to sponsor a symposium whose goal was "to provide a starting place for librarians and IT staff at the Five Colleges to learn about and explore research and scholarship in the Digital Humanities in liberal arts settings. The symposium included a panel followed by breakout sessions to explore topics around the broad question *'What does it take to become an effective digital humanities community of practice in the Five Colleges?'*"[14]

Imagining a Community of Practice

The DEDCC librarians solicited proposals nationally to help the group reflect on what it would take to become an effective community of practice. The committee selected speakers to represent a variety of perspectives: Joanne Schneider, library director at Colgate University; Laura McGrane, a faculty member at Haverford College; Jen Rajchel, a post-baccalaureate resident for the Tri-Co DH Initiative (at Haverford, Swarthmore, and Bryn Mawr Colleges); Laurie Allen at Haverford, who had transformed from a traditional reference and instruction librarian into Digital Scholarship Coordinator; Alston Brake, the very first Digital Scholarship Librarian at Washington and Lee University; and Brandon Bucy, an Academic Technologist at Washington and Lee. Each speaker saw changes in their titles and responsibilities to meet new challenges presented by the digital humanities. The panels were excellent object lessons in how to transform libraries to meet the evolving needs of digital scholarship in small organizations. Often, these transformations were accomplished without adding new positions, which is always a challenge in waging organizational change.

The 5CollDH event was a one-day symposium that began with the usual mix of coffee and mingling followed by presentations from invited speakers and discussions of digital scholarship. Following lunch, the group of archivists, librarians, instructional technologists, and administrators broke out for an "unconference" of active conversations, brainstorming, and small-group exercises. What might work at Colgate or Haverford or Washington and Lee would not necessarily work at Smith, Mount Holyoke, Hampshire, Amherst, or the University of Massachusetts, so the afternoon's work session was intended to envision DH in the local context. Armed with a range of brightly colored sticky notes, pens, and enthusiasm, participants went to work brainstorming about how to facilitate a DH community of practice in the Five Colleges.

Active facilitation of these conversations was key to identifying themes and ideas that resonated across and within libraries and units. In unconference mode, participants voted on the top priorities within their groups. Themes included budgets, "special collections," "updated position descriptions," and "compelling vision." Soon, participants covered the white butcher paper with many brightly colored sticky notes. Following the conclusion of that exercise, facilitators began grouping the Post-it notes together in themes: relationships, communication, funding, skills, definitions of DH, and creating an inventory of 5CollDH projects. Groups gathered around butcher paper to meditate on these themes. Eventually, facilitators provided orange dots for participants to use in voting on common themes that emerged to help work toward the goal of defining our community of practice. Themes emerged, such as "who else is working on an area of interest," "who is this for," "common set of principles." Once the votes were tallied, the facilitators compiled the results to act as action steps for the committee to consider for future programming. While the consortial perspective was critical for the success of the event, the local context was equally critical for our day-to-day work. We also considered how we would do digital humanities at our individual campuses. The facilitated discussions were excellent, but raised additional questions: How could we bring these conversations into our local institutional contexts? How should we create working groups on our campuses and beyond to integrate this work into our existing practices?

An opportunity to do digital humanities at Mount Holyoke College soon presented itself. The professor of the first-year connections course, a one-credit course designed to acclimate first-year students to college learning, approached the college archivist about an assignment focusing on college traditions. The objective was to inculcate first-year students with a sense of Mount Holyoke history and to allow them to learn about the traditions that make Mount Holyoke College unique. We eventually decided to create a digital exhibit that incoming students and their families could view and enjoy before they arrived on campus. The exhibit would also serve the library as a large-scale teaching tool, engaging a variety of students over the long term. And so began the first iteration of RAD: Research and Instructional Support, Archives and Special Collections, and Digital Assets and Preservation Services.

A Cross-Functional Community at Mount Holyoke

One subject liaison, one metadata librarian, or one archivist cannot play hero to the digital humanities endeavor. In our case at Mount Holyoke, we recognized that our cohort would take the form of working groups formed under the charge of producing certain projects. Our cohort coalesced in an informal but powerful way. In one example, we built an Omeka site for the first-year seminars program to empower new students to transition to college and cultivate resilience in a new community. The Omeka site would not have been possible without the collaborative efforts of everyone involved in the project, especially the students who were at the center of the research, development, and deployment stages.

Our cross-functional work is not a monument to digital scholarship or to collaboration; we fully expect that our working group will evolve to meet new challenges and reflect constructively on past work. We organized new configurations of people to attend to new tasks, but we recognized the impermanence of these configurations and our need to be open to shifting responsibilities. Positions in libraries cannot be monuments to the past or to the already completed work of other people. Libraries themselves cannot simply be static monuments to past work; we cannot rely on grand architecture to remind our funders and our constituents to care about the future of libraries in higher education. While we must remember our past to understand our present and plan for the future, we need to be nimble and sensitive to local organizational contexts.

Cross-Functional Individuals: Queering the Subject Librarian

If this generation of librarians must choose between disrupting and being disrupted, there are exciting possibilities ahead for us. Today's information professionals can disrupt the information professional binary that divides librarians and archivists, subject liaisons and metadata librarians. These binaries obscure the remarkable commonalities and complementary skill sets that make academic library communities stronger, nimbler, and ready for future challenges. Successful digital humanities work depends upon effective cross-functional collaboration. I readily and enthusiastically identify as a *librarchivist*; a franken-professional who is part archivist and special collections professional and part librarian, heir of information, collection development, instruction, and liaison to faculty, curriculum, and student research needs. While my professional identity as a "specialized generalist" empowers me to participate in a range of conversations and projects,

I recognize that I need the expertise and skills of my community of allies and collaborators. Ideas that can shape our scholarly future can come from any of us. Can they come from you? We should disrupt toward solidarity and innovate toward communities of practice in the digital humanities. These communities have the potential for positive, lasting disruption in the academy, as Roxanne Shirazi has argued: "Let's join our colleagues who are struggling with the narrow system of rewards that favors individual research over (collaborative) service work. The same system in which women, people of color, and queer scholars disproportionately shoulder the burden of committee work, community building, and 'service work' that reproduces the academy."[15] If the library of the past was a monument to the past, perhaps digital humanities can create a counter-monument, disrupting the landscape towards a new future.

Notes

1. James E. Young, "The Counter-Monument: Memory against Itself in Germany Today," *Critical Inquiry* 18, no. 2 (January 1, 1992): 271.
2. Murray Roston, quoted in Natasha Vargas-Cooper, *Mad Men Unbuttoned: A Romp through 1960s America* (New York: Collins Design, 2010), xii.
3. Jill Lepore, "The Disruption Machine," *New Yorker*, June 30, 2014, accessed February 4, 2015, http://www.newyorker.com/magazine/2014/06/23/the-disruption-machine.
4. Caro Pinto, "Creative Destruction in Libraries: Designing Our Future," *In the Library with the Lead Pipe* (blog), November 20, 2013, www.inthelibrarywiththeleadpipe.org/2013/creative-destruction-in-libraries-designing-our-future.
5. Adam Kirsch, "Technology Is Taking Over English Departments: The False Promise of the Digital Humanities," *New Republic*, May 2, 2014, www.newrepublic.com/article/117428/limits-digital-humanities-adam-kirsch.
6. Five College Consortium home page, accessed October 25, 2014, https://www.fivecolleges.edu.
7. Johanna Drucker, "The University as a Fully Integrated and Distributed Platform: A Vision," *portal: Libraries and the Academy* 14, no. 3 (2014): 326.
8. Joshua Wolf Shenk, "The End of 'Genius,'" Sunday Review, *New York Times*, July 19, 2014, www.nytimes.com/2014/07/20/opinion/sunday/the-end-of-genius.html.
9. Caro Pinto, "Digital Humanities Is a Team Sport: Thoughts on #DHTNG," *dh + lib* (blog), April 10, 2013, http://acrl.ala.org/dh/2013/04/10/digital-humanities-is-a-team-sport-thoughts-on-dhtng.

10. Laurie Taylor and Blake Landor, "Intertwingularity with Digital Humanities at the University of Florida," *dh + lib* (blog), July 23, 2014, http://acrl.ala.org/dh/2014/07/23/intertwingularity-digital-humanities-university-florida.

11. Thomas Padilla, "Digital Humanities Librarianship: Year 1," *Thomas Padilla* (blog), July 13, 2014, www.thomaspadilla.org/2014/07/13/digital-humanities-librarianship-year-one.

12. William Pannapacker, "Stop Calling It 'Digital Humanities,'" *Chronicle of Higher Education*, February 18, 2013, http://chronicle.com/article/Stop-Calling-It-Digital/137325.

13. Five College Digital Humanities, "About" page, accessed July 30, 2014, http://5colldh.org/about.

14. Digital Humanities for Liberal Arts Colleges Symposium home page, accessed July 30, 2014, https://sites.google.com/a/mtholyoke.edu/digital-humanities-for-liberal-arts-colleges-symposium.

15. Roxanne Shirazi, "Reproducing the Academy: Librarians and the Question of Service in the Digital Humanities," *Roxanne Shirazi* (blog), July 15, 2014, http://roxanneshirazi.com/2014/07/15/reproducing-the-academy-librarians-and-the-question-of-service-in-the-digital-humanities.

Bibliography

Association of College and Research Libraries. "Keeping Up With…." Accessed October 25, 2014. www.ala.org/acrl/publications/keeping_up_with.

Bennett, Hannah. "The Psyche of the Library: Physical Space and the Research Paradigm." *Art Documentation* 32, no. 2 (Fall 2013): 174–85. www.jstor.org/stable/10.1086/673511.

Digital Humanities for Liberal Arts Colleges Symposium home page. Accessed July 30, 2014. https://sites.google.com/a/mtholyoke.edu/digital-humanities-for-liberal-arts-colleges-symposium

Drucker, Johanna. "The University as a Fully Integrated and Distributed Platform: A Vision." *portal: Libraries and the Academy* 14, no. 3 (2014): 325–28.

Five College Consortium home page. Accessed October 25, 2014. https://www.fivecolleges.edu.

Five College Digital Humanities. "About" page. Accessed July 30, 2014. http://5colldh.org/about.

Kirsch, Adam. "Technology Is Taking Over English Departments: The False Promise of the Digital Humanities." *New Republic*, May 2, 2014. www.newrepublic.com/article/117428/limits-digital-humanities-adam-kirsch.

Lepore, Jill. "The Disruption Machine." *New Yorker*, June 30, 2014, , http://www.newyorker.com/magazine/2014/06/23/the-disruption-machine.

One Week | One Tool homepage. Accessed October 25, 2014. http://oneweekonetool.org.

Padilla, Thomas. "Digital Humanities Librarianship: Year 1." *Thomas Padilla* (blog), July 13, 2014. www.thomaspadilla.org/2014/07/13/digital-humanities-librarianship-year-one.

Pannapacker, William. "Stop Calling It 'Digital Humanities.'" *Chronicle of Higher Education*, February 18, 2013. http://chronicle.com/article/Stop-Calling-It-Digital/137325.

Pinto, Caro. "Creative Destruction in Libraries: Designing Our Future." *In the Library with the Lead Pipe* (blog), November 20, 2013. www.inthelibrarywiththeleadpipe.org/2013/creative-destruction-in-libraries-designing-our-future.

———. "Digital Humanities Is a Team Sport: Thoughts on #DHTNG." *dh + lib* (blog), April 10, 2013. http://acrl.ala.org/dh/2013/04/10/digital-humanities-is-a-team-sport-thoughts-on-dhtng.

Shenk, Joshua Wolf. "The End of 'Genius.'" Sunday Review, *New York Times*, July 19, 2014. www.nytimes.com/2014/07/20/opinion/sunday/the-end-of-genius.html.

Shirazi, Roxanne. "Reproducing the Academy: Librarians and the Question of Service in the Digital Humanities." *Roxanne Shirazi* (blog), July 15, 2014. http://roxanneshirazi.com/2014/07/15/reproducing-the-academy-librarians-and-the-question-of-service-in-the-digital-humanities.

Taylor, Laurie, and Blake Landor. "Intertwingularity with Digital Humanities at the University of Florida." *dh + lib* (blog), July 23, 2014. http://acrl.ala.org/dh/2014/07/23/intertwingularity-digital-humanities-university-florida.

Vargas-Cooper, Natasha. *Mad Men Unbuttoned: A Romp through 1960s America*. New York: Collins Design, 2010.

Young, James E. "The Counter-Monument: Memory against Itself in Germany Today." *Critical Inquiry* 18, no. 2 (January 1, 1992): 267–96.

CHAPTER FOUR

Distant Reading, Computational Stylistics, and Corpus Linguistics

The Critical Theory of Digital Humanities for Literature Subject Librarians

David D. Oberhelman

FOR LITERATURE librarians who frequently assist or even collaborate with faculty, researchers, IT professionals, and students on digital humanities (DH) projects, understanding some of the tacit or explicit literary theoretical assumptions involved in the practice of DH can help them better serve their constituencies and also equip them to serve as a bridge between the DH community and the more traditional practitioners of literary criticism who may not fully embrace, or may even oppose, the scientific leanings of their DH colleagues.* I will therefore provide a brief overview of the theory

---

* Literary scholars' opposition to the use of science and technology is not new, as Helle Porsdam has observed by looking at the current debates over DH in the academy in terms of the academic debate in Great Britain in the 1950s and 1960s between the chemist and novelist C. P. Snow and the literary critic F. R. Leavis over the "two cultures" of science and the humanities (Helle Porsdam, "Too Much 'Digital,' Too Little 'Humanities'? An Attempt to Explain Why Humanities Scholars Are Reluctant Converts to Digital Humanities," Arcadia project report, 2011, DSpace@Cambridge, www.dspace.cam.ac.uk/handle/1810/244642).

behind the technique of DH in the case of literature—the use of "distant reading" as opposed to "close reading" of literary texts as well as the use of computational linguistics, stylistics, and corpora studies—to help literature subject librarians grasp some of the implications of DH for the literary critical tradition and learn how DH practitioners approach literary texts in ways that are fundamentally different from those employed by many other critics.[†] Armed with this knowledge, subject librarians may be able to play a role in integrating DH into the traditional study of literature.

Attempts to define DH in the modern academy tend to focus on DH as more of a series of practices and methods that utilize computer technology to examine objects studied by humanities such as literary texts.[‡] As Kathleen Fitzpatrick, Director of Scholarly Communication for the Modern Language Association, has defined DH, it is "a nexus of fields within which scholars use computing technologies to investigate the kinds of questions that are traditional to the humanities, or, as is more true of my own work, ask traditional kinds of humanities-oriented questions about computing technologies."[1] The *Digital Humanities Manifesto 2.0* issued by several UCLA researchers maintains that DH is "an array of convergent practices" in which print is no longer the privileged medium of knowledge and "digital tools, techniques, and media have altered the production and dissemination of knowledge in the arts, humanities, and social sciences."[2] DH emerged out of what had been loosely called humanities computing starting in the 1940s and 1950s and extending through the early TEI

[†]   There have not been many studies of how literature librarians can benefit from learning the basics of literary theory (apart from overall studies of the value of understanding the information needs of literary scholars), but Stephanie M. Mathson has argued that understanding and applying literary theory such as Wolfgang Iser's reader-response theory to librarian/patron service encounters can be beneficial (Stephanie M. Mathson, "Engaging Readers, Engaging Texts: An Exploration of How Librarians Can Use Reader Response Theory to Better Serve Our Patrons," *Library Philosophy and Practice* [August 2011]: 589, http://digitalcommons.unl.edu/libphilprac/589).

[‡]   For this study I will confine my exploration of DH projects to those dealing with literary topics that are textual in nature. There are many that examine the geography of regions associated with authors, historical content, economic data in literary texts, and many other aspects, but here I am concerned with projects that chiefly focus on the language and textual analysis of literary works.

encoding initiatives of the Internet age[3] and as such is usually described in terms of its practical applications.[§] Central to most definitions of DH is the basic tenet that DH is a dynamic process or methodology of using digital tools to study the humanities more than a systematic theory of how to study the humanities or, in the case of literature, how to study literary texts. Yet to understand the role of DH in literature departments, it is necessary to explore the relationship between DH and the critical theories that inform how literary scholars approach texts. Although DH may appear to be more practice than theory, it is closely related to new theoretical trends with which literature librarians should become familiar so they can better work with their patrons.

Literary Theory in the Twentieth Century: A Brief Overview

Literary critical theory, which investigates the aesthetic, philosophical, political, and cultural assumptions underlying various techniques of reading and interpreting literary texts, has been an important aspect of study in English, foreign language, and comparative literature programs in American universities. Indeed, scholars and students of literature, including literature librarians who work with them, have since the mid–twentieth century had to contend with a multitude of theoretical schools of thought or the so-called "isms" (feminism, Marxism, structuralism/poststructuralism, etc.),[**] and debates over theories of reading have been featured prominently in courses, conference papers, and publications.

---

§   The loose and somewhat informal process by which DH received its name is indicative of its practice-based and experimental foundations; it was a term suggested by John Unsworth in coming up with a title for the 2004 Blackwell *Companion to Digital Humanities* because the editors and publisher wanted to avoid *humanities computing* or *digitized humanities* (Matthew G. Kirschenbaum, "What Is Digital Humanities and What's It Doing in English Departments?" *ADE Bulletin*, no. 150 [2010]: 55–61).

**   For concise, helpful overviews of history and concepts underlying the different schools of literary theory, see Terry Eagleton, *Literary Theory: An Introduction* (Minneapolis: University of Minnesota Press, 1983) and Paul H. Fry, *Theory of Literature*, Open Yale Course Series (New Haven, CT: Yale University Press, 2012).

Many academics regard DH as an alternative to the theoretical, qualitative approaches to literature, one which brings the humanities more in line with the quantitative methods of other fields such as the social sciences and STEM disciplines. As Patricia Cohen has commented in a 2010 *New York Times* arts column, digital humanists often argue that data and big data sets should replace the competing political or philosophical systems as the key to approaching the humanities.[4] Literary theory, some DH proponents contend, is too narrow and inward-focused in its perspective on texts and therefore misses the big picture that DH methods can sketch by means of technology. Despite the insistence of DH practitioners that they are more concerned with practice than with theorizing about it, there are some fundamental theoretical presuppositions that inform the methods employed in the DH field, particularly in its literary application— presuppositions that in some way represent a theoretical paradigm shift of sorts for many critics that may explain why there is some hesitation about DH among humanities scholars (other than its obvious use of computers and scientific principles).

Central to the theory behind DH is the somewhat controversial theory the Italian-born critic Franco Moretti has termed "distant reading." In his theoretical texts and DH projects at the Stanford Literary Lab he co-founded with Matthew Jockers, Moretti articulates and models a framework for studying literature that breaks from over fifty years of theoretical tradition of close scrutiny of single texts or a delimited canon of literary works. I will offer a short summary of the theories based on close reading first, and then examine some of Moretti's theoretical pronouncements to illustrate how the "big data" approach DH takes to literature stems from a movement away from the privileging of close analysis of a single or limited group of texts.

From Close Reading to Distant Reading

Literary studies in the early decades of the twentieth century often focused on literary history, situating authors and texts in movements and establishing the canon of British, American, and other literatures. By the middle of the century, though, a group of Anglo-American literary critics such as I. A. Richards, William Empson, John Crow Ransom, and Cleanth Brooks theorized that the literary text should be studied as an object of art with laws governing its aesthetic integrity. This formalist school, which looked at how literary meaning is conveyed by or is created by the form of the text (such as the poem), became known as the New Criticism, and it ushered in a theory of close reading that would, despite changes and the advent of French philosophical and linguistic theory in the latter decades of the century, become the basic theoretical model that several generations of critics and students in American literature classes learned. Perhaps the best example of their theoretical notions appears in Brooks's 1947 collection *The Well Wrought Urn*,[5] a volume containing essays that give detailed close readings of poems by John Donne, John Keats (whose "Ode on a Grecian Urn" gives the book its title), Shakespeare, and others. The New Critical technique of close reading, which outlines the carefully balanced tensions in meaning held together by symmetry in the poetic form, reflects the theoretical premise that the critic should give a detailed, almost microscopic analysis of the literary text to find its meaning. Subsequent generations of American literary critics, many of whom were trained in close reading, argued that the New Critics divorced literary works from their historical or cultural contexts and thereby ignored important layers of meaning, but the basic belief that texts should be closely examined in terms of their own structure or logic persisted.

The appearance of French schools of literary criticism such as the structuralism of Roland Barthes, a school derived from the linguistic study of signs or semiotics of Ferdinand de Saussure and the anthropological study of myth as a system by Claude Lévi-Strauss, marked a point at which literary critics began to look at larger assemblages of texts, but close reading continued to be the dominant form of critical engagement with texts. In the 1970s and 1980s, deconstruction, the poststructuralist theory of reading texts based on the philosophical work of Jacques Derrida, had critics read for gaps, aporias (irresolvable contradictions), or traces of other concepts within their seemingly well-wrought tension of opposites that unhinge the integrity of the textual construct. For deconstructionist critics there is no "outside the text," meaning all ideas and concepts are bound to the faulty vehicle of (written) language that conveys them.†† Although Derridan theory does not look just at one book—his notion of the text covers many writings beyond the covers of one book—its central premise is that the reader must turn a critical gaze to one instance of text at a time and read it closely. Although deconstruction represented a great departure from the New Critics' view that literary works are perfect, balanced objects of art, it, as Jonathan Culler and others have noted, takes some of the New Critics' approaches to reading to their ultimate conclusion,[6] and both theories are predicated upon an intense, microscopic attention to, or perhaps dissection of, a particular text or texts. In that sense, it is not surprising that American literary critics in particular picked up many of the deconstructive processes of close reading much like they had embraced the New Criticism decades earlier.

Other schools of literary theory emerged in that period that regarded close reading of texts to be too constraining, divorcing them from the culture and the political institutions that created them. Marxist theory, feminist theory, cultural materialism, and other more engaged schools also appeared, some using psychoanalysis, political philosophy, or the discourse analysis of philosopher Michel Foucault, but in the American university setting, the close reading of texts in the literary canon, even if that canon was changed, reinvented, or expanded, was still dominant. Indeed, many of these schools, or "isms" as they are often somewhat dismissively labeled, still rely upon a close encounter with specific texts, often read in terms of different, interdisciplinary perspectives.

The dominance of close reading has been challenged in the twenty-first century, however, by the work of the DH circles that study vast assemblages of texts rather than home in on a single text. Franco Moretti, a Marxist scholar of the European novel born and trained in Italy prior to a distinguished academic career at Columbia and then Stanford University, has become the critical theorist most associated with the rise of DH

---

†† Derrida's famous aphorism in the original French is *il n'y a pas d'hors-texte*—literally, there is no outside-text, no meaning that transcends the imperfect text that expresses it (Jacques Derrida, *De la grammatologie* [Paris: Les Éditions de Minuit, 1967], 227).

and is the figure who best articulates the radical change in the approach to literary texts that the practice of DH entails. His concept of "distant reading" stands in marked opposition to the tradition of close reading, and his championing of a quantitative approach to texts that, in essence, does not involve having an individual critic read them at all gives a theoretical foundation to the disparate projects and data analyses that fall under the general moniker of DH.

Moretti's six books and numerous articles on different national traditions of the novel, the history of publishing, and related fields all reflect his conviction that literary scholars should not study individual great novels or even a narrow canon of novels, which is inevitably selective and omits the vast majority of the artistic output of any given literary time period, but rather should utilize computers to study large numbers of novels to gain a broader understanding of the genre and produce a better literary history. His seminal essay "Conjectures on a World Literature," reprinted in Moretti's award-winning 2013 collection *Distant Reading*, outlines the broad strokes of his critical theory of reading.[7] In it, Moretti questions whether scholars of literature should continue the vain task of trying to become well-read, for they will never be able to read but a miniscule, highly selective portion of the literary output of a given culture. Close reading may even be, by extension, an exercise in futility for Moretti, for picking one text to analyze or even deconstruct means hundreds of thousands have been left unread, so general conclusions about the concerns or thematic patterns in a literary age cannot legitimately be drawn. He changes the critical lens by rejecting the microscopic close reading of a single text and, instead, regards very large constellations of many literary works, which he describes a "planetary system," requiring a macroscopic approach.[8] The sheer number of texts— planets with their satellites and other bodies—defies the ability of any one critic to read them all, so Moretti calls for a new approach using alternate means to process and analyze the vast quantity of now-forgotten or unread books produced in a period or national literature. Readers must look at the big picture to discern how this system operates, and thus distant reading gives a broader perspective on literary interpretation. As a result,

Moretti hearkens back to the early theoretical aim to map out the historical contours of *Weltliteratur*, "world literature,"\" recalling the style of literary history of the pre–New Critical era, albeit using the scientific principles of the twenty-first century to survey and categorize numbers of books that would have been impossible for the earlier literary historians to read and synthesize.

Moretti's 2005 book *Graphs, Maps, and Trees* explains how his theory of distant reading can construct a large-scale literary history from models derived from quantitative history (the graphs), geography (maps), and evolutionary theory (trees).[9] Here he shows his debt to the French Marxist *Annales* school of historiography, which focuses not on extraordinary events but on the *longue durée*, or long duration, of gradual historical change coming from the bottom up rather than from the great figures down. Here, as in other works on the novel in particular, Moretti uses computer data and digitized texts to construct graphical charts out of data from several thousand texts to trace massive patterns in book history, in the development of genres, titles, characters, and other features of novels in various national literature, all rendered in graphs, charts, and other graphical forms. He has extended this work into the DH projects he has worked on for the Stanford Literary Lab (http://litlab.stanford.edu) such as *Network Theory, Plot Analysis*, a comparison of dramatic patterns from over 300 Western plays, and "The Emotions of London," a project to create an emotional map of London derived from characters' emotional states in an array of novels from the 1700s to the 1800s.[10] Here the importation of social science methods of data manipulation into the literary critical domain becomes evident.

Moretti's vision of distant reading and his approach to literary study has been criticized for its faith in a scientific method, most notably by fellow Marxist scholar Christopher Prendergast.[11] The noted critical commentator Alan Liu has pointed out in a critique of Moretti and DH that even if we accept distant reading as a theoretical paradigm, digital humanists still need to formulate a "close reading 2.0" or "a method of micro-analysis in an era of big humanities"[12]—some provision for approaching individual texts while still regarding them as parts of big planetary systems. Other theorists, nevertheless, have embraced Moretti's big data concept of literary history and find his approach liberating, an invitation to move beyond the fear of not having read "everything" (or even enough) that so frequently haunts literary scholars, and consequently allows them to seek out new ways to approach the enormity of past and present literary output. The DH critic Stephen Ramsay, noting how critics today are faced with the old dilemma, so many books, so little time, posits what he dubs the "hermeneutics of screwing around" to characterize how the great proliferation of online texts in the Internet age allows readers to engage in interpretive activity by just dipping in, following hyperlink trails, and exploring the various pathways through the mazes of webpages.[13] Moretti and his followers thus lay a foundation for DH practice that signals a departure from the literary critical theories based upon close reading and other theories that depend upon narrower canons of works rather than the enormous body of poems, plays, novels, and other literary output, most of which is now lost or forgotten.

Stylistics and Corpora

The other major theoretical foundation upon which DH rests is one that is largely derived not from literary studies per se, but from the importation of quantitative, especially computational linguistic models into the realm of literature. Language study and linguistics have long played a key role in literary criticism—and in late-twentieth-century theoretical circles, Saussure and other anthropological linguists were commonly read—but much of the data analysis that goes into the study of grammar, stylistics, and other aspects of linguistics has not been traditionally used for examining literary texts. Stylistics, the study of literary style (for author studies, period studies, and other applications), is one area in which some of the technical procedures of linguistics have been brought to bear upon creative texts and has gained greater importance with the rise of DH and its ability to let critics study the language of a text in a nonlinear fashion (as they must be in reading a printed book). In his 1986 book *Linguistic Criticism*, the noted British linguist Roger Fowler called for the application of linguistic stylistic analysis, especially the quantitative analysis of elements of language, to literary texts, arguing that there is no inherent distinction between "ordinary" uses of language and literary usage.‡‡

Linguistic studies of literary stylistics are frequently associated with analyses of a linguistic "corpus" or large, usually digital, collection of texts as data to be scrutinized. Douglas Biber and Randi Reppen (2012) outline how "corpus stylistics" makes use of computational methods and computer technology to subject literary texts, either works of one author or a larger constellation of texts in a corpus, to lexical, grammatical, and other linguistic investigation.[14] DH projects frequently create corpora for study and thus ally themselves with the computational linguists, who can provide a vocabulary and a theoretical underpinning for their work on stylistics. DH studies utilizing corpus stylistics can concentrate upon single authors, looking at their texts as whole body, or in distant reading fashion tackle the stylistic categories of a big array of digital texts much like the immense corpora of natural language gathered by linguists. One representative DH project currently under development that brings together the various strands of linguistic theory is the Tolkien Corpus Project, in which Robin Reid, an English faculty member specializing in literary stylistics, and Christian Hempelmann, a computational linguist, are in the process of creating a corpus database of the works of J. R. R. Tolkien to subject to corpus stylistics analysis.§§ Such work will be able to extend the research on Tolkien's style by putting his texts into a new framework for analysis and thus using computational linguistics to explore his syntax, grammar, and other elements, parsing the vast number of words and sentences of Tolkien

---

‡‡ Roger Fowler, *Linguistic Criticism* (Oxford: Oxford University Press, 1986). For an early application of linguistic theory to prose literary texts, see also Geoffrey Leech and Mick Short, *Style in Fiction: A Linguistic Introduction to English Fictional Prose*, English Language Series (London: Longman, 1981).

§§ Robin Anne Reid and Christian Hempelmann, "The Tolkien Corpus Project," posted April 8, 2013, on the Tolkien Scholarship Project website, http://earendel. net/?q=node/4. Reid has also published some detailed analyses of Tolkien's style using the principles of linguistic stylistics and is extending her work by the development of a true corpus of many of Tolkien's writings to facilitate a larger, big-data study of his stylistics (Robin Anne Reid, "Mythology and History: A Stylistic Analysis of *The Lord of the Rings*," *Style* 43, no. 4 [Winter 2009]: 517–38).

into units that can be scrutinized. In their collection *Digital Literary Studies*, David L. Hoover, Jonathan Culpepper, and Kiernan O'Hallaran describe their corpus stylistics projects on Shakespeare, Henry James, Wilkie Collins, and other, larger groupings of novelists.[15] They make the case that corpus stylistics is a linguistic theory that is, compared to other linguistic theories, easy to master and light on jargon; they even provide a glossary of terms at the end of the volume. These approaches demonstrate how computational linguistics and corpus stylistics can provide a theoretical support digital humanists can turn to in their mining of the textual data they have amassed.

Conclusion: Literature Librarians and Theory

Moretti's theories of distant reading and computational corpus linguistics both represent realignments in the critical approach to literary texts and a movement away from the concentrated attention to the interplay of language, its structures, and their breakdowns in a limited number of texts toward a much grander playing field in which big quantities of textual data are now the focus of study. These theories come into play in various forms for digital humanists collecting and analyzing their own databases, assemblages of texts, or other electronic objects. Literature subject librarians are generally trained in the social science and computer-based data analysis techniques of the LIS field with its own rules for gathering and interpreting information sets, but they also pay close attention to bibliographic detail in working with texts. In that sense, subject librarians, who frequently must shift between library jargon or theories of patrons' information-seeking behavior and the language of scholars or students as they conceptualize their own research methods, are adept at code switching—to use the terms Thomas Bartscherer and Roderick Coover employ to characterize interdisciplinary dialogue in the DH world[16]—so they may be able to promote code switching among their patrons who have their own divergent theoretical approaches to literature.

Thus understanding some of the literary critical theory behind DH and how it embodies a different relationship between critic and text can be very beneficial to subject specialists, for they can help serve as intermediaries or even interpreters who stand between the DH scholars and practitioners and their world of planetary systems and big data and the other literary scholars trained in the "isms" and focused on the close reading of texts, seeking to find ways to bridge the divide between these scholars as they do with collection- and item-level bibliographic control. By knowing the respective theoretical universes from which their various constituencies come, subject librarians can help find ways to encourage the ongoing integration of DH in its many forms into the literature and language departments with which they work.

Notes

1. Kathleen Fitzpatrick, "The Humanities, Done Digitally," in *Debates in the Digital Humanities*, edited by Matthew K. Gold (Minneapolis: University of Minnesota Press, 2012), 12.
2. *Digital Humanities Manifesto 2.0*, posted June 22, 2009, on *Humanities Blast* (blog) by Todd Presner, 2, www.humanitiesblast.com/manifesto/Manifesto_V2.pdf.
3. Susan Hockey, "The History of Humanities Computing," in *A Companion to Digital Humanities*, edited by Susan Schreibman, Ray Siemens, and John Unsworth (Oxford: Blackwell, 2004), www.digitalhumanities.org/companion.
4. Patricia Cohen, "Digital Keys for Unlocking the Humanities' Riches," *New York Times*, November 10, 2010, C1.
5. Cleanth Brooks, *The Well Wrought Urn: Studies in the Structure of Poetry* (New York: Harcourt, Brace and World, 1947).
6. Jonathan Culler, *On Deconstruction: Theory and Criticism after Structuralism* (Ithaca, NY: Cornell University Press, 1982).
7. Franco Moretti, "Conjectures on a World Literature," in *Distant Reading* (London: Verso, 2013), 43-62.
8. Ibid., 45.
9. Franco Moretti, *Graphs, Maps, and Trees* (London: Verso, 2005).
10. Franco Moretti, *Network Theory, Plot Analysis,* pamphlet 2 (Stanford, CA: Stanford Literary Lab, May 1, 2011), http://litlab.stanford.edu/LiteraryLabPamphlet2.pdf; "The Emotions of London," Stanford Literary Lab website, Projects page, accessed December 22, 2014, http://litlab.stanford.edu/?page_id=13.
11. Christopher Prendergast, "Evolution and Literary History: A Response to Franco Moretti," *New Left Review*, no. 34 (July–August 2005), http://newleftreview.org/II/34/christopher-prendergast-evolution-and-literary-history.
12. Alan Liu, "The State of Digital Humanities: A Report and Critique," *Arts and Humanities in Higher Education* 11, no. 1–2 (February/April 2012): 26.
13. Stephen Ramsay, "The Hermeneutics of Screwing Around; or What You Do with a Million Books," in *Pastplay: Teaching and Learning History with Technology*, edited by Kevin Kee (Ann Arbor: University of Michigan Press, 2014), 111–120.

14. Douglas Biber and Randi Reppen, "Corpus Linguistics," in *Corpus Linguistics*, edited by Douglas Biber and Randi Reppen (London: Sage, 2011), xix-vliii.
15. David L. Hoover, Jonathan Culpepper, and Kieran O'Hallaran, *Digital Literary Studies: Corpus Approaches to Poetry, Prose, and Drama*, Routledge Advances in Corpus Linguistics (New York: Routledge, 2014).
16. Thomas Bartscherer and Roderick Coover, "Introduction," in *Switching Codes: Thinking through Digital Technology in the Humanities and the Arts*, ed. Thomas Bartscherer and Roderick Coover (Chicago: University of Chicago Press, 2011), 1–11.

Bibliography

Bartscherer, Thomas, and Roderick Coover. "Introduction." In *Switching Codes: Thinking through Digital Technology in the Humanities and the Arts*, edited by Thomas Bartscherer and Roderick Coover, 1–11. Chicago: University of Chicago Press, 2011.

Biber, Douglas and Randi Reppen, eds. *Corpus Linguistics*. London: Sage, 2011.

Brooks, Cleanth. *The Well Wrought Urn: Studies in the Structure of Poetry*. New York: Harcourt, Brace & World, 1947.

Cohen, Patricia. "Digital Keys for Unlocking the Humanities' Riches." *New York Times*, November 10, 2010, C1.

Culler, J. D. *On Deconstruction: Theory and Criticism after Structuralism*. Ithaca, NY: Cornell University Press, (1982).

Derrida, Jacques. *De la grammatologie*. Paris: Les Éditions de Minuit, 1967.

Digital Humanities Manifesto 2.0. Humanities Blast (blog), posted June 22, 2009 by Todd Presner. www.humanitiesblast.com/manifesto/Manifesto_V2.pdf.

Eagleton, Terry. *Literary Theory: An Introduction*. Minneapolis: University of Minnesota Press, 1983.

Fitzpatrick, Kathleen. "The Humanities, Done Digitally." In *Debates in the Digital Humanities*, edited by Matthew K. Gold, 12–15. Minneapolis: University of Minnesota Press, 2012.

Fowler, Roger. *Linguistic Criticism*. Oxford: Oxford University Press, 1986.

Fry, Paul H. *Theory of Literature*, Open Yale Course Series. New Haven, CT: Yale University Press, 2012.

Hockey, Susan. "The History of Humanities Computing." In *A Companion to Digital Humanities*, edited by Susan Schreibman, Ray Siemens, and John Unsworth. Oxford: Blackwell, 2004. www.digitalhumanities.org/companion.

Hoover, David L., Jonathan Culpepper, and Kieran O'Hallaran. *Digital Literary Studies: Corpus Approaches to Poetry, Prose, and Drama*, Routledge Advances in Corpus Linguistics. New York: Routledge, 2014.

Kirschenbaum, Matthew G. "What Is Digital Humanities and What's It Doing in English Departments?" *ADE Bulletin*, no. 150 (2010): 55–61.

Leech, Geoffrey, and Mick Short. *Style in Fiction: A Linguistic Introduction to English Fictional Prose*, English Language Series. London: Longman, 1981.

Liu, Alan. "The State of Digital Humanities: A Report and Critique." *Arts and Humanities in Higher Education* 11, no. 1–2 (February/April 2012): 8–41.

Mathson, Stephanie M. "Engaging Readers, Engaging Texts: An Exploration of How Librarians Can Use Reader Response Theory to Better Serve Our Patrons." *Library Philosophy and Practice* (August 2011): 589. http://digitalcommons.unl.edu/libphilprac/589.

Moretti, Franco. *Distant Reading*. London: Verso, 2013.

———. *Graphs, Maps, and Trees: Abstract Models for a Literary History*. London: Verso, 2005.

———. *Network Theory, Plot Analysis*, pamphlet 2. Stanford, CA: Stanford Literary Lab, May 1, 2011. http://litlab.stanford.edu/LiteraryLabPamphlet2.pdf.

Porsdam, Helle. "Too Much 'Digital,' Too Little 'Humanities'? An Attempt to Explain Why Humanities Scholars Are Reluctant Converts to Digital Humanities." Arcadia project report, 2011. DSpace@Cambridge. www.dspace.cam.ac.uk/handle/1810/244642.

Prendergast, Christopher. "Evolution and Literary History: A Response to Franco Moretti." *New Left Review*, no. 34 (July–August 2005). http://newleftreview.org/II/34/christopher-prendergast-evolution-and-literary-history.

Ramsay, Stephen. "The Hermeneutics of Screwing Around; or What You Do with a Million Books." In *Pastplay: Teaching and Learning History with Technology*, edited by Kevin Kee, 111–20. Ann Arbor: University of Michigan Press, 2014.

Reid, Robin Anne. "Mythology and History: A Stylistic Analysis of *The Lord of the Rings*." *Style* 43, no. 4 (Winter 2009): 517–38.

Reid, Robin Anne, and Christian Hempelmann. "The Tolkien Corpus Project." Posted April 8, 2013, on the Tolkien Scholarship Project website. http://earendel.net/?q=node/4.

Stanford Literary Lab. "The Emotions of London." Stanford Literary Lab website, Projects page. Accessed December 22, 2014. http://litlab.stanford.edu/?page_id=13.

Digital Humanities

IN THE LIBRARY:

PART 2

Getting Involved in Digital Humanities

CHAPTER FIVE

Digital Humanities Curriculum Support inside the Library

Zoe Borovsky and Elizabeth McAulay

Introduction

As we entered a presentation room in the UCLA Library in June 2013, we passed library spaces overflowing with students feverishly studying and completing final papers. We were attending the end-of-term presentations for the class Ancient Near East 105: Archaeology of Egypt and Sudan, an undergraduate course taught by Professor Willeke Wendrich with which we both had been closely involved. In Spring 2013, the course was cross-listed as a qualifying elective for students pursuing a minor in digital humanities. We were excited to see the students' final projects, but we did not anticipate that this finals session would be as rigorous as a professional conference panel, and we were completely unaware that we would be observing a vibrant celebration of learning, including students' emotional displays of excitement and pride.

As we watched, we were thrilled at the level of engagement these students demonstrated, and we realized that we had contributed to a transformative learning experience. Something special had happened in this course. We knew instantly that we wanted to do more work like this, and we wanted to understand why this course had resonated so much with the students. Soon after, we learned that Wendrich planned to teach the course in the same way the following year—as a digital humanities elective and within the library. We deemed the course a success and began a more thorough analysis of which factors had contributed to that success.[*] This chapter presents our findings from this analysis as a case study and concludes with suggestions for using this model in other environments. We also note the further development that we plan to undertake in the upcoming academic year.

What Makes For Success

Through our analysis, we identified two key elements that contributed to the course's success.[†] The first, most important factor was that the subject matter was the central concern of the course rather than digital methodology.[‡] The second factor was that the course was located in the library, both physically and intellectually. Several library staff members participated in different activities to teach specific skills, provide appropriate research materials, and support student work. The staff included a subject specialist in Middle Eastern Studies (Hirsch), a subject specialist in art and architec-

---

[*] We have not yet collected quantitative indicators of the course's success, and our evaluation at this point is preliminary. Our future work will include developing instruments to allow for quantitative assessment.

[†] We presented preliminary findings on the role of instructional space for this course during a panel discussion at the Digital Library Forum 2013 in Austin, Texas (see Trevor Muñoz et al., "Past the First Bend in the Road: Reflections on the Development of Digital Scholarship Programs from Five Institutions" [panel presentation, DLF Forum, Austin, TX, November 4–6, 2013]). We are grateful to our co-panelists and to Trevor Muñoz, who moderated the session, for their observations and helpful cross-pollination.

[‡] During an informational interview with Alex Gil of Columbia University Libraries following the first iteration of the course, he confirmed that he too had found that subject specialization was key to making digital humanities activities within the library successful.

ture (Henri), a digital humanities librarian (Borovsky), a digital librarian (McAulay), a programmer/analyst (Chiong), and student staff to assist with technology support. These two critical elements to success indicated that the library's role in this course was much more than support or provision of technical assistance. Instead, subject librarians were critical partners in expanding this collaboration.

In this chapter, we present a methodology and a rationale for collaborating with faculty in digital humanities (DH) curriculum development and classroom instruction. We begin by presenting the details of the course, and then we discuss ways in which librarians and library staff are qualified for this type of engagement, no matter their DH experience level. In addition, we outline a wide range of methods for engagement with DH that can be pursued in many different settings. In conclusion, we present some suggestions of how to measure more effectively the impact of collaboration and how to scale this type of work to a larger number of courses.

The Course and the Methodology

The University of California, Los Angeles is a large, public research institution with 109 academic departments and 42,000 students. The UCLA Library is an academic research library, currently ranked eleventh among its peers. The library has a staff of circa three hundred working in several buildings. The Charles E. Young Research Library is one of the largest libraries on campus and houses collections and staff related to the humanities, arts, and social sciences. The Young Research Library was built in 1964 and underwent a significant renovation of its first floor and the floor below in 2009 and 2010. One key component of the renovation was a remodel of the first floor to include a conference center and a large space called the Research Commons. The Research Commons includes small-group study rooms, a laptop-lending office, a traditional classroom, and a large open area furnished with a variety of group work areas for Edigital collaboration. The group work areas all have digital displays that can connect to multiple laptops at a time, each with lounge or table seating arranged around the displays—we call these work areas "pods."

At the same time that the Research Commons was being designed and built in the library, several UCLA faculty members were at work establishing an official DH curriculum, which included a new academic minor for undergraduates and a certificate program for graduate students. The DH program launched in Fall 2011 and has a core faculty of thirty-five. Since that time, faculty have taught undergraduate and graduate classes in the Research Commons, and each class has been an experiment to discover the best uses for the new space.

Wendrich offered the course in the DH format for the first time in Spring 2013 and subsequently in Winter 2014.[§] In this DH-oriented course, students were organized into groups to produce a sophisticated digital encyclopedia article with cross-references, illustrations, and semantic encoding. The underlying digital architecture for the course was a web application cloned from the *UCLA Encyclopedia of Egyptology* (*UEE*). The clone web application was dubbed "Shadow UEE," and students were introduced to this publication tool very early in the term.[**]

Wendrich is the editor-in-chief of the *UEE* and served as co-principal investigator on two grants from the National Endowment for the Humanities that were instrumental in developing the *UEE* publication as both a scholarly endeavor and a web application. Therefore, when Wendrich had the idea to reuse the *UEE* infrastructure for teaching, she drew together the project team that created the *UEE* and enlisted their support to implement the Shadow UEE.[††] Programmers worked in advance of the spring term to

---

[§]   The syllabi for Spring 2013 and Winter 2014 are available at "Ancient Near East M105: Archaeology of Egypt and Sudan," UCLA Library website, last updated July 28, 2014, http://guides.library.ucla.edu/anne-m105.

[**]   The *UCLA Encyclopedia of Egyptology* is available online at www.uee.ucla.edu. Access to the articles and different browse pages is open, but a user needs to log in using one of numerous ID services (Google, Yahoo, etc.) to see those pages. The Shadow UEE is available at http://shadowuee.idre.ucla.edu.

[††]   The project, which began officially in 2006, was funded by two grants from the National Endowment of the Humanities and contributions from UCLA's Digital Library Program, the Center for Digital Humanities and Academic Technology Services. Although the *UEE* was designed as a professional scholarly publication platform, Wendrich was involved in other projects, such as Digital Karnak, that focused on creating classroom materials. Since Borovsky worked as *UEE*'s project coordinator and McAulay worked as markup specialist, we were familiar with those roles and had taught these skills to graduate students working on the project.

clone the web application and prepare it for students to use. Meanwhile, Borovsky collaborated with Wendrich to develop the group assignment, the course syllabus, and the logistics of the course, including where the class would be held and which library resources could be used to enhance the lab time. Then Wendrich requested that an art history and architecture librarian, Janine Henri, teach a special session on methods for finding images to illustrate the students' articles. Henri also taught students how to evaluate copyright status and how to seek permission from publishers or creators. Another guest speaker was McAulay, who lectured on the Text Encoding Initiative (TEI) and demonstrated the way it is used in the *UEE*. Thus, the course design and instruction were truly collaborative, and no one instructor was an expert on all the concepts and methods that the students were learning.

This collaboration was an essential component of the course's success for several reasons. During a retrospective review of the two courses,[‡‡] Wendrich identified one of our most important decisions as actually being Borovsky's suggestion. Wendrich planned to divide the class into groups, with each group focused on a topic from a list that she and the TA prepared in advance. In order to divide up the work within each of the groups, Borovsky suggested that each member of the group assume a role. The roles were modeled upon ones from the *UEE*: a project coordinator, a content developer, a copy editor, an image coordinator, a metadata specialist, and a markup specialist. Wendrich opted to allow the students to choose roles within their groups.

In addition, since several librarians contributed to the course, each librarian was able to provide a specialized instructional session, which meant more librarians could participate and divide the work. In particular, the course benefited from having three different subject librarians involved. Their subject knowledge was crucial to providing students with the resources and methods they needed to do their research. Meanwhile, metadata, instructions on how to use the *UEE* web application, databases,

---

[‡‡] We met with Wendrich in May 2014 to review our observations about the two iterations of the course.

and TEI markup were handled by McAulay. This specialization allowed for significant DH engagement between the library and the faculty without having every librarian trained in DH.

Another important feature of the course was that it was taught inside the library. Lectures were held one morning a week in the research library's newly renovated conference room, and later that day, students met for a three-hour lab in the library's Research Commons. This environment allowed students to collaborate with each other, Wendrich, the teaching assistant, and the librarian liaisons to make progress on their digital research projects. During lab time, students had access to a special book cart of reserve materials (selected before the term began by Hirsch), and laptops from the lending service. By holding the class and lab in the library, we were able to consistently highlight services and collections that were available.

Having the physical setting of the course in the library, as well as having undergraduates publish their essays online, helped to embed students in the research process and scholarly workflow. They were not merely consumers of scholarly products—with librarians to assist in that transaction—but were deeply engaged with their peers, faculty, and librarians in the process of learning and producing digital research projects. Although the students' articles were published online in a separate version of the *UEE*, their process closely mirrored the production cycle of the scholarly *UEE*, from commissioning articles from authors, through peer-review, and finally, publication. Students voiced their pride and enthusiasm for their projects, and we hypothesized that sentiment arose in part from giving their articles the same presentation on the web in the Shadow UEE as the expert scholars received in the main *UEE*.[§§] In addition, students were better able to perceive scholarship as a conversation in which they could

---

§§ The *UEE* articles are written by international experts, and thus, the students' articles could not replicate the same depth. Therefore, the articles were not integrated with the full *UEE*, but they were published in the clone platform. The student UEE, though, is not restricted and is as widely available as the main *UEE*. The student work is visible to everyone in the class, and was throughout the development process, and students and others can easily alert friends, family, and colleagues about their work. While the online publication might not have been significant to students who are "digital natives," the unique opportunity to work with the application that had been designed for scholars seemed to bestow on the students a sense of worth on their work that was unfamiliar.

participate. With this realization, they started to see the library as more than a mere repository of books and a quiet place to study. It was a site of both discovery and production. Librarians were viewed not merely as gate-keepers, but as active partners in producing scholarship.

Impact and Innovation

As we watched students present their work in Spring 2013, their engagement with the course content and with their fellow students, faculty, librarians, and the tools was evidence enough to convince us that our effort had been worth the time we had invested in realizing the course. We marveled at the students' ability to take the eccentricities of TEI markup in stride and with passion. Even more astonishing was their willingness, after an introduction to finding images that included the complexities of copyright, to write to publishers seeking permission to use images in their projects. It was gratifying that our colleagues also thought that the library's effort had been worthwhile. They, too, remarked that the final presentations demonstrated that students had a deeper understanding of the research process and scholarly communication.

At the outset, we feared that providing an on-site print collection and no formal instruction of how to make use of the material might discourage students from finding resources on their own. However, students began retrieving books from the stacks and taught others in their pods to do the same. Students were also surprised to learn about the roles the library played in digitizing resources, making those resources discoverable, and developing projects such as the *Encyclopedia of Egyptology*. Holding the final presentations in the main conference room of the library and inviting other faculty, librarians, and the students' friends to the presentations was a powerful demonstration of connecting and opening the classroom to the broader community. Just as students valued making their essays available online to the public, they viewed the library as an open space for creating and displaying scholarly works and discussions.

We realized, however, that the amount of time we spent on this course was more than librarians usually spend on instructing undergraduates in courses focused on a traditional research paper. We discussed whether this approach was scalable, and those discussions informed our plans for the course the following year. When the course was offered in Winter 2014, the TA for the course taught the guest lecture on TEI markup. While McAulay still attended some lab sessions for troubleshooting, we were able to reduce the amount of time spent preparing and the need for our physical presence during lab sessions. The TA, an Egyptology graduate student who had learned TEI markup to work as a content editor for the *UEE*, was now teaching those skills as part of an undergraduate course in her subject area. Rather than viewing those skills as separate from her academic training, the course provided her with an opportunity to integrate her digital skills with instruction and research.

We also began to assess and articulate the benefits of the course from the librarian perspective. In addition to measuring the impact on student learning, we saw a value in longer-term engagements with librarians outside our home departments. While we had worked together in a production environment on the *UEE*, our work was inward-facing and shared largely with the project team. The course, in contrast, made our teamwork very visible and demonstrated the productive partnerships among faculty, graduate students, librarians, and technologists. By making the final presentations open and extending invitations to all librarians, we worked to alleviate anxieties that participation in DH projects devalued the traditional skills of subject librarians. Several of our library colleagues have expressed dismay when an article or report mentions "re-skilling" or "re-tooling" librarians to meet the needs of scholars doing digital projects.*** Instead, we

---

*** For example, see Mary Auckland, *Re-skilling for Research* (London: Research Libraries UK, January 2012), www.rluk.ac.uk/wp-content/uploads/2014/02/RLUK-Re-skilling. pdf.Our approach aligns with Posner's suggestion that librarians participate in "targeted, collaborative, project-based training in a relatively low-stakes, supportive environment" (Miriam Posner, "No Half Measures: Overcoming Common Challenges to Doing Digital Humanities in the Library," *Journal of Library Administration* 53, no. 1 [2012]: 50, doi:10.1080/01930826.2013.756694). Others (e.g., Trevor Muñoz, "Digital Humanities in the Library Isn't a Service," *Trevor Muñoz: Writing* [blog]. August 19, 2012, http://trevormunoz.com/notebook/2012/08/19/doing-dh-in-the-library.html) have sought to reframe the issue by advocating for library-initiated projects, i.e., ones that are led by librarians.

encouraged librarians to participate as an extension of their subject exper-tise and offered a chance to learn more about digital scholarship methods.

Moreover, we fostered the idea that investing time in longer-term curricular engagements provides cross-training opportunities that would build toward a more diverse and sustainable ecosystem of librarians. Li-brarians do not need to learn DH skills to be involved in DH courses. We are working in increasingly collaborative methods, and digital scholarship is an excellent area to bring differently skilled team members together. Librarians can work with a team engaged in digital research without be-ing DH-trained or even digitally inclined. At most institutions, there are willing collaborators who can provide the technology expertise while li-brarians can provide research guidance, curricular input, and curation of research materials. Librarians can seek out these opportunities as part of their usual outreach, while library leaders should foster collaboration and team-based approaches to curricular support.

Variations

While we have presented a detailed case study of the way this course col-laboration worked, we also are interested in sharing some ways we feel this approach can be varied and still yield significant benefits. It is pos-sible to teach a similar course in a classroom or lab outside the library. The decision to host the course in the library was a strategic step that we decided to take. Because both labs and lectures for the course were located in the library, students and librarians benefited. Students' notions of the library transformed, and librarians' notions of digital scholarship became more informed. We were pleased and astonished by the former, which en-couraged us to take bolder strides towards the latter. In doing so, we first realized that in designing the UCLA Library Research Commons for digi-tal scholarship, we had created a "digital divide" that affected how students and librarians viewed these recently renovated spaces. As we planned the lab sessions in the pod area, we realized there were no bookshelves in the Research Commons. Across the hall in the Reading Room, students could bring their laptops and work alongside the reference collection. To integrate books into the digital environment of the pods, we opted for a mobile book cart that could be wheeled in each week.

Secondly, hosting the course in the library brought librarians, even those not involved in the course, into contact with students, faculty, and librarians engaged in digital scholarship. Because the class met every week in the pod area—a location that is not only open and visible, but also conveniently located near a very popular cafe—librarians who would not otherwise work closely with a DH course could pass through and see students working in the pods, using the collection, and engaging their peers to produce digital projects. Hosting the course in the library reduced anxieties about digital scholarship and, through the students, demonstrated the value of DH.

Finally (and this was an unexpected outcome), we saw that the undergraduate student employees in the Research Commons connected the work they were being paid to perform—helping students check out laptops and use the pods—to learning and the library. These students began to view themselves as partners in the process of performing digital scholarship in the Research Commons.

Conclusion and Recommendations

Based on our experience with this course at UCLA, we believe there are several avenues for adapting this method to a wide range of other library and DH collaborations. We will conclude by suggesting a few different approaches to achieving similar results in other institutions as well as presenting the future activities we intend to undertake at UCLA to continue this collaboration with undergraduate instruction.

For ANE 105, we converted a DH research project into a platform for undergraduate instruction. While this exact scenario may be rare, the general principle is widely applicable: repurpose pre-existing web or software applications for use in the classroom. When the *UEE* was under development, the project team did not intend it to be used for instruction. Yet the web application turned out to be a perfect framework for students to use for complex group projects. We also believe that by reusing a scholarly platform, the students felt that their projects were more meaningful and that they were getting access to an authentic publishing experience. There are many small and large technology tools or frameworks that are used for normal workflow or for research projects, and these frameworks can serve as tools to enable students to do more sophisticated work.[†††]

Prior to Spring 2013, we had been running workshops in the library and teaching special sessions for DH courses. In those instances, students were learning about DH methodology, but they often struggled to understand its utility because they were not assigned projects that required them to apply what they had learned. These workshops and even special class presentations felt ancillary to the work of the course itself. In Wendrich's class, though, Ancient Egypt's 25th Dynasty was the focus, and the DH methods were a way to engage with the subject matter rather than vice versa. Subject knowledge, therefore, was more important than the DH skills. In addition, the non-DH subject librarians were an integral part of making this course a success because they could select the right resources and guide students in doing online research.

In our case, both subject and digital librarians supported the course. However, we believe that the same success could be achieved without any digital specialists from the library. Digital expertise or technical support could be provided by other campus partners. The best approach is to work in a team that has both subject expertise and digital experience.

As we have noted earlier, this course took a significant dedication of time from multiple librarians and additional university staff. We were motivated to experiment with that level of commitment because it was also an opportunity to host a class in the library's new study space, the Research Commons. Hosting the class in the library has many advantages. Most notably, it made the library physically the center of students' research and

---

††† We view the development of workshops or sessions that focus on pedagogy at digital humanities institutes and conferences as evidence that other examples of integrating digital humanities research projects into courses are emerging at other institutions. See, for example, information on the Digital Humanities Summer Institute (DHSI) on the Digital Pedagogy website (Katherine D. Harris, Diane Jakacki, and Jentery Sayers, Digital Pedagogy home page, 2012, http://web.uvic.ca/~englblog/pedagogydhsi.)

class work, and with the variety of staff supporting the class, the students got to experience the wide range of services available from the library.

Having a new, inviting space for students to work in was just incidental. We believe that students will still gain a greater understanding of the library and its services if a class is hosted in the library in any type of space. We posit that the number of resources and the time dedicated to the course could also be scaled back and it could still be effective. Staff or librarians could drop in on the course rather than staying for the full lab period and still give students the sense that they were working in a place where staff members were interested in helping. Likewise, one of the simplest services we provided was a book cart of relevant materials, like a moveable reserves shelf. Whether there were one hundred or twenty books on the cart was somewhat immaterial; the fact that the books came to the students encouraged them to use the reserves materials more heavily and to pursue additional resources on their own. One student exclaimed during a lab session after searching the library catalog, "They have the book right upstairs! I'm going to go get it!" This moment was one of many where a student showed true enthusiasm for his or her work and shared it openly with the rest of the class.

After the course was held for the second time, we met with Wendrich and compared our observations. We all agreed that the course had been a tremendous success. In our discussions, we worked together to isolate which features had made the biggest impact. We also made plans to do further quantitative and qualitative analysis to gain a better insight into the impact the course has on students' learning and research experiences. From further work, we plan to develop a set of new measurements for recording librarian impact on undergraduate instruction. Currently, library instructional metrics are biased toward transactional statistics—how many thousands served?—as opposed to measures of student impact or student success. Following students' progress after the course by reconvening their project teams as focus groups would allow us to better measure the impact of this type of course. We believe that these types of initiatives will be exciting avenues for subject librarians, who can bring core research content to students and enable active learning that digital humanities experts alone cannot support.

Bibliography

Auckland, Mary. *Re-skilling for Research*. London: Research Libraries UK, January 2012. www.rluk.ac.uk/wp-content/uploads/2014/02/RLUK-Re-skilling.pdf.

Harris, Katherine D., Diane Jakacki, and Jentery Sayers. Digital Pedagogy home page. 2012. http://web.uvic.ca/~englblog/pedagogydhsi.

Muñoz, Trevor. "Digital Humanities in the Library Isn't a Service." *Trevor Muñoz: Writing* (blog), August 19, 2012. http://trevormunoz.com/notebook/2012/08/19/doing-dh-in-the-library.html.

Muñoz, Trevor, Jennifer Guiliano, Andrew Ashton, Zoe Borovsky, Elizabeth McAulay, Devin Becker, Annie Gaines, and Allan Tullos. "Past the First Bend in the Road: Reflections on the Development of Digital Scholarship Programs from Five Institutions." Panel presentation, DLF (Digital Library Foundation) Forum, Austin TX, November 4–6, 2013.

Posner, Miriam. "No Half Measures: Overcoming Common Challenges to Doing Digital Humanities in the Library." *Journal of Library Administration* 53, no. 1 (2012): 43–52. doi:10.1080/01930826.2013.756694.

UCLA Library. "Ancient Near East M105: Archaeology of Egypt and Sudan." UCLA Library website. Last updated July 28, 2014. http://guides.library.ucla.edu/anne-m105.

Wendrich, Willeke. "Shadow UEE." Accessed January 28, 2015. http://shadowuee.idre.ucla.edu.

———, ed. *UCLA Encyclopedia of Egyptology*. Los Angeles: UCLA, 2008. www.uee.ucla.edu.

CHAPTER SIX

A Checklist for Digital Humanities Scholarship

Elizabeth Lorang and Kathleen A. Johnson

WITH VARIED training, experience, and interest, and working at widely different colleges and universities, subject librarians may be well prepared or utterly at sea when students and faculty ask for help with creating digital humanities scholarship. But as subject specialists increasingly connect patrons to resources both within and outside the library for developing digital humanities scholarship or collaborate in creating projects, they must have a core of knowledge and practical resources for working with their researchers. To help develop this core of knowledge, this chapter addresses foundational issues that arise in the process of creating digital humanities scholarship and offers some practical guidance. Specifically, this chapter provides a checklist for managing crucial points throughout the scholarship life cycle—whether the project is an undergraduate's class activity, a

We would like to thank Katherine Walter, Chair of Digital Initiatives and Special Collections and Co-Director of the Center for Digital Research in the Humanities at University of Nebraska–Lincoln, and the fellows of the UNL Digital Scholarship Incubator—Rebecca Ankenbrand, Geraldine Dobos, Kevin McMullen, and Brian Sarnacki—for their input on this essay and checklist.

graduate student's first foray into digital scholarship, or a new or experienced faculty member's enterprise, and whether or not one's institution has an established support structure for digital scholarship. This chapter has emerged in part from discussions at a range of professional conferences and meetings, in which subject librarians have expressed significant concern about not knowing where to begin when researchers ask for assistance in their digital humanities research and scholarship. The goal of this chapter is to provide subject librarians a compact, streamlined resource to consult when approached by researchers whose scholarly questions require an engagement with digital humanities methods. This checklist does not endeavor to be a detailed how-to, but rather to develop a framework within which subject specialists can work with researchers.

Why create a checklist for digital humanities scholarship, and what is the place of a checklist in an enterprise that depends so heavily on innovation and creativity? In developing a checklist for digital humanities scholarship, we draw on Dr. Atul Gawande's *Checklist Manifesto*. Gawande is a surgeon who was asked by the World Health Organization to help develop an approach to reduce surgical errors.[1] To learn more about how other professions avoid errors, he consulted with construction engineers and aviation specialists. *The Checklist Manifesto* details the process by which Gawande came to value and then develop a checklist to improve patient outcomes worldwide in surgery and to advocate for the use of checklists in any complex endeavor. "[T]he reliable management of complexity… ," Gawande writes, "requires balancing a number of virtues: freedom and discipline, craft and protocol, specialized ability and group collaboration."[2] He goes on to explain how checklists can help manage complexity and strike a balance between the sometimes competing virtues (e.g., freedom and discipline): "They supply a set of checks to ensure the stupid but critical stuff is not overlooked, and they supply another set of checks to ensure people talk and coordinate and accept responsibility while nonetheless being left the power to manage the nuances and unpredictabilities the best they know how."[3] Following Gawande's model, this chapter aims to help manage the complexities of digital humanities scholarship to ensure that critical steps are not overlooked. In documenting the critical steps that cut across projects, the checklist also enables scholars to focus their energy on creativity, craft, and imagination—other key features of successful scholarship.

The umbrella term *digital humanities* covers a wide variety of approaches and types of projects, and digital humanities' definition as a field, a set of methodologies, a community of practice, a movement, or something else altogether remains an ongoing point of discussion.* Digital humanities writ large includes research and pedagogical activities, as well as public programming, and the boundaries between these activities are fluid. While subject librarians should be aware of the unfixed nature of definitions for digital humanities, the indefinite nature of the terminology ultimately is not crucial to the work of this chapter. This chapter focuses on scholarly projects in the humanities that further conversations in the researchers' fields of study and for which digital methodologies are a critical component of research, analysis, or dissemination.

In constructing a checklist for digital humanities scholarship, our goal has been to focus rather than to exclude. Our checklist endeavors to fit a wide range of digital humanities scholarship, from Web-based projects to large-scale data mining. While the sources, methods, and products of these scholarly endeavors will vary, certain key activities must be accomplished for successful digital humanities scholarship across the spectrum.† To that end, we are interested not in what is the same or what is different in the digital or in claiming any kind of shift—epistemological, paradigmatic, or otherwise—but rather in documenting what is necessary for creating successful digital humanities scholarship in a very practical sense.

Background: Lessons on Digital Humanities

The University of Nebraska–Lincoln (UNL) is a land-grant research university of 25,000 students with very high research activity and is a member of the Committee on Institutional Cooperation (CIC).[4] Before getting to

---

* For a sampling of pieces that take up defining digital humanities and digital scholarship, see "Readings on Defining Digital Humanities" at the end of this chapter.

† For a selection of pieces that discuss the work of building in digital humanities, see "Readings on Doing Digital Humanities" at the end of this chapter.

the checklist proper, we want to reflect on a few lessons learned at UNL regarding digital humanities work over the past fifteen-plus years. These lessons continue to guide the efforts of the UNL Libraries and the Center for Digital Research in the Humanities to develop digital humanities scholarship in the present, and they form a backbone for the checklist that follows. Although these lessons come out of our specific institutional context, they apply broadly to the creation of digital humanities scholarship.

Lesson One

Space and equipment are not the only—nor even the most important—requirements for successful digital scholarship. Developing a knowledge base is far more crucial than physical space or technical infrastructure. Although UNL Libraries set up an E-Text Center with new desktop computers and some cutting-edge digitization equipment in the later 1990s, the library staff as well as the humanities and social science researchers had not yet developed a solid understanding of what digital scholarship might entail. In the years since, as UNL founded and developed the Center for Digital Research in the Humanities (CDRH) as a joint initiative of the University Libraries and College of Arts and Sciences, library leaders and others learned from the early experience of the E-Text Center. The E-Text Center was incorporated into the CDRH with a far more robust vision of the potential for digital humanities research and scholarship and with the necessary intellectual frameworks and staff in place. Now nearly two decades and many projects later, the CDRH launched a pilot program called the Digital Scholarship Incubator in spring 2014. Although a small, designated space with basic computing equipment is part of the Incubator, its most important characteristic is knowledge exchange: graduate student fellows agree to develop their projects in the co-working space, so that they can take advantage of the group's collective knowledge. In addition, the Incubator director works to connect the students with individuals inside the library and elsewhere on campus, as well as with information resources. The emphasis in this space is not on high or bleeding-edge technology. Rather, the space is about collective knowledge and relationships. This first lesson is significant for subject librarians because they may see the first move within institutions, or the desires of their patrons, to be for space and equipment; what is most crucial, however, is connecting individuals or groups with information, serving as a liaison for users both within the library and between the library and other campus entities, and connecting people with resources and with one another.

Lesson Two

As with scholarship in any form or medium, the researcher must be able to articulate the scholarly conversation in which her project participates, and the project should create new knowledge. Some digital projects are routine digitization endeavors: they create digital resources that are fundamentally about access to materials. These more routine digitization initiatives can usefully be compared with the electronic scholarly editions published in the open-access journal *Scholarly Editing* or the multimodal scholarship of the journal *Vectors*.[5] All of these projects involve digitization at some level, but the difference is not simply one of scale, the large-scale versus the "boutique."

In the case of editions in *Scholarly Editing*, the digitization of a text through page images and transcription is often one component of the work. In proposing an edition for *Scholarly Editing*, however, the editor must craft both a statement of significance for the edition as well as a statement of editorial approach—an editorial policy and editorial philosophy. Thus, in his "Introduction to '*Avisos a pretendientes para Indias*,'" Clayton McCarl offers a lengthy discussion of the editorial philosophy underlying the preparation of the edition, and he connects that philosophy of the edition to all of its components, including transcription, encoding, annotation, and web display. He writes, in part, "A guiding principle behind this project has been a desire to exploit the possibilities of TEI XML to document and reveal the various levels of editorial and translational decisions involved."[6] Likewise, in the Fall 2013 issue of *Vectors*, contributor Emily Thompson, creator of "The Roaring 'Twenties: An Interactive Exploration of the Historical Soundscape of New York City," wrote to introduce her project, "The aim here is not just to present sonic content, but to evoke the original contexts of those sounds, to help us better understand that context as well as the sounds themselves. The goal is to recover the meaning of sound, to undertake a historicized mode of listening that tunes our modern ears to the pitch of the past. Simply clicking a 'play' button will not do."[7] Digital humanities scholarship requires an intellectual engagement with how the methods, form, and medium of the scholarship further the argument the scholar seeks to advance. As Thompson's description of her work makes clear, digital humanities scholarship may grow out of digitization— the digitization of a corpus of texts or images, for example, may lead to research questions or allow one to make the critical point. Especially when working with undergraduate students, it is valuable for a subject librarian to help them understand the difference between routine digitization and the development of a project that seeks to address a research question.

Lesson Three

While nearly all scholarship in any form requires collaboration, a remarkable feature of digital humanities scholarship is the way it foregrounds collaboration, often through the formation of interdisciplinary research groups. Such a group might include scholars from one or more disciplines, graduate or undergraduate students, librarians, and technologists. Various articles have commented on the ways in which such collaborations may blur the roles of the participants and how collaborative engagement in a research question or project may result in more satisfying results. Any such endeavor requires commitment of team members to listen to one another's opinions and to value the different skills and knowledge of the individuals within the group. It also requires that the project director recognize when the group's collective opinions should supersede personal inclinations. This can actually be crucial to the research.‡

Subject Librarians and the Digital Humanities

As a subject librarian, you already have many of the tools necessary, and you know more than you think you do, to be able to assist researchers in the development of digital humanities scholarship. Knowing what is

---

‡ For a selection of pieces that deal with collaboration in digital humanities, see "Readings on Collaborating in Digital Humanities" at the end of this chapter.

happening in the departments you serve as well as knowing your institution's collections remains critical and will allow you to be proactive in your support of digital humanities scholarship. Being aware of the interests and strengths of researchers in your departments allows you to connect them with archival or special collections from which digital humanities scholarship might emerge. It also puts the subject librarian in a position to advocate within the library and elsewhere for resources to meet researchers' needs, whether content and materials or technology. Developing and maintaining relationships with vendors also remains important. For data-mining projects, researchers sometimes need access to the underlying data of a service rather than access via the product's typical web interface. The subject librarian may serve as a liaison between the researcher and the vendor, potentially working also with acquisitions staff or legal departments. In this scenario as well, the subject librarian serves as an advocate for the information needs of the researcher. Subject librarians might also raise matters of copyright, preservation, and archiving of the project or of elements of data in the project, as well as offering traditional reference assistance and alerting people to the existence of relevant resources outside of one's home library. Beyond these specific kinds of assistance, by drawing on the checklist in this chapter, you will provide your faculty and students with a larger framework to think through the entire process and to see how your knowledge and skills fit into the big picture.

With a major digital humanities unit already in place at our institution, subject librarians have played many roles in the development of various projects. In several cases, subject librarians have served as the project director or principal investigator and have guided the intellectual pursuits and outcomes of their projects.[§] More frequently, however, UNL subject librarians have served in supporting roles: they have helped with early digital humanities project development; served on a joint library and

---

§   Two examples of digital humanities projects created by UNL librarians are the *American Indian Treaties Portal,* headed by UNL Documents Librarian Professor Charles Bernholz (University of Nebraska–Lincoln website, accessed July 21, 2014, http://treatiesportal.unl.edu), and Architecture Librarian Professor Kay Logan-Peters's *Architectural Tour of Historic UNL* (*see* "About the Project," accessed July 21, 2014, http://historicbuildings.unl.edu/about).

college advisory committee centered on digital humanities, alerted faculty members to the existence of relevant collections within a larger special collection, purchased microfilms needed for a digital project, connected faculty members to resource people who could provide the underlying data for data mining, encouraged graduate students and faculty to follow standards and best practices, developed metadata frameworks according to community standards, and helped to assess the usability and enhancement of completed projects. At institutions without an established digital humanities program, the subject librarian might well find himself or herself called to provide more extensive assistance. Regardless of the level of involvement subject librarians may have in digital humanities at different institutions, as the most successful subject librarians do, continue to perform environmental scans and develop habits of mind for working with your researchers in their specific areas. The following annotated checklist articulates many of the habits of mind a subject librarian needs to use in working with any digital humanities project.

Annotated Checklist

As noted above, the goal of this checklist is to provide a framework within which subject specialists can work with researchers. This checklist is not intended to capture every contingency or to explain how to perform each step, but to raise foundational issues in creating successful digital humanities scholarship. This document is designed for subject specialists to use as they consult with the researchers they assist in connecting scholars with information, opportunities, and possibilities, but also as they develop their own scholarly projects. Ultimately, it is the scholar, or a designated member of the project team, who is responsible for completing each of the items in the checklist. Thus, the "you" referenced in the checklist items refers to the researcher or scholar.

☑ **Articulate the project's research question and the scholarly conversation being entered.**

The boundaries between "routine" digitization and scholarship are not hard and fast, of course, but within a scholarly project it is fundamental from the outset that the scholar be able to articulate the research question and the scholarly conversations in which the project participates. Over time, the argument or thesis should develop.

☑ **Research other projects with similar research aims or methodologies.**

This step is analogous to performing a literature review before starting research and writing. Doing so ensures you do not pour your heart and soul into something someone has already done, and it may suggest possible collaborators.

☑ **Define the scope of the project.**

Set out the boundaries for the project, including the beginning and ending of the project, what it will accomplish, and the primary audience. If you fail to define a project, you risk struggling with a scope that continually changes and, consequently, never finishing the project.

You need a base project to build on first. It is best to keep track of good ideas, but to stick to the boundaries. At the same time, be prepared to evaluate progress toward your stated goal. Before revising the scope of the project, carefully consider the consequences of scope change, and remember that resources—including time— are finite. If the scope must change for a legitimate reason, reassess whether the project can be completed with the resources you have or can draw on.

☑ **Evaluate needed and available resources.**

Determine what resources are necessary to complete the project (hardware, software, content, expertise). Perform this evaluation early to get a handle on what it will take to complete the project. Assess what resources are available at your institution, both within and outside the library, as well as in the community. If you do not have access to all of the necessary resources, how might the problem be solved (changing the project scope, partnering with another institution or bringing additional collaborators on board, employing a different technological solution)? Bear in mind that sometimes a lack of resources leads to creative solutions.

The resource evaluation may indicate that funding (whether internal or external) is needed in order to complete the project work. If the project requires funding, at what stage is funding needed and at what level? Where might this funding be secured? If you think the project needs funding, does that suggest a need to reconceptualize the project to complete it with resources at hand? If you need outside funding, what does that mean for the timeline of the project? Is it more important to get something done now, or can you wait for grant funding that may or may not come through? If funding is necessary, factor in the time involved to research funding opportunities, write proposals, and wait on funding decisions.

☑ Identify project participants.

Digital humanities projects regularly involve a range of participants, including scholars and librarians as well as students, information technology professionals, and people from outside of the academic community. Assess early in the project who these participants should be. You cannot develop your project further without the right team. Have a frank discussion about what it means to have each person involved in the project. Include in this discussion participant roles and how people will be credited and acknowledged.[8]

☑ Develop a communication plan.

A communication plan articulates the etiquette for how the team will communicate with one another and externally about the project. Within the team, what is a reasonable time to wait for an answer from another project participant? The communication plan may state that a lack of response is agreement and that the person asking for input will then be able to take action.

The communication plan should spell out not only how creators of the project will communicate, but also how inquiries will be handled once the project or project results are public. What is an acceptable time frame to respond? How will you document your response? Will other project members need to receive a copy of the response?

☑ **Investigate issues regarding intellectual property.**

There are a host of issues to consider regarding intellectual property and digital humanities scholarship. Before proceeding with the project, have clarity about copyright and fair use for any intellectual property used by the project. Always articulate why you have the right to use content, even if the justification seems obvious. For intellectual property created for the project, investigate issues relating to development of potentially marketable products (such as software). Who—an individual, the team, the institution—will own the scholarship and any products? Under what terms will the project's intellectual property be made available? Document all of the decisions made about intellectual property both used by and created for the project.

☑ **Develop a project work plan.**

Identify the order of activities and the critical paths. What must happen before or after something else? What things can be done concurrently? Break the project into smaller pieces and establish milestones and benchmarks for each of these pieces as well as for the overall project. Set deadlines for the goals and monitor progress in order to avoid scope creep and project drift.

The work plan should also include a budget. You may not have a pool of money with which to work, but participants' time should be included in the budget. Remember, no one has limitless time to work on a project. Treating time as money will help to evaluate whether the goals and timeline are reasonable.

☑ **Develop a data management plan.**

Determine what project materials will need to be maintained beyond the research stage, by whom, and for how long. Project data might include source code, incoming data being processed, data results of running software, and analyses. Not everything has to be saved or maintained, but for parts of the project for which long-term use is possible, what must you do to assure that others will be able to access and use those materials? Start planning for data management at the beginning of the project because your choices will affect what data will be retained and how the data can be managed. Funding agencies increasingly require thinking about these issues before they will provide support.**

☑ **Assess project development.**

Regularly assess whether actual project work matches with the scope, timeline, goals, and budget articulated in the project initiation phase. Respond to changes as necessary. Repeat this step throughout the project work stage.

Stay alert to mission creep. Work plans are projections. You may not have the timeline right for some elements. You may have to take longer on one aspect than planned but still have a fixed deadline. What do you do to complete the work in light of change in available time? Figure out how you can respond to unexpected roadblocks.

☑ **Document project work.**

Document work throughout the entire project. With multiple people working on most digital humanities projects, turnover happens.

** For examples of data management plans submitted for NEH-funded digital humanities projects, see National Endowment for the Humanities, "Digital Humanities Start-up Grants," accessed July 15, 2014, www.neh.gov/grants/odh/digital-humanities-start-grants.

Without documentation, a new person coming into a crucial role might have to start fresh. He or she may have to piece together the past and may make wrong assumptions; moreover, it is a waste of time to have to recreate and backtrack. Even without staff turnover, with any digital humanities project, you might step away for a few weeks to work on other responsibilities; upon return, it is hard to remember even a short time later what you did or how you did it.

Later, writing up project results also requires good documentation, and you will need detailed, sound documentation for peer review. Document both the humanities content and that you have used best practices for your field.

☑ **Seek evaluation and peer review.**

At the outset of the research endeavor, members of the project team should discuss requirements and options for evaluation of their scholarship. A host of issues, including status and rank of the scholars, requirements of sponsoring institutions and organizations, team members' ideals, and the project's purpose, may affect decisions about what form and level of evaluation is necessary. While all scholarship benefits from evaluation, for faculty seeking tenure or promotion, evaluation and peer review are especially crucial.

Time-tested methods of peer review remain viable for some forms of digital humanities scholarship: data and results of a data-mining project, for example, may be presented in a peer-reviewed journal article or in an essay collection or monograph from an academic publisher. For other scholarly products, such as websites, databases, and software code, structures for evaluation and peer review in the humanities may be less fixed.[9] Professional organizations and less formal communities of practice can offer valuable information and resources as you consider your options for evaluation.

At the conclusion of the project, follow up on the evaluation plan.

☑ **Disseminate results.**

Project results may culminate in an article, book, series of blog posts, website, source code, or input and output data, in a combination of these elements, or in completely different forms. Depending on the final forms, strategies for dissemination and promotion may be well established, such as with a book, or require more legwork on the part of the team, such as with project data made available through a data repository.

Beyond getting the results in their final form and making them available, explore possibilities for increasing the findability of your scholarship. Scholars should also work with librarians on project metadata since having good metadata is crucial to findability. Work with librarians at your institution to have websites cataloged and submitted to WorldCat, for example. Similarly, work with your institutional repository and data management librarians, if available. Promote and share project results on Listservs and social media and at conferences, as appropriate. University communications offices can also help to publicize projects in local, national, and international media.

☑ **Perform project closedown procedures.**

Taking the time to formally conclude a project is a crucial final step. Closedown procedures include completing any remaining documentation as well as following through on the data management plan. In addition, the project closedown phase is an opportunity to thank everyone who has contributed to the project. Even—or especially—for very large research initiatives that might extend over many years, conceptualizing the initiative as a sequence of projects, each of which can be initiated, completed, and closed down, is important to long-term success.

Conclusion

With this annotated checklist, our aim has been to provide practical guidance for developing digital humanities scholarship at all scales. We hope that readers will use this checklist as a foundation to build on. We also hope that subject specialists involved in advising about or creating digital humanities scholarship will draw on other chapters in this collection, which offer a variety of case studies illustrating the development of digital humanities projects within the library and partnerships among a variety of participants. Those chapters might usefully be read as illustrations to many of the key ideas set out in the checklist.

Suggested Readings

Readings on Defining Digital Humanities

For a sampling of pieces that take up defining digital humanities and digital scholarship, see Matthew K. Gold, ed., *Debates in the Digital Humanities* (Minneapolis: University of Minnesota Press, 2012), open-access edition: http://dhdebates.gc.cuny.edu; Clifford A. Lynch, "The 'Digital' Scholarship Disconnect," *EDUCAUSE Review* 49, no. 3 (May/June 2014), www.educause.edu/ero/article/digital-scholarship-disconnect; Bethany Nowviskie, *Bethany Nowviskie* (blog), accessed July 15, 2014, http://nowviskie.org; Ted Underwood, "You Can't Govern Reception," *The Stone and the Shell* (blog), May 3, 2014, http://tedunderwood.com/2014/05/03/you-cant-govern-reception.

Readings on Doing Digital Humanities

This chapter and its checklist participate in developing discussions about documenting a set of practices for "doing" digital humanities, however one may define digital humanities and whatever form that doing takes. See, for example, Anne Burdick et al., *Digital_Humanities* (Cambridge, MA: MIT Press, 2012), http://mitpress.mit.edu/sites/default/files/titles/content/9780262018470_Open_Access_Edition.pdf, which includes the chapters "Questions and Answers" (with the sections "Digital Humanities Fundamentals" [pp. 122–23], "The Project as Basic Unit" [pp. 124–25], and "Institutions and Pragmatics" [pp. 126–27]) and "Specifications" (with the sections "How to Evaluate Digital Scholarship" [pp. 128–29], "Project-Based Scholarship" [pp. 130–31], "Core Competencies in Processes and Methods" [pp. 132–33], "Learning Outcomes for the Digital Humanities" [p. 134], and "Creating Advocacy" [p. 135]). Similarly, the Fall 2012 issue of *Journal of Digital Humanities* (Daniel J. Cohen and Joan Fragaszy Troyano, eds., *Journal of Digital Humanities* 1, no. 4, http://journalofdigitalhumanities. org/1-4) is dedicated to "Closing the Evaluation Gap." Examples of webpages, blog posts, and other web resources concerned with practices for creating, sustaining, and maintaining digital projects include Association for Computers and the Humanities, "Digital Humanities Questions and Answers," accessed July 15, 2014, http://digitalhumanities.org/answers; LAIRAH (Log Analysis of Internet Resources in the Arts and Humanities), "The LAIRAH Digital Humanities Checklist," University College London website, last updated July 4, 2013, www.ucl.ac.uk/infostudies/research/ circah/lairah/features; 4Humanities, "Check IT Out!" accessed July 15, 2014, http://4humanities.org/check-it-out; Paige Morgan, "How to Get a Digital Humanities Project off the Ground," personal website, June 5, 2014, www.paigemorgan.net/how-to-get-a-digital-humanities-project-off-the-ground; and Cheryl Klimaszweski, "Digital Project Checklist," last modified November 23, 2011, https://docs.google.com/document/ d/1dnKMwiUR-evkcNQDEbJMMBrhIICVH_J14ku5VsmCKog/edit. Likewise, Rebecca Frost Davis has created a "Process Checklist for Integrating Digital Humanities Projects in Courses" (September 13, 2012, http://rebeccafrostdavis.wordpress.com/2012/09/13/process-checklist-for-integrating-digital-humanities-projects-into-courses). The resources included here are not intended to comprise a comprehensive list, but to give a sense of what is out there and where the present checklist fits in.

Readings on Collaborating in Digital Humanities

Some readings that deal with collaboration in digital humanities projects include Amy E. Earhart, "Challenging Gaps: Redesigning Collaboration in the Digital Humanities," in *The American Literature Scholar in the* Digital

Age, ed. Andrew Jewell and Amy E. Earhart (Ann Arbor: University of Michigan Press, 2011), 27–43; Julia Flanders, "Time, Labor, and 'Alternate Careers' in Digital Humanities Knowledge Work," in *Debates in the Digital Humanities*, ed. Matthew K. Gold (Minneapolis: University of Minnesota Press, 2012), open-access edition: http://dhdebates.gc.cuny.edu; Bethany Nowviskie, "Evaluating Collaborative Digital Scholarship (or, Where Credit Is Due)," *Journal of Digital Humanities* 1, no. 4 (2012), http://journalofdigitalhumanities.org/1-4/evaluating-collaborative-digital-scholarship-by-bethany-nowviskie; Lynne Siemens, "'It's a Team If You Use "Reply All"': An Exploration of Research Teams in Digital Humanities Environments," *Literary and Linguistic Computing* 24, no. 2 (2009): 225–33, doi:10.1093/llc/fqp009; and Lynn Siemens et al., "A Tale of Two Cities: Implications of the Similarities and Differences in Collaborative Approaches within the Digital Libraries and Digital Humanities Communities," *Literary and Linguistic Computing* 26, no. 3 (2011): 335–48, doi:10.1093/llc/fqr028. See also Gawande, *Checklist Manifesto*, 46, 68, 70.

Checklist

- ☑ Articulate the project's research question and the scholarly conversation being entered.
- ☑ Research other projects with similar research aims or methodologies.
- ☑ Define the scope of the project.
- ☑ Evaluate needed and available resources.
- ☑ Identify project participants.
- ☑ Develop a communication plan.
- ☑ Investigate issues regarding intellectual property.
- ☑ Develop a project work plan.
- ☑ Develop a data management plan.
- ☑ Assess project development.

☑ Document project work.

☑ Seek evaluation and peer review.

☑ Disseminate results.

☑ Perform project closedown procedures.

Notes

1. Atul Gawande, *The Checklist Manifesto: How to Get Things Right* (New York: Metropolitan Books, 2010), 86–87.
2. Ibid., 79.
3. Ibid.
4. University of Nebraska–Lincoln, "About UNL," accessed July 15, 2015, www.unl.edu/aboutunl; University of Nebraska–Lincoln, "Biggest Freshman Class in 35 Years Pushes UNL's Enrollment Past 25,000," news release, September 8, 2014, http://newsroom.unl.edu/releases/2014/09/08/
5. Amanda Gailey and Andrew Jewell, eds., *Scholarly Editing: The Annual of the Association for Documentary Editing*, accessed July 15, 2014, www.scholarlyediting.org; *Vectors Journal: Introduction*, accessed July 15, 2014, http://vectors.usc.edu/journal/index.php?page=Introduction.
6. Clayton McCarl, "Introduction to '*Avisos a pretendientes para Indias*,'" *Scholarly Editing: The Annual of the Association for Documentary Editing* 35 (2014), www.scholarlyediting.org/2014/editions/intro.avisos.html.
7. Emily Thompson, "Author's Statement," The Roaring 'Twenties: An Interactive Exploration of the Historical Soundscape of New York City, *Vectors* 4, no. 1 (Fall 2013), http://vectors.usc.edu/projects/index.php?project=98&thread=AuthorsStatement.
8. Adam Crymble and Julia Flanders, "FairCite," *Digital Humanities Quarterly* 7, no. 2 (2013), www.digitalhumanities.org/dhq/vol/7/2/000164/000164.html; Anne Burdick, Johanna Drucker, Peter Lunenfeld, Todd Presner, and Jeffrey Schnapp, *Digital_Humanities* (Cambridge, MA: MIT Press, 2012), 15, http://mitpress.mit.edu/sites/default/files/titles/content/9780262018470_Open_Access_Edition.pdf.
9. Daniel J. Cohen and Joan Fragaszy Troyano, eds., *Journal of Digital Humanities* 1, no. 4 (Fall 2012), http://journalofdigitalhumanities.org/1-4.

Bibliography

ACH (Association for Computers and the Humanities). "Digital Humanities Questions and Answers." Accessed July 15, 2014. http://digitalhumanities.org/answers.

Bernholz, Charles. *American Indian Treaties Portal.* University of Nebraska–Lincoln website. Accessed July 21, 2014. http://treatiesportal.unl.edu.

Burdick, Anne, Johanna Drucker, Peter Lunenfeld, Todd Presner, and Jeffrey Schnapp. *Digital_Humanities*. Cambridge, MA: MIT Press, 2012. http://mitpress.mit.edu/sites/default/files/titles/content/9780262018470_Open_Access_Edition.pdf.

Cohen, Daniel J., and Joan Fragaszy Troyano, eds. *Journal of Digital Humanities* 1, no. 4 (Fall 2012). http://journalofdigitalhumanities.org/1-4.

Crymble, Adam, and Julia Flanders. "FairCite." *Digital Humanities Quarterly* 7, no. 2 (2013). www.digitalhumanities.org/dhq/vol/7/2/000164/000164.html.

Davis, Rebecca Frost. "Process Checklist for Integrating Digital Humanities Projects into Courses." September 13, 2012. http://rebeccafrostdavis.wordpress.com/2012/09/13/process-checklist-for-integrating-digital-humanities-projects-into-courses.

Earhart, Amy E. "Challenging Gaps: Redesigning Collaboration in the Digital Humanities." In *The American Literature Scholar in the Digital Age*, edited by Andrew Jewell and Amy E. Earhart, 27–43. Ann Arbor: University of Michigan Press, 2011.

Flanders, Julia. "Time, Labor, and 'Alternate Careers' in Digital Humanities Knowledge Work." In *Debates in the Digital Humanities*, edited by Matthew K. Gold. Minneapolis: University of Minnesota Press, 2012. Open-access edition: http://dhdebates.gc.cuny.edu.

4Humanities. "Check IT Out!" 4Humanities website. Accessed July 15, 2014. http://4humanities.org/check-it-out.

Gailey, Amanda, and Andrew Jewell, eds. *Scholarly Editing: The Annual of the Association for Documentary Editing*. Accessed July 15, 2014. www.scholarlyediting.org.

Gawande, Atul. *The Checklist Manifesto: How to Get Things Right*. New York: Metropolitan Books, 2010.

Gold, Matthew K., ed. *Debates in the Digital Humanities*. Minneapolis: University of Minnesota Press, 2012. Open-access edition: http://dhdebates.gc.cuny.edu.

Klimaszweski, Cheryl. "Digital Project Checklist." Last modified November 23, 2011. https://docs.google.com/document/d/1dnKMwiUR-evkcNQDEbJMMBrhIICVH_J14ku5VsmCKog/edit.

LAIRAH (Log Analysis of Internet Resources in the Arts and Humanities). "The LAIRAH Digital Humanities Checklist." University College London website. Last updated July 4, 2013. www.ucl.ac.uk/infostudies/research/circah/lairah/features.

Logan-Peters, Kay. "About the Project." *An Architectural Tour of Historic UNL website*. Accessed July 21, 2014. http://historicbuildings.unl.edu/about.

Lynch, Clifford A. "The 'Digital' Scholarship Disconnect." *EDUCAUSE Review* 49, no. 3 (May/June 2014). www.educause.edu/ero/article/digital-scholarship-disconnect.

McCarl, Clayton. "Introduction to '*Avisos a pretendientes para Indias*.'" *Scholarly Editing: The Annual of the Association for Documentary Editing* 35 (2014). www.scholarly-editing.org/2014/editions/intro.avisos.html.

Morgan, Paige. "How to Get a Digital Humanities Project off the Ground." Personal website. June 5, 2014. www.paigemorgan.net/how-to-get-a-digital-humanities-project-off-the-ground.

NEH (National Endowment for the Humanities). "Digital Humanities Start-up Grants." Accessed July 15, 2014. www.neh.gov/grants/odh/digital-humanities-start-grants.

Nowviskie, Bethany. *Bethany Nowviskie* (blog). Accessed July 15, 2014. http://nowviskie.org.

———. "Evaluating Collaborative Digital Scholarship (or, Where Credit Is Due)." *Journal of Digital Humanities* 1, no. 4 (2012). http://journalofdigitalhumanities.org/1-4/evaluating-collaborative-digital-scholarship-by-bethany-nowviskie.

Siemens, Lynne. "'It's a Team If You Use "Reply All"': An Exploration of Research Teams in Digital Humanities Environments." *Literary and Linguistic Computing* 24, no. 2 (2009): 225–33. doi:10.1093/llc/fqp009.

Siemens, Lynne, Richard Cunningham, Wendy Duff, and Claire Warwick. "A Tale of Two Cities: Implications of the Similarities and Differences in Collaborative Approaches within the Digital Libraries and Digital Humanities Communities." *Literary and Linguistic Computing* 26, no. 3 (2011): 335–48. doi:10.1093/llc/fqr028.

Thompson, Emily. "Author's Statement." The Roaring 'Twenties: An Interactive Exploration of the Historical Soundscape of New York City. *Vectors* 4, no. 1 (Fall 2013). http://vectors.usc.edu/projects/index.php?project=98&thread=AuthorsStatement.

Underwood, Ted. "You Can't Govern Reception." *The Stone and the Shell* (blog), May 3, 2014. http://tedunderwood.com/2014/05/03/you-cant-govern-reception.

UNL (University of Nebraska–Lincoln). "About UNL." Accessed July 15, 2014. www.unl.edu/aboutunl.

"Biggest Freshman Class in 35 Years Pushes UNL's Enrollment Past 25,000." News release, September 8, 2014. http://newsroom.unl.edu/releases/2014/09/08/Biggest+freshman+class+in+35+years+pushes+UNL%27s+enrollment+past+25,000.

———. "The Big Ten Conference, CIC and APLU." Accessed July 15, 2014. www.unl.edu/aboutunl/big10.shtml.

Vectors Journal. Introduction. Accessed July 15, 2014. http://vectors.usc.edu/journal/index.php?page=Introduction.

CHAPTER SEVEN

In Practice and Pedagogy
Digital Humanities in a Small College Environment

Christina Bell

HOW DOES digital humanities (DH) work fit into the teaching mission of a liberal arts college? While DH at large research universities has certainly been the focus of attention, there are many possibilities in smaller, more individualized environments. This chapter will explore the place of digital humanities in the small college library and how subject librarians can become collaborative practitioners in digital scholarship. In a place where most staff carry multiple roles and responsibilities, the small college librarian and library play integral roles in the implementation of digital humanities work in partnering with faculty, managing ongoing projects, and bringing digital methodologies to the classroom.

The small college subject librarian's responsibilities are many. I, for example, serve as liaison librarian to all the humanities disciplines, including languages, literatures, history, and some area studies at Bates College, a highly selective, residential liberal arts college in Central Maine. My duties include collection management, reference, instruction, research support for both students and faculty, and service to the college at large. It is then no small task to add digital scholarship to such a workload, but, as I will discuss, the undertaking would be well placed with the subject specialist. This chapter will attempt to offer some "getting started" tips for both subject librarians and new DH communities on campus, using my own experience as a librarian at Bates for context.

By virtue of size, small colleges are characteristically collaborative places. Faculty and staff must work closely and cooperatively to create projects, develop courses and curriculum, and provide service to the college at large. The library is a natural place to form the type of collaborative team that can bring the methods, practices, and tools of digital scholarship to a small college. In a small college setting, DH can provide new modes of innovation in teaching, creative platforms for student and faculty projects, collaborative research partnerships, and an introduction to the types of digital literacies expected of a twenty-first-century education.

The best kind of digital humanities practice grows from the mission of the college in which it is situated, to meet the needs of the campus research and teaching community. Digital scholarship is not a new practice at Bates, but faculty and staff are considering better ways to organize the ad hoc services distributed across campus, to create a more robust and cohesive group to further advance DH in our research community. In a liberal arts college, it is vital that these efforts incorporate student research and learning and have a place in the classroom and pedagogical mission of the institution.

Differences in Practice: Digital Humanities at Research Institution versus Small College

A review of much of the DH-related literature, conference presentations, project releases, and online media reveal a strong trend: most DH projects and practitioners are affiliated with research institutions or large universities.[1] The most common model for DH engagement in larger universities is the digital humanities center. A number of studies have examined how such centers are organized, funded, and integrated with the mission and culture of the larger institution.[2] Functionally, the purpose of such centers is to enable interdisciplinary and interdepartmental collaboration, as well as to bring in project participants from outside a department.[3]

Given the success of the model of housing DH projects in a center, a study by OCLC asked a simple question: Does every research library (or academic institution) *need* a digital humanities center? The executive summary of the OCLC study indicates that the center model is "appropriate in relatively few circumstances," yet it has become the most visible standard for the practice of digital humanities.[4] The model of the DH center is "predicated on a campus being large and resourced well enough to allocate significant funds to what may be perceived as a niche effort."[5] However, large universities are more likely to produce content for wider audiences, both academic and nonacademic, outside their institutions. Faculty surveyed at large schools indicate that they want interoperable tools and repositories, materials in various formats, and easy online access to these materials. Faculty also need help for themselves and their students in learning new skills, methods, and tools, as well as support in integrating them into their work.[6] Thus the center model fits for research institutions, as these activities and the staff needed to both support faculty and participate in collaborative projects are likely widely distributed across a large campus and staff.

A small college, by contrast, has no need for the center model of DH so common in larger institutions. In an environment where collaborative work is necessary for success in any initiative, the centralizing purpose of a dedicated center is redundant. The very nature of DH work facilitates nonlocal collaboration and allows small schools to forge new relationships outside of traditional academic organizational divisions. Small colleges are often part of consortia within their region or with similar schools. They may be a part of a network of campuses or partnered with a nearby research institution. These types of partnerships allow for collaborative projects and enterprises and access to networking and professional development opportunities. Bates is a member of networks regional to New England, and our library has strong partnerships with our sister schools in Maine, Bowdoin College and Colby College. We look both to our existing relationships and to new endeavors as digital scholarship moves forward at Bates. DH practice is not defined by location, and further projects may allow us to expand into new partnerships.

Digital Scholarship in a Small College

Pursuing the digital humanities at a small liberal arts college is not easy, but then, it's not easy at research universities, either.

—William Pannapacker[7]

There are many types of small colleges, and many already have established DH practices and presences, but these may differ from what we find at larger research institutions. At a casual glance, small colleges and universities that are focused on traditional-age undergraduate education, often with teaching-focused missions, have apparently played a much smaller part in the DH movement. The pedagogical focus of many small schools is one possible obstacle to the formation of a traditional DH center.[8] But as the OCLC report and others have made clear, a center is not the only or even the best way to integrate DH into a college campus. In a liberal arts setting specifically, a digital scholarship lab or center can develop innovative DH projects that contribute to research and teaching. Most existing examples occur where IT and the library are a merged organization with central leadership or where there is already a close working relationship between these departments. At Bates, Information and Library Services (ILS) has long been a merged organization, although units are distributed across campus. Despite this physical separation, ILS staff have engaged in collaborative partnerships in support of student and faculty research. A digital initiative group (affectionately called DigIn) is now in place to bring a new level of organization to this work—to, it is hoped, engage in larger and more complex projects. While this group may seem like a centralizing force, the purpose is to better advertise existing units and expertise in the context of digital scholarship and move forward in more deliberate, less ad hoc manner.

It is common to hear from faculty, "I didn't know I was doing digital humanities."[9] I heard this from several people when I started at Bates. While the work they were doing was not on a scale of large, outward-facing projects, many Bates faculty incorporate digital methodologies into their classrooms and in their own scholarship. For example, there are ongoing projects that use advanced GIS mapping to trace rebellion movements in medieval England or that ask students to incorporate multiple types of media to create a theory-based narrative argument built across exhibits in Omeka.[10] As technology is more integrated into our classrooms, communication, and even everyday lives, researchers may not realize that their incorporation of digital methodologies may fall under "digital humanities." Many institutions have had various levels of DH engagement without calling it that or without offering specifically marketed DH service and support. The simplest way to creating a DH community on campus is to package and market existing services that are valuable to DH scholars.[11]

Teaching-focused colleges have significant advantages over research universities in pursuing DH. A smaller college can innovate more rapidly and at lower cost. It is easier to build coalitions and organize project teams at small colleges. Faculty members are more likely to be able to experiment with projects that may not lead to traditional scholarly publications, perhaps because the continual pressure to publish is not as prevalent. William Pannapacker has argued that the practices and process of DH are an enhancement of the core methods of an ideal liberal arts education.[12] The traditional liberal arts emphasis on involving undergraduates, local communities, and multiple campuses in scholarship might contribute to a sense of humanities belonging to everyone, not just trained professionals. Including undergraduates in DH provides them with applied or problem-based learning, and the project and the classroom community benefit from the real-world skills the students have acquired. Student/faculty collaboration in DH also enhances project scalability; students are learning by contributing to faculty projects, and faculty do not have to separate their time so rigidly between teaching and research.[13]

There are a number of small colleges already successfully engaged with DH in different ways. Hamilton College and Occidental College have created DH initiatives that support both faculty and student work. Hamilton requires all DH projects to have a curricular element and have hired additional programming support specifically for these projects. The mission of the DH center at Occidental explicitly focuses on the process of undergraduate education rather than on producing projects. Bates's efforts in DH have not been to create large end projects, but rather to provide a knowledge base on campus as people engage in digital scholarship in different ways. Several individual departments have brought in speakers to address DH in a disciplinary context, and a faculty-led project pedagogical initiative seeks to incorporate technology into existing faculty workflows.[14] In the classroom, a number of Bates courses incorporate video projects, data visualizations, GIS and mapping, and platforms like Omeka in student work. These are only a few examples of small colleges engaged in digital humanities, but they show how the tradition of interdisciplinary work and the incorporation of digital methodologies are linked to the values of liberal education.

Digital Humanities in the Library

> *The experience of the digital humanities shows that the digital can also bring scholars into ever closer and more substantive collaboration with librarians. It is no accident that many if not most successful digital humanities centers are based in university libraries. Much of digital humanities is database driven, but an empty database is a useless database. Librarians have the stuff to fill digital humanists' databases and the expertise to do so intelligently.*
>
> —Tom Scheinfeldt[15]

As there is no singular way to practice DH, there is then no one true way for libraries to be involved with DH. The OCLC report concluded that libraries can engage with DH along a continuum of investment.[16] Yet while many libraries, at research institutions or small colleges, have maintained visibility in DH, the Library (writ large) has yet to fully understand itself as essential to the goals of digital humanities.[17]

DH scholars require everything libraries already provide for the humanities, along with support in leveraging computational methods for their research, publication of that research in publicly accessible forms, and long-term archiving and preservation of their work. Traditional humanities scholars and DH practitioners share a need for these services. In many ways, librarianship and the work done in academic libraries already overlaps with the practice of DH. A number of the core competences of librarianship listed by the American Library Association (ALA) are interlinked with DH competencies, including access to information and digital resources, knowledge organization (classification, metadata), user services, and technological knowledge (e.g., content management tools and data visualization).[18] These are obviously very broad categories, in which any number of library or information technology staff members may be engaged. Existing skill sets common to librarians, such as support in copyright and licensing issues, collection management, project management, and application of metadata also overlap with DH practices.[19]

Library- or information services–wide staffing for new initiatives requires a very clear message about priorities and goals for the organization, the departments, and the individuals involved, addressing such questions as: How do the new services build on existing work? What new skills are staff expected to acquire? What current work can become a lower priority or be reassigned? Who has the authority to delegate new work to staff across various departments?[20] Questions such as these often stymie the growth of digital humanities in the library as librarians grapple with the introduction of a new field in which they are active participants at the same time as the library profession undergoes its own change with advances in technology. These questions are especially important in a small college environment, where a librarian, and a subject specialist in particular, has more than one responsibility.

Subject Specialists and the Digital Humanities

Traditionally, librarianship has focused on the fundamental aspects of acquiring, organizing, tracking, and protecting resources. To this list, modern librarianship also adds reference, instruction, outreach, programming, technological innovation, and knowledge of scholarly communication issues. The liaison or subject specialist role in an academic library can include all of these tasks, in addition to service to the college on committees and other governing bodies, support for multiple disciplines and departments, and one-on-one work with students in research. While large research libraries may have a robust staff and specialists for one or very few subject areas, in small colleges librarians are more likely to have broad responsibilities across whole divisions such as humanities, social sciences, sciences, and so on. When the liaison role is compounded across many disciplines and responsibilities are shared by a smaller staff, how then can a librarian effectively add digital scholarship to an already robust position description?

Most subject librarians oversee multiple disciplinary areas, with collection development, reference and instruction, outreach, professional development, and administrative responsibilities. This amount of work quickly adds up. The role of the research librarian is evolving in order to effectively integrate the library as a partner in DH scholarship.[21] A white paper completed by members of the Digital Librarians Initiative includes an extensive list of tasks in which a librarian can engage in DH.[22] The specific ways in which an individual librarian can participate depends on the needs of his or her institution. Digital humanities and its associated tool sets and investigative processes are typically anchored in three broad areas: textual analysis, spatial analysis, and media studies.[23] A faculty member in an English department may be text mining a literary corpora, while a history professor may use GIS and spatial analysis, and a sociologist may draft a critique of social media relationships. These are all general examples of proposals I've seen at Bates, and they rely upon different technological skill sets from collaborators. No one person can or should be the expert in all these things, but librarians can be willing partners in learning and the experimental practice of DH work.

Librarians bring expertise in both content and the process in working with DH projects and centers.[24] A Council on Library and Information Resources (CLIR) report on digital humanities centers suggests four kinds of library expertise required in DH projects: subject (domain), analytical, data management, and project management.[25] It is unreasonable to assume that a single person can encompass all of these, but librarians are well suited to tasks such as project management. This especially true in a small college, where the scale of the project and budget may not have room for additional staff hires. Librarians may require training in other areas to supplement their knowledge, but the core library and information science competencies provide a solid foundation upon which to build. It is up to individual librarians and their institutions to determine what support and skills meet institutional goals and how to best bring about the changes that allow librarians to contribute to those goals.

It is not practical or realistic to expect one person to "do all the digital stuff."[26] This is particularly true in a small college environment, for the reasons already stated. Librarians—and importantly, library administrators—have to take a close look at the workload of any staff engaged in DH work and make appropriate changes.[27] The emphasis that this is not a one-time organizational change is an important message to campus and library leaders. Digital humanities cannot be an add-on to current library positions, but must include a rethinking of the ways in which libraries receive staff and resource allocations.[28] As Miriam Posner of UCLA eloquently points out, "Building a DH-friendly library environment often leans too hard on individual librarians, without taking into account the set of institutional supports, incentives, and rewards that will allow DH to flourish in a sustained way (without librarian burnout)."[29] She goes on to say, "DH is not, and cannot be, business as usual for the library. To succeed at DH, a library must do a great deal more than add 'digital scholarship' to an individual librarian's long string of subject specialties."[30]

There are two related challenges librarians face when actually engaging in DH work: authority and service ethic. A librarian might be tasked with supporting a particular project, but without the authority to collate the additional resources and staff it would take to make the project successful. It can be difficult, if not impossible, for a librarian assigned to "supporting" a project to dissuade a faculty member from barreling forward with a half-formed idea. Most librarians do not have the authority to make the necessary pieces fall into place, whether that involves assigning additional staff, allocating server space, buying hardware and software, and so on.[31] Regarding a service ethic, the service model common in academic librarianship is built on a support or client relationship between librarians and faculty researchers that is often hierarchical.[32] Most DH projects do not need supporters, or staff in service of a researcher. The project and research-ers need collaborative partners.[33] In this, the small college environment may be at an advantage, depending on the local culture. In a school with a small faculty and staff, the tradition of collaborative work, flexibility, and nonhierarchical partnerships is already in place.

This may all seem doom-and-gloom for subject specialists interested in or tasked with digital scholarship, but ultimately librarians have an in-trinsic position in the practice of DH. The role of the liaison librarian is changing throughout academia, not just by or within small colleges or digi-tal humanities. An Association of Research Libraries (ARL) report released in 2013, *New Roles for New Times: Transforming Liaison Roles in Research Libraries,* includes digital humanities as only one of a number of growing areas to meet "changing user needs."[34] While the focus of this report is the research library, it has implications for smaller colleges. Subject special-ist roles share many commonalities regardless of school size and mission. Trends of flexibility, collaboration, digital scholarship, and intellectual property are concerns for liaisons at colleges large and small. While much of the library and DH literature may focus on the research institution, this does not exclude a small college or small library. The approach suggested by ARL is for a hybrid model of librarianship, where one is mostly a sub-ject specialist with a portion of time devoted to others areas of expertise or demand.[35] This model works for digital humanities, scholarly commu-nication, or any other area of developing skill sets within librarianship. This model is also highly adaptable for small-college librarians, as a hybrid model creates a more flexible description of how they are already working.

Functioning without a Dedicated Digital Humanities Center or Librarian

As we have seen, the library and subject specialist librarian are key partners to a sustained digital humanities presence on campus. While research institutions and large DH centers get the greatest representation in scholarly and online publications, many small colleges are successfully engaged in digital humanities. As the center model is not ideal for most situations, colleges must thus consider the best way to organize DH activity on their campus. DH is not a solitary or passive process. It is collaborative and requires active participation. Even if you are not involved in a specific project, you can still engage with the DH community and introduce DH to your campus.

Whatever model for DH support is chosen, it needs to be appropriate and customized to the needs of the institution. A one-size-fits-all approach to digital scholarship support never fits all (or anyone). There is no one set of services that must be offered by a library or DH center. Rather, services are determined by the needs of the community.[36] Ultimately, the majority of campuses can engage in successful digital humanities without a DH center, and even without a dedicated DH staff. In many cases, the necessary personnel, technology, and project support are already extant, but not organized or publicized as specific to digital humanities. When I was hired at Bates, I was told by a number of my new colleagues that the college was interested in advancing a practice of digital scholarship for faculty and student research. I was pleasantly surprised to find staff dedicated to GIS and mapping, imaging, and data visualization through our Imaging Center, and in video and multimedia creation through the Digital Media Studio, among other practice areas.[37] Faculty had already incorporated digital methodologies and theories into a number of courses, so much so that a new program in digital and computational studies is under review.[38] The challenge was not to create the infrastructure to begin DH work, but to organize the already robust and specialized units in such a way as to be more deliberate in our engagement with digital scholarship. While ad hoc support has worked to date, it is ultimately not a sustainable model for developing a more cohesive DH practice.

Most library-based DH work is being done in a very piecemeal fashion. Responding to a survey, 48 percent of research libraries report providing "ad hoc" type support.[39] The result is that the success of DH efforts in the library often depends on the energy, creativity, and goodwill of a few overextended library and IT professionals and the services they can throw together. At present, most libraries create processes on the fly for each project individually.[40] The downside to ad hoc support is that it does not consider organizational goals, staff time, funding, or campus skill sets in creating a portfolio of projects. Without clear selection criteria and processes and project management that includes service oversight, an institution is likely to take on more than it is able to support and have difficulty completing the work on time, if at all.[41] In many ways, it is more common to find ad hoc services at a small school. Without effective communication to organize DH participation in a deliberate manner, ad hoc support is the default, in many ways the opposite of the center model. It is important especially for small colleges to find the appropriate middle ground, to invest in DH in an intentional way without overextending the people or resources of the school.

The typical small college cannot afford the money or time to dedicate much staff to a niche effort. The very collaboration that fosters DH work can also inhibit it at a small school. It is difficult to argue for dedicated staff in one area, in a place where most staff fill a number of roles. A hybrid model, somewhere between a totally separate center and ad hoc staff support, relies on a few existing staff or new hires to oversee initiatives, drawing in other support as needed from subject specialists, archivists, technologists, and so on. This is the most scalable option for a small college, as it draws on existing expertise without overwhelming any one person. Any hybrid model requires clear direction from library leadership about expectations and priorities. At the institutional level, long-term investment in the professional staff will enable more robust and successful support and collaborative partnerships. Within the library, collaboration and partnerships are necessary at every level, not just in DH work. Support for digital scholarship more broadly relies upon collaborative, nonhierarchical team environments, areas in which librarians excel.[42]

To be successful, libraries need to create a well-thought-out process for how partnerships work. This includes discussing intellectual property and scholarly communication; considering capacity (storage space, staff time, prioritizing collections, etc.); finding the smallest number of tools you can offer while satisfying the most needs; and determining the afterlife of a project in terms of hosting and preservation.[43] A library interested in adding DH must be prepared to make hard decisions about what they are not going to do as well as what they will. At New York University, librarians created a hybrid model structure for scalable and sustainable services, tiered from widely adaptable tools and services to applied development. This attention to scalability indicates the entire structure can be scaled down to suit institutions significantly smaller than NYU. NYU defines services as sustainable "when they can be efficiently maintained over time" and as scalable "when they can be provided effectively as demand increases."[44] Levels of support are described on a tiered scale that ranges from basic computing and enhanced research support to custom-built tools. These services can be offered at a school large or small; they are in no way inherent only in a research library. Implementing scalable and sustainable services has certain programmatic and strategic requirements without which these initiatives will fail. Solutions that are too narrowly focused, short-lived, or difficult to maintain will fail. Solutions also must be reusable for other projects, or interoperable. In the same way that an institution should not "do" DH for the sake of doing it, it should not approve every project just to show progress. Fewer and smaller projects that are carefully selected, are properly staffed and funded, and fit the mission and culture of the institution are more likely to succeed. This is exactly the type of hybrid model that is the most easily adapted to the small college environment, as it relies on people and services already in place on campus. While new staff may be needed in the course of time, it is possible to begin by investing in engaged and enthusiastic staff already committed to the institution.

Getting Started: Suggestions for the Interested Librarian

As previously stated, there is no one way to practice or support digital humanities. That being said, what follows are various tips and suggested reading for getting started, gathered both from other librarians in the field and from my own experience. DH is an experimental field; many in the community are self-taught or gained knowledge through work on projects rather than formal training.[45] Just because you may not have a background in technology, don't have an established career in more "traditional" librarianship, or don't know anyone who does DH doesn't mean you can't learn as you go. The DH community is largely welcoming, even to novices, and excited to have people interested in what they do and how they do it.

As librarian Josh Honn notes, "Any librarian charged with engaging with digital services or scholarship will confront a vast ecosystem of digital tools and methods for a variety of purposes; from doing library outreach via popular social media platforms to collaborating with scholars working with obscure or difficult digital tools."[46] Do not be afraid that you need a computer science degree in order to work on DH projects. There is a continuum of engagement for both institutions and individuals, and no one type of practice makes something DH. The following is a series of suggestions, practices and readings that will get you up to speed on the history of DH, its community, the myriad of practices, and where you can go to learn more.

A good place to start is by reframing things you may already be doing: go to events and meetings hosted by the departments you support; be a fountain of information in new topics, resources, and events for your departments, including digital scholarship; start exploring what DH work, however minor, is being done on your campus. There is probably more going on than you realize, and as you start establishing yourself as someone interested in and knowledgeable on the subject of DH, you make yourself visible as a potential resource and collaborator.

This list offers some beginning ways to connect to the larger DH community.

- Get on DH-identified social networks. Twitter is one of the largest means of communication in the digital humanities world. Accounts (denoted by @) and hashtags (#) are created for conferences and events so that you may follow what people are saying even if you cannot be present.

- Follow Twitter accounts such as Digital Humanities Now (@dhnow), the Q&A account of the Association for Computing in the Humanities (@DHAnswers), and dh + lib (@DHandLib). A casual search in Twitter for people with "DH" and "digital humanities" will create lists of active practitioners.

- Join e-mail discussion lists such as the ACRL DH discussion group (http://lists.ala.org/wws/info/acrldigitalhumanitiesig), Humanist (http://dhhumanist.org), and DH Now (http://digitalhumanities-now.org).

- DHCommons (http://dhcommons.org) is a great hub for finding projects and people seeking partners.

- If you can afford it or get funding, go to a THATCamp (http://thatcamp.org). These small-scale and often local or regional "un-conferences" are great places to meet others in the DH community, acquire new skills, learn about new tools, or get some free software.

- Familiarize yourself with available tools via something like DiRT: Digital Research Tools (http://dirtdirectory.org). This site organizes and explains a variety of tools, both free and paid, by activity type.

- There are many regional digital humanities groups, such as NYC Digital Humanities (@NYCDH on Twitter) or Boston DH Consortium (@Boston_DH on Twitter), which loosely covers all New England). In addition to being present on Twitter and e-mail discussion lists, these groups often have local events and informal meetups.

- Besides Twitter, the blogosphere is a great way to read about nearly every aspect of digital humanities, from project announcements to critique and theory. As you find practitioners on Twitter, their accounts will link to their blogs.

- Consider engaging with professional organizations, including Digital Library Federation (www.diglib.org), HASTAC (www.hastac.org), NITLE (www.nitle.org), and the Alliance of Digital Humanities Organizations (http://adho.org), which will give you membership to the North American group, the Association for Computers in the Humanities.

- The Digital Library Federation (DLF) has a cohort engaged in an ongoing discussion of digital scholarship and liberal arts colleges (www.diglib.org/archives/5383).

There are a number of articles and journals for background and additional reading. Fortunately, open access is an important tenet in DH, and so much of the scholarship is freely available online.

- For background reading, Miriam Posner offers on her blog a broad bibliography (http://miriamposner.com/blog/digital-humanities-and-the-library) organized by topic.

- The CUNY Digital Humanities Resource Guide (http://commons.gc.cuny.edu/wiki/index.php/The_CUNY_Digital_Humanities_Resource_Guide) is one of the more comprehensive lists of DH content online, also organized by type. The emphasis is on larger schools, but small college participants are not absent.

- Lisa Spiro wrote an article for the *Journal of Digital Humanities*, "Getting Started in the Digital Humanities" (http://journalofdigitalhumanities.org/1-1/getting-started-in-digital-humanities-by-lisa-spiro), that covers a variety of definitions, people and areas of study to acquaint the newcomer with both the DH community and scholarship.

- The *Journal of Library Administration* devoted a special issue to "Digital Humanities in Libraries," available free online (https://micahvandegrift.wordpress.com/2013/01/30/proof). This issue offers a broad view of challenges and ideas specifically for DH in the library, and for including librarians as DH practitioners.

- *Debates in the Digital Humanities* (http://dhdebates.gc.cuny.edu/debates) is an excellent source of reading to understand the faculty side of DH and how scholars contextualize their work in broader academic structures. There is one chapter devoted to liberal arts colleges, by Brian Alexander and Rebecca Frost Davis, that speaks to the small college environment in particular.

- *A Companion to Digital Humanities* (www.digitalhumanities.org/companion) is the most complete and descriptive history of DH and includes excellent descriptions and examples of different types of DH practice or topical areas of study.

This is by no means a comprehensive list that will make you into a digital humanist. It will, however, get you started in learning new skills, seeing what has already been done, and connecting to the existing DH community. It may feel overwhelming at first, but no one DH practitioner can "do" all the things that make a DH practice or project. With these suggestions, you can begin to see where you as an individual and where your institution can fit in the larger scheme.

Organizing Digital Humanities on Campus

Think of your main duty as providing a place where others can grow and exceed their goals. Invest as much as you can in the success of your colleagues and students, while keeping in mind the benefit of their service to the larger institution.

—William Pannapacker[47]

As you begin, it is important to consider both "Why digital humanities?" and "How do you do digital humanities?" in the context of your institution. Do not get into DH just for the sake of doing something new or keeping up with big trends. This is a difficult thing to consider, especially for campus and library leadership. The more DH becomes a buzzword for innovation, schools clamor to show they are on board without considering the why, how, and who questions. In getting started with DH at the institutional level, it is vitally important to keep the mission and culture of the college at the core of the effort. Without this consideration and integration, developing a successful initiative will become a challenge.

There is some difference of opinion among practitioners on the next steps to getting started. William Pannapacker advises investing as much as possible in one collaborative, multidisciplinary flagship project, ideally one with strong ties the most distinctive qualities of the institution.[48] Bucknell University has created an interdisciplinary public humanities project centered on its geographical home, the Susquehanna River, which incorporates student, faculty, and staff contribution.[49] Dartmouth College has developed a project around Samson Occom and the Occom Circle, based on historical ties to the local Native American community and original documents housed at Dartmouth.[50] Bethany Nowviskie cautions that DH is not always a response to specific demand. Sometimes the best introduction is to start a workshop, bring in a speaker, or give staff the time to develop their own trial project to spur further interest across campus.[51] Miriam Posner states that issuing a faculty call for digital projects is a poor way to start. The power imbalance between faculty and library staff makes it difficult to say no to a poorly planned project, and novice faculty likely underestimate how much time and staff commitment a digital project will take. She suggests rather than call for projects, issue a call for people willing to commit to training on new technology. Such an introduction may lead to a better ability to plan a project in the future.[52] Bates has thus far taken the path of introducing small measures, as Nowviskie suggests. This includes sponsoring talks within academic departments and partnering with CLIR in the spring of 2014 to host a one-day regional symposium on digital scholarship. This event fostered an interesting discussion on the presence of liberal arts colleges in DH, particularly those in the Northeast and New England. Regardless of what is the best "first thing," DH is not technology for the sake of technology, or just to try something new. Any DH endeavor should be driven by a research question, intellectual passion, or a pedagogical goal.[53]

Beginning any new project or initiative will require the support of campus leadership and the leadership of every department involved. Pannapacker suggests raising your own money, keeping costs for experimental work low, and demonstrating how digital methods enhance the college mission and promote its image. Faculty support will be essential to long-term success, so show how digital technologies support faculty research by introducing new tools and highlighting what new results are possible.[54] Tri-Co Digital Humanities, a group formed by Bryn Mawr, Haverford, and Swarthmore, has established a workshop series to offer faculty, staff, and librarians training in new skills where they can practice on actual DH tools.[55] This model is employed at a number of institutions, and provides training for staff while also "beta testing" the ability of the campus network to successfully create a project. This is a concept Bates is also considering, in allowing staff from disparate units the time to create a project utilizing material from our archives. This will create a product serviceable to the college, and also give staff the opportunity to work together in expanding and sharing our collective knowledge. As Nowviskie points out, "When a library can create a critical mass of staffing and intellectual energy, then it has set the conditions for the advancement of knowledge itself, through the fulfillment of research desires unknown."[56]

Conclusion

In planning to offer services in digital humanities, institutions must be guided by local considerations such as user needs, strategic priorities, and existing organizational structures and services. DH takes time and an investment in relationships across the campus. Ultimately it is the people who will bring about a successful project, not the technology, methodologies, processes, or products. Since there is no one way to define what DH is and no one model in which to engage in DH, there remains creative space to develop a practice uniquely suited to the local community. The small college environment is a natural situation for digital humanities to flourish, with existing complementary structures such as collaborative research partnerships and strong pedagogy. Libraries and librarians have an invaluable role in both the development and the sustainability of DH on any campus. When libraries do DH, they are in it for the long term.

Notes

1. Bryan Alexander and Rebecca Frost Davis, "Should Liberal Arts Campuses Do Digital Humanities? Process and Product in the Small College World," in *Debates in the Digital Humanities*, ed. Matthew K. Gold, Part VI: Teaching the Digital Humanities (Minneapolis: University of Minnesota Press, 2012), 368, http://dhdebates.gc.cuny.edu/debates.

2. See Diane M. Zorich, "Digital Humanities Centers: Loci for Digital Scholarship," in *Working Together or Apart*, ed. Kathlin Smith and Brian Leney (Washington, DC: Council on Library and Information Resources, 2009), 70–78, www.clir.org/pubs/pubs/reports/pub145/pub145.pdf, and Miriam Posner, "No Half Measures: Overcoming Common Challenges to Doing Digital Humanities in the Library," *Journal of Library Administration* 53, no. 1 (2013), open-access copy at www.escholarship.org/uc/item/6q2625np.

3. Alexander and Davis, "Should Liberal Arts Campuses Do Digital Humanities?" 369.

4. Jennifer Schaffner and Ricky Erway, *Does Every Research Library Need a Digital Humanities Center?* (Dublin, OH: OCLC Research, 2014), 5, http://oclc.org/content/dam/research/publications/library/2014/oclcresearch-digital-humanities-center-2014.pdf.

5. Alexander and Davis, "Should Liberal Arts Campuses Do Digital Humanities?" 370.

6. Jennifer Vinopal and Monica McCormick, "Supporting Digital Scholarship in Research Libraries: Scalability and Sustainability," *Journal of Library Administration* 53, no. 1 (2013): 1, open-access copy at http://hdl.handle.net/2451/31698.

7. William Pannapaker, "Stop Calling It 'Digital Humanities,'" *Chronicle of Higher Education*, February 18, 2013, http://chronicle.com/article/Stop-Calling-It-Digital/137325.

8. Alexander and Davis, "Should Liberal Arts Campuses Do Digital Humanities?" 370.

9. Ibid., 375.

10. Bates College, "Material Culture Omeka," 2013, http://omeka-archive.bates.edu/201309.

11. Schaffner and Erway, *Does Every Research Library Need a Digital Humanities Center?* 14.

12. Pannapacker, "Stop Calling It 'Digital Humanities.'"

13. Alexander and Davis, "Should Liberal Arts Campuses Do Digital Humanities?" 381.

14. Bates College, PiCTR, accessed September 29, 2014, http://pictr.bates.edu.

15. Tom Scheinfeldt, "Nobody Cares about the Library: How Digital Technology Makes the Library Invisible (and Visible) to Scholars," *Found History* (blog), February 22, 2012, www.foundhistory.org/2012/02/22/nobody-cares-about-the-library-how-digital-technology-makes-the-library-invisible-and-visible-to-scholars.

16. Schaffner and Erway, *Does Every Research Library Need a Digital Humanities Center?* 7.

17. Micah Vandegrift, "What Is Digital Humanities and What's It Doing in the Library?" *In the Library with the Lead Pipe* (blog), June 27, 2012, www.inthelibrarywiththeleadpipe.org/2012/dhandthelib.

18. Chris Alen Sula, "Digital Humanities and Libraries: A Conceptual Model," *Journal of Library Administration* 53, no. 1 (2013), 4, open-access copy at http://chrisalensula.org/digital-humanities-and-libraries-a-conceptual-model.

19. Janice M. Jaguszewski and Karen Williams, *New Roles for New Times* (Washington, DC: Association of Research Libraries, August 2013), 9, www.arl.org/storage/documents/publications/NRNT-Liaison-Roles-final.pdf.

20. Vinopal and McCormick, "Supporting Digital Scholarship in Research Libraries," 12.

21. Micah Vandegrift and Stewart Varner, "Evolving in Common: Creating Mutually Supportive Relationships between Libraries and the Digital Humanities," *Journal of Library Administration* 53, no. 1 (2013): 1, open-access copy at http://pid.emory.edu/ark:/25593/cwzbf.

22. Tim Bryson et al., "Roles of Librarians in Digital Humanities Centers," Research Commons White Paper, Digital Librarians Initiative (DLI), September 2010, https://docs.google.com/document/edit?id=1tch6xW7bh_vbJOzG7xYs9z6yX-ATC68x-Fg-BRVD298.

23. Donald J. Waters, "An Overview of the Digital Humanities," *Research Library Issues* 284 (2013): 6, http://publications.arl.org/rli284/3.

24. Bryson et al., "Roles of Librarians in Digital Humanities Centers."

25. Jennifer L. Adams and Kevin B. Gunn, *Keeping Up With… Digital Humanities*, Association of College and Research Libraries (ACRL) website, April 2013, www.ala.org/acrl/publications/keeping_up_with/digital_humanities.

26. Schaffner and Erway, *Does Every Research Library Need a Digital Humanities Center?* 8.

27. Vandegrift and Varner, "Evolving in Common," 13.

28. Barbara A. Rockenbach, "Digital Humanities in Libraries: New Models for Scholarly Engagement," *Journal of Library Administration* 53, no. 1 (2013): 6, open-access copy at http://hdl.handle.net/10022/AC:P:18892.

29. Posner, "No Half Measures," 2.

30. Ibid., 9.

31. Ibid., 3, 5.

32. Rockenbach, "Digital Humanities in Libraries," 3.

33. Posner, "No Half Measures," 3.

34. Jaguszewski and Williams, *New Roles for New Times*, 8–12.

35. Ibid., 7.

36. Schaffner and Erway, *Does Every Research Library Need a Digital Humanities Center?* 15.

37. Bates College, Imaging Center, accessed September 23, 2014, www.bates.edu/imaging; Bates College, Digital Media Studios, accessed September 23, 2014, www.bates.edu/digital-media.

38. Bates College, "Courses Related to Digital and Computational Studies 2014/2015," Imaging Center website, accessed September 23, 2014, www.bates.edu/imaging/dcs-courses-ay14-15.

39. Posner, "No Half Measures," 2.

40. Vandegrift and Varner, "Evolving in Common," 7.

41. Ibid., 11.

42. Jaguszewski and Williams, *New Roles for New Times*, 13.

43. Vandegrift and Varner, "Evolving in Common," 7.

44. Vinopal and McCormick, "Supporting Digital Scholarship in Research Libraries," 4.

45. Lisa Spiro, "Getting Started in Digital Humanities," *Journal of Digital Humanities* 1, no. 1 (Winter 2011), http://journalofdigitalhumanities.org/1-1/getting-started-in-digital-humanities-by-lisa-spiro.

46. Josh Honn, "Never Neutral: Critical Approaches to Digital Tools and Culture in the Humanities" (paper presented at Digital Humanities Speaker Series, University of Western Ontario, London, Ontario, Canada, October 16, 2013), http://joshhonn.com/?p=1.
47. Pannapacker, "Stop Calling It 'Digital Humanities.'"
48. Ibid.
49. Bucknell University, Stories of the Susquehanna website, accessed September 20, 2014, http://susquehannastories.blogs.bucknell.edu.
50. Dartmouth College, The Occom Circle website, accessed September 20, 2014, www.dartmouth.edu/~occom.
51. Bethany Nowviskie, "Asking for It," *Bethany Nowviskie* (blog), February 8, 2014, http://nowviskie.org/2014/asking-for-it.
52. Miriam Posner, "Commit to DH People, Not DH Projects," *Miriam Posner's Blog*, March 18, 2014, http://miriamposner.com/blog/commit-to-dh-people-not-dh-projects.
53. Spiro, "Getting Started in Digital Humanities."
54. Pannapacker, "Stop Calling It 'Digital Humanities.'"
55. Tri-Co Digital Humanities, "Faculty and Staff Seminars," accessed November 6, 2014, http://tdh.brynmawr.edu/faculty-staff-seminars.
56. Bethany Nowviskie, "Asking for It."

Bibliography

Adams, Jennifer L., and Kevin B. Gunn. *Keeping Up With... Digital Humanities.* Association of College and Research Libraries (ACRL) website, April 2013. www.ala.org/acrl/publications/keeping_up_with/digital_humanities.

Alexander, Bryan, and Rebecca Frost Davis. "Should Liberal Arts Campuses Do Digital Humanities? Process and Product in the Small College World." In *Debates in the Digital Humanities*, edited by Matthew K. Gold. Part VI: Teaching the Digital Humanities. Minneapolis: University of Minnesota Press, 2012. http://dhdebates.gc.cuny.edu/debates.

Bates College. "Courses Related to Digital and Computational Studies 2014/2015." Imaging Center website. Accessed September 23, 2014. www.bates.edu/imaging/dcs-courses-ay14-15.

———. Digital Media Studios. Accessed September 23, 2014. www.bates.edu/digital-media.

———. Imaging Center. Accessed September 23, 2014. www.bates.edu/imaging.

———. "Material Culture Omeka." 2013. http://omeka-archive.bates.edu/201309.

———. PiCTR. Accessed September 29, 2014. http://pictr.bates.edu.

Bryson, Tim, Miriam Posner, Stewart Varner, Michael Page, Kim Durante, and Alain St. Pierre. "Roles of Librarians in Digital Humanities Centers." Research Commons White Paper. Digital Librarians Initiative (DLI), September 2010. https://docs.google.com/document/edit?id=1tch6xW7bh_vbJOzG7xYs9z6yX-ATC68x-Fg-BRVD298.

Bucknell University. Stories of the Susquehanna website. Accessed September 20, 2014. http://susquehannastories.blogs.bucknell.edu.

Dartmouth College. The Occom Circle website. Accessed September 20, 2014. www.dartmouth.edu/~occom.

Honn, Josh. "Never Neutral: Critical Approaches to Digital Tools and Culture in the Humanities." Paper presented at Digital Humanities Speaker Series, University of Western Ontario, London, Ontario, Canada, October 16, 2013. http://joshhonn.com/?p=1.

Jaguszewski, Janice M., and Karen Williams. *New Roles for New Times: Transforming Liaison Roles in Research Libraries.* Washington, DC: Association of Research Libraries, August 2013. www.arl.org/storage/documents/publications/NRNT-Liaison-Roles-final.pdf.

Nowviskie, Bethany. "Asking for It." *Bethany Nowviskie* (blog), February 8, 2014. http://nowviskie.org/2014/asking-for-it.

Pannapaker, William. "Stop Calling It 'Digital Humanities.'" *Chronicle of Higher Education,* February 18, 2013. http://chronicle.com/article/Stop-Calling-It-Digital/137325.

Posner, Miriam. "Commit to DH People, Not DH Projects." *Miriam Posner's Blog,* March 18, 2014. http://miriamposner.com/blog/commit-to-dh-people-not-dh-projects.

———. "No Half Measures: Overcoming Common Challenges to Doing Digital Humanities in the Library." *Journal of Library Administration* 53, no. 1 (2013): 43–52. Open-access copy at www.escholarship.org/uc/item/6q2625np.

Rockenbach, Barbara. "Digital Humanities in Libraries: New Models for Scholarly Engagement." *Journal of Library Administration* 53, no. 1 (2013): 1–9. Open-access copy at http://hdl.handle.net/10022/AC:P:18892.

Schaffner, Jennifer, and Ricky Erway. *Does Every Research Library Need a Digital Humanities Center?* Dublin, OH: OCLC Research, 2014. http://oclc.org/content/dam/research/publications/library/2014/oclcresearch-digital-humanities-center-2014.pdf.

Scheinfeldt, Tom. "Nobody Cares about the Library: How Digital Technology Makes the Library Invisible (and Visible) to Scholars." *Found History* (blog), February 22, 2012. www.foundhistory.org/2012/02/22/nobody-cares-about-the-library-how-digital-technology-makes-the-library-invisible-and-visible-to-scholars.

Spiro, Lisa. "Getting Started in Digital Humanities." *Journal of Digital Humanities* 1, no. 1 (2011). http://journalofdigitalhumanities.org/1-1/getting-started-in-digital-humanities-by-lisa-spiro.

Sula, Chris Alen. "Digital Humanities and Libraries: A Conceptual Model." *Journal of Library Administration* 53, no. 1 (2013): 10–26. Open-access copy at http://chrisalensula.org/digital-humanities-and-libraries-a-conceptual-model.

Tri-Co Digital Humanities. "Faculty and Staff Seminars." Accessed November 6, 2014. http://tdh.brynmawr.edu/faculty-staff-seminars.

Vandegrift, Micah. "What Is Digital Humanities and What's It Doing in the Library?" *In the Library with the Lead Pipe* (blog), June 27, 2012. www.inthelibrarywiththeleadpipe.org/2012/dhandthelib.

Vandegrift, Micah, and Stewart Varner. "Evolving in Common: Creating Mutually Supportive Relationships between Libraries and the Digital Humanities." *Journal of Library Administration* 53, no. 1 (2013): 67–78. Open-access copy at http://pid.emory.edu/ark:/25593/cwzbf.

Vinopal, Jennifer, and Monica McCormick. "Supporting Digital Scholarship in Research Libraries: Scalability and Sustainability." *Journal of Library Administration* 53, no. 1 (2013): 27–42. Open-access copy at http://hdl.handle.net/2451/31698.

Waters, Donald J. "An Overview of the Digital Humanities." *Research Library Issues* no. 284 (2013): 3–22. http://publications.arl.org/rli284/3.

Zorich, Diane M. "Digital Humanities Centers: Loci for Digital Scholarship." In *Working Together or Apart: Promoting the Next Generation of Digital Scholarship, edited by Kathlin Smith and Brian Leney,* 70–78. Washington, DC: Council on Library and Information Resources, 2009. www.clir.org/pubs/pubs/reports/pub145/pub145.pdf.

Digital *Humanities*

IN THE LIBRARY:

PART 3

Collaboration, Spaces, and Instruction

CHAPTER EIGHT

Digital Humanities for the Rest of Us

Judy Walker

Introduction

Recently there has been a push to hire digital humanities librarians and establish big flashy digital humanities centers. This chapter discusses how J. Murrey Atkins Library at the University of North Carolina at Charlotte (UNC Charlotte) has worked collaboratively to provide digital humanities services and resources on a relatively low budget.

In 2009, the American Library Association Council approved and adopted "ALA's Core Competences for Librarianship." A close look at the competences suggest there is some overlap with the issues and needs of digital humanities scholarship. Some of the more obvious are the competences concerning information resources, knowledge organization, technological knowledge and skills, and user services.[1] Because of these similarities, there appears to be a logical connection between libraries, librarians, and digital humanities, and it is this connection librarians at J. Murrey Atkins Library at the University of North Carolina at Charlotte are trying to establish. Like Vandegrift and Varner, we believe we should be building on the strengths of librarianship to supplement and reflect the essential elements of digital humanities.[2] What we are doing is merely an extension of what we have been doing for years. None of the activities discussed in this chapter is drastic, but they will be far-reaching. They are also being done in collaboration with a number of different constituencies within the library, across campus, and in the community. To paraphrase Sula, seeing the obvious overlap of interests, competences, and structure, the library stopped wondering if it should be involved in the field of digital humanities and started strategizing how the library would be involved.[3]

Cast of Characters

Before discussing what is happening at J. Murrey Atkins Library, it will be helpful to know a bit about the cast of characters involved in supporting digital humanities on our campus. All of these units are committed to enhancing the instruction and research mission of the university and are involved with digital humanities scholarship and teaching. Establishing collaborative relationships between these entities has been a key to the successful implementation of services to those students and faculty involved in digital humanities projects.

The University of North Carolina at Charlotte is the region's premiere, urban research institution. A relatively young institution compared to others in the University of North Carolina system, it was established in the late 1940s to serve returning veterans from World War II. In the past two decades, it has seen tremendous growth and now enrolls over 27,500 students. Its seven colleges offer eighty bachelor's, sixty-three master's, and twenty-one doctoral degrees. The majority of its facilities have been built in the last twenty years, so it has the infrastructure to support the increasing technological demands for supporting robust digital humanities activities.

J. Murrey Atkins Library (http://library.uncc.edu) is the largest urban research library in the region and the only one serving the Charlotte metropolitan area. Physically, the library, like the university itself, has recently undergone major renovations. The renovations, based on ethnographic studies of student and faculty use and needs, have greatly expanded the collaborative space as well as overhauled the building's infrastructure to accommodate the greater technological demands being placed on it.

Of the eighty-five full-time staff members, thirty are professionals and are considered members of the university faculty. Although they are not tenure-tracked faculty, they have a robust retention and promotion track that parallels the responsibilities of the tenure-tracked faculty. They are required to do research and outreach. Fourteen of the librarians are considered liaisons with specific discipline expertise. Their responsibilities include instruction, research assistance, collection development, and outreach. It should be noted no one in the library currently has the title Digital Humanities Librarian. Activities in this area are being pursued by a variety of professionals and staff from a number of different units.

Atkins Library has always had an outstanding reputation among faculty and students when it comes to providing research and basic digital production services. From its inception, the library's information commons area has always had an area where students could edit video and audio projects required by a number of humanities courses. For a time, the library also circulated digital still and video cameras. But with the proliferation of mobile devices with excellent cameras for taking both still photos and video, the library has suspended that service.

The Special Collections unit (http://specialcollections.uncc.edu) was established in 1973 to manage the library's rare book and manuscripts collection and the university's archives. A key element of its mission is to collect, create, curate, and disseminate rare, historical, and digital materials for research. Its services, which are available to the community as well as to faculty and staff, include instruction, reference, and tools to support digital research.

In the fall of 2010, the library began discussions with university faculty and students to address current and future digital scholarships needs. As a result, in 2011 the Digital Scholarship Lab (DSL) was established to provide support to faculty and students in the production and management of digital scholarship. The phrase *digital scholarship* was used because it was broad in scope and would include a variety of digital research methods, as well as providing for the digital dissemination of scholarship. Thus digital humanities projects and scholarship are included within its purview. Services of the unit include but are not necessarily limited to the establishment and promotion of a digital repository, hosting open-source research journals, instruction and assistance in data management, copyright advisement, and usability testing. The unit also works closely with the Special Collections department to provide instruction and assistance in development of digital collections and exhibits using Omeka. Because the staff of the unit is small, it relies on the involvement of library liaisons to support, promote, and integrate their services into the curriculum. How the liaisons provide this support will be discussed in more detail shortly. At the moment, there is no physical space allocated specifically for the unit, but the library is currently renovating an area to provide easier access to the unit's technologies, expertise, and services.

The Center for Teaching and Learning (CTL; http://teaching.uncc. edu) is a department within the university's Information Technology unit. Its primary responsibilities are to provide professional development opportunities for faculty to ensure quality teaching and to provide technological support for campus-wide instructional technology systems such as Moodle and Mahara. CTL offers faculty workshops, online resources, and consultations with instructional designers for course design and access to a variety of learning technologies. Although CTL focuses on instruction and work with faculty, it has found itself working with faculty wanting to incorporate digital humanities projects into their courses.

The university has a number of specific initiatives to enhance teaching and student learning in addition to the Center for Teaching and Learning. The Center for Communications across the Curriculum is one such initiative that assists faculty with developing a communication-enhanced curriculum that includes oral and written communication outcomes and provides students with frequent opportunities for writing and speaking across the curriculum. A small staff provides mini-workshops and discussions on various topics, best practices, and techniques for integrating oral and written communications and critical-thinking skills into courses.

Getting Started

The library's first significant foray into working with faculty and students in the area of digital humanities occurred in the early 2000s, when the Special Collections department received a grant for a local history project called New South Voices (http://nsv.uncc.edu). The project was originally supported in part with federal LSTA funds made possible through a grant from the Institute of Museum and Library Services and administered by the State Library of North Carolina, a division of the Department of Cultural Resources. It was developed further as part of North Carolina ECHO (Exploring Cultural Heritage Online), a collaborative project providing access to special collections throughout the state. New South Voices provides access to more than 700 transcripts of interviews, narratives, and conversations documenting life in the Charlotte, North Carolina, region in the twentieth century, including the experiences and language of recent immigrants to the area. UNC Charlotte faculty, students and staff as well as several community organizations conducted the interviews. Many transcripts have audio recordings, and new recordings continue to be added individually as the quality of each is checked.

The New South Voices project is an excellent example of collaboration. It included librarians, students, faculty, and community organizations. The librarian managing the project worked with faculty and students to conduct the interviews. Students from the departments of history, English, Africana studies, and computing science were responsible for transcribing, editing, meta tagging, copying, and digitizing the interviews. The community partners, such as the Museum of the New South and the Carolina Agency for Jewish Education, identified key people in the community to be interviewed. Since the technologies for developing this project have been constantly evolving, the staff of Special Collections has worked closely with the Center for Teaching and Learning to update equipment and digitalization techniques. The key to the success of this project was maintaining communications between the diverse members of the team.

The project is also a good example of both creation and curation of knowledge. The interviews provide new insights into understanding the history of the region. They provide a wide variety of points of view and details about life in the twentieth century that was not available previously. The new knowledge was then analyzed and classified for dissemination to scholars and the community at large. Students and scholars can now analyze these documents through a variety of means, such as textual analysis or cultural analytics, to create additional knowledge.

Creation, curation, and analysis are all key components of digital humanities. This project demonstrates how librarians can be an integral part of the process. Libraries and librarians have always been good mediators between users and resources, and this project demonstrates how they can be the link between faculty, students, and the community. Since one of the primary elements of the Special Collections unit mission is to collect and provide access to local community history, the library became the locus of activity because we had the storage capability and directive to collect the resources. But we didn't have the staff support to properly collect and organize them. The faculty member wanted his students to have the experience of collecting, curating, and analyzing primary resources—in this case, interviews—but didn't have access to the resources or tools. The local community organizations also wanted to collect these histories but didn't have the capacity to store them. They could, however, provide access to the actual primary sources—the people to be interviewed. The librarians also had the expertise in using the digital tools to collect and curate the resources, which they shared with the students to develop public access to the collection. It was a librarian who identified the different needs of the library, faculty, students, and community and was able to bring these groups together to collaborate on the project.

This project would be very easy to duplicate in just about any library setting. Libraries are part of a community and have traditionally gathered resources about that community as part of their mission. This project goes beyond just collecting secondary resources to creating primary sources for students and scholars to use. The possibilities for this type of collaboration are almost limitless.

The New South Voices project proved to be somewhat of a watershed project for the library, the university faculty and students, and community organizations. Librarians started looking at the library's resources in a different way, especially the primary resources in the collection. Everyone started thinking and experimenting with new ways to curate and disseminate resources beyond listing them in a catalog. Digitization projects began to spring up. Liaisons to the humanities, especially history, began to collaborate more with the librarians and staff in the Special Collections unit to integrate resources (print and digital) into the courses they were teaching. Liaisons also began to realize the technologies used for digital humanities scholarship were many of the same technologies we were using for instruction. We found ourselves suggesting not only new resources but also new technologies to the faculty with whom we were collaborating.

Although the number of faculty and students involved in this project was small, they came away from the endeavor with a new appreciation of what the library could do improve their scholarship and teaching. They discovered a new breed of librarian with knowledge and skills beyond how to find a resource in the catalog. In reality this was the best advertising the library could create for itself because the faculty went back to their respective departments and spread the word. And as the word spread, additional professors began to see the library as a partner in their research endeavors as well as instruction.

The project also elevated our stature in the community. The library has collaborated with a number of other community organizations to develop both physical and digital exhibits. Currently we are collaborating with NASCAR to digitize photographs, press kits, and other memorabilia chronicling its history and make it available to the public. The collection also includes papers and memorabilia of several drivers as well. Resources from the library are also being used by the Levine Museum of the New South's exhibit *LGBTQ Perspectives on Equality*. Although this is not specifically a digital project, it demonstrates how one project can lead to another.

Next Steps

With the success of the New South Voices, it became apparent the library needed to have some type of organized effort to promote its new capabilities. To address this need, the Digital Scholarship Lab (DSL) was created. Because there was no budget to create a completely new unit, the DSL was more a reorganization of existing staff expertise and rebranding. Although it was not created strictly for digital humanities projects, many of its activities are directly related to the field. DSL staff act like a matchmaker, connecting faculty and students with liaisons and other library staff with the skills they need. The process works both ways, with liaisons referring faculty and students to DSL staff when necessary.

Because the DSL is a new library service, its staff knows collaborating with other units in the library and the university will be the key to its success. They have established strong relationships with both the Center for Teaching and Learning (CTL) and the Center for Communication across the Curriculum (CCAC). One of the first major collaborations was with the CCAC. It was looking for a tool that would allow students and faculty in a course to asynchronously collaborate verbally and not just in writing. The DSL staff knew the education liaison had been working with several professors in the College of Education on the same issue. As a result, the education liaison teamed up with DSL staff to conducted a workshop on VoiceThread, an asynchronous, collaborative application that encourages students and faculty to discuss a topic verbally, a topic that is usually presented as some type of visual, set of visuals, or video. This tool proved invaluable to the faculty in the dance department as they started using it to evaluate student work. This workshop helped establish in the minds of faculty that librarians understood what went on in their classrooms and were a valuable resource in the area of technology as well as books. Librarians continue to do workshops addressing specific needs of faculty involved with the CCAC.

The DSL staff was also instrumental in establishing a positive relationship with the staff of the Center for Teaching and Learning. Since this unit was originally part of the library when it was first established in the late 1990s, some individual relationships were established during that time period. But when it was moved to the Information Technology unit in the early 2000s, unit relationships cooled a bit, especially since the primary function of CTL at that time was to implement and support the university course management system. As CTL matured and turned its attention to assisting faculty with course design, links between CTL and the library began to strengthen again. Many librarians take workshops offered by CTL to keep up-to-date on the technologies being used by the faculty and to improve their own instruction. While taking the workshops, we often find ourselves suggesting additional resources and technologies, which are often incorporated into subsequent workshops. In recent years, CTL staff have found themselves working with faculty who want to incorporate digital humanities projects into their courses. DSL staff and liaisons are helping CTL address issues such as copyright and curation through workshops and online tutorials.

Addressing DH Directly

In an effort to address digital humanities issues directly in the spring of 2013, Atkins Library, under the leadership of the DSL, staff hosted THATCamp Piedmont (http://piedmont2013.thatcamp.org). *THATCamp* stands for "The Humanities and Technology Camp." It is an "unconference," which is an open, free meeting where humanists and technologists of all skill levels learn and build together in sessions proposed on the spot by the attendees. THATCamp Piedmont was a free two-day workshop open to professors, students, technologists, librarians, K–12 educators, and archivists who work in the humanities. Since this was our first attempt at this type of conference, we decided the first day would have a more formal schedule with hands-on workshops for Omeka, WordPress, screencasting, digital storytelling, Zotero, concordances, and peer collaboration. The workshops were presented by librarians, professors, and CTL staff. The second day was much more fluid, with the participants suggesting and then voting on the topics to be discussed. Topics on the second day included agent modeling, data visualization, gamification, Google apps, carpentry, VDO collaboration around digital artifacts, hacker space, and more. Some of the participants gave on-the-spot presentations on the topics or shared what they were doing with their projects.

Hosting this type of unconference took minimal effort and nominal funding. We advertised on local and regional e-mail discussion lists plus sent direct invitations to libraries and academic institutions. Word of mouth was probably the most effective means of advertisement. There was no formal registration, so we really didn't know how many folks would show up, which was a bit unnerving. When participants arrived, they picked up a very simple schedule with a list of workshops and their locations and a blank name tag. Everyone was on their own for food, and participants came and went as needed. It was both a very relaxed and a stimulating atmosphere.

However, the benefits of hosting the event were tremendous. It again placed librarians at the forefront of the discussion. The mix of attendees was very interesting, including archivists, teaching faculty, academic librarians, IT staff, and even a few public librarians. The participants were primarily from the North Carolina Piedmont region, but there were a few participants from further afield. The interaction between the participants was energizing and very informative. It also encouraged collaboration among a number of local institutions. The responsibility of hosting these "camps" on an annual basis is now being shared with another local institution, Davidson College. And although THATCamp is a formal organization (http://thatcamp.org), the structure of the conference could be adapted to any situation. Faculty and librarians have discussed doing unconferences related to specific areas of digital humanities, but these are still in the planning stages. The faculty in the history department, the library's history liaison, and members of Special Collections are thinking about developing an unconference as part of their preparation for the regional National History Day competition (http://www.ncdcr.gov/historyday/Home.aspx).

Additional Support for DH Scholarship

Part of the Digital Scholarship Lab's mission is to assist students and faculty in disseminating their research. To accomplish this task, the library established two new services—open-access journal publication and a digital repository. About a decade ago when the idea of scholarly repositories first became prominent, the library tried to create a "home-grown" repository but really didn't have the staff expertise to develop a quality product. It was also very difficult to convince faculty of the need for such a repository. However, times have changed. Younger faculty members have a different mind-set and are highly collaborative. Sharing their ideas and research is very important to them. The university IT unit does provide secure servers for faculty to store their research, but the folks in IT do not understand how to make information accessible in meaningful ways. So the library has stepped in to provide that type of access. But this time, because of budget restraints, instead of trying to develop our own product, we have joined forces with sister institutions to create a consortium to make the scholarly output of the University of North Carolina system more available to the world. The end product is NC DOCKS (North Carolina Digital Online Collection of Knowledge and Scholarship; http://libres.uncg.edu/ir), which includes text articles, audio recordings, dissertations, and other formats. All materials are indexed by Google and are freely available to scholars and researchers worldwide. The response to this new service has been very positive. Faculty in the anthropology and English departments were the first to take advantage of the service, but other departments are quickly catching up. Although NC DOCKS supports a wide variety of formats, the library also decided to partner with an established data repository provider within the UNC system. As a result of that partnership, faculty also have access to a secure (and backed-up) Dataverse server.

In the spring of 2013, the library launched its first open-access journal, *Urban Education Research and Policy Annuals*. Although this is not specifically a digital humanities project, it was quickly followed by the publication of an undergraduate psychology journal and two additional education-related journal. The library is now working with several other departments to begin similar publications. It should be noted DSL staff work with the individual departments to set up the publications and train members of the departments (usually graduate or doctoral students) on maintaining the production of the journal. The librarians are not involved in the reviewing process or the routine publication processes.

Recently the library received additional funds from the university's Office of Academic Affairs to purchase equipment for a digital visualization lab. Currently there is no central location on campus to make this type of equipment and software available to the faculty as a whole. Several departments, mostly in the engineering and computing sciences, have this type of technology for their own faculty members. However, faculty in the humanities and social sciences do not have access to this high-end equipment and software. Since the library provides access to a wide variety of data sources and already has staff to support the manipulation of data, a digital visualization lab is a logical extension of its current services. Although there will be staff dedicated to supporting the technical aspects of the lab, the liaisons will be expected to become familiar with the technologies in order to promote the services to their faculty. They will also be able to use it for their own research.

From the Lab to the Liaisons

From the brief descriptions above of project activities, it would appear the DSL staff are the primary purveyors of digital humanities work at Atkins Library. As mentioned earlier, the Digital Scholarship Lab has a very small staff. They are primarily responsible for the technical aspects of their services. The mission of the Digital Scholarship Lab cannot be accomplished without the support of other librarians, particularly those in Special Collections and the subject liaisons. Atkins Library's approach to supporting digital humanities on campus is a team effort. No one unit within the library has sole responsibility for its success. Librarians throughout the library work to promote the services, and many provide direct input to a variety of projects.

It is relatively easy to describe the activities of the Digital Scholarship Lab and its important role in establishing the library as a credible partner in the field of digital humanities. What is much more difficult to describe is how individual librarians are making substantial contributions to the effort. Subject liaisons act as point persons guiding faculty and students to the necessary services. We advertise the services to our respective disciplinary departments, and like most good liaisons, we often know what is needed before the faculty members realize they need it. Some of what we are doing would be considered traditional liaison responsibilities, such as making faculty aware of new data sources and digital humanities technologies. Others are a bit "out of the box" for liaisons, such as actually teaching students how to use the digital tools or being embedded in a class project.

Librarians have been assisting faculty and students with their research for decades. But helping them, especially students, go beyond finding the five to ten peer-reviewed articles for a research paper can be a real challenge. UNC Charlotte has recently implemented a program called Prospect for Success, designed to improve student success during the freshman year. One of the components of the program includes an inquiry project. Every department has to integrate some type of inquiry project into a freshman-level course. Many of the humanities and social sciences have incorporated this project in their general education courses. The development and implementation of the program has been a great opportunity for liaisons to work collaboratively with faculty in developing assignments. The challenge, however, has been to encourage faculty to go beyond the traditional research paper and create assignments that incorporate aspects of digital humanities pedagogy. As a result of this program, liaisons are helping students and faculty discover new types of resources, such as using social media to investigate current issues, and introducing them to new tools of inquiry as simple as using Wordle for text analysis. This same type of collaboration is occurring in upper-level courses as well. Some of this work is being done in collaboration with CTL through sponsored workshops, but much of it is on a one-to-one basis with the faculty. The one advantage that library liaisons have over the CTL staff is that we are actually in the classroom with the students and see what is going on. We can be proactive in suggesting resources and technologies based on what we see in the classroom.

Another traditional role of librarians is that of aggregator and curator. Librarians are great at finding and organizing information and resources. What we haven't done in the past, though, is share our tools and expertise. The New South Voices mentioned earlier in this chapter is a great example of sharing that expertise, and of course the special collection provides a wealth of primary resources. Subject liaisons are doing the same thing on an individual basis. Several professors in the history department are now having their students create projects in Omeka, which would not have happened without the assistance of the history liaison. On a smaller scale, the education liaison encouraged faculty teaching a multicultural course to incorporate simple tools like Glogster and VoiceThread into her multi-genre assignment. With the integration of these types of tools into course curriculum, students not only have to do the research to discover valuable content, they also have to analyze and synthesize it to create new knowledge. Thus they are contributing to the discipline's knowledge base.

The librarians in the Special Collections unit have been aggregating and making primary resources accessible to students and faculty for years. It has only been recently that they have taken those resources and created digital exhibits. Most of these exhibits have related directly to the university or the Charlotte region. However, recently, an instruction librarian discovered the comic book collection housed in Special Collections. He has a passion for comic books and decided to create a digital exhibit of his own—*Heroes and Villains: Silver Age Comics* (http://silveragecomics. omeka.net). The exhibit highlights comics of the era published by industry leaders DC Comics and Marvel Comics from the mid-1950s to the early 1970s and includes background information, a timeline, video, and illustrations from the comics. As a result of this exhibit, the librarian has had the opportunity to present at several local and national venues. This is a good example of how a librarian can go beyond what would be considered traditional library research to contribute to another discipline's knowledge base; it is being now being used in the English department's curriculum. Several other liaisons are considering doing similar projects in their subject disciplines.

Today, academic librarians with subject expertise are often called liaisons. A better title might be mediator. For decades, librarians have been connecting people with print resources. In today's high-tech digital environment, librarians not only have to connect faculty and students with the traditional resources, but we also have to connect them with the digital tools to understand those resources. Databases help find the traditional resources and data, but what tools do the students and professors need to interpret that data and then communicate their analysis of the data? Connecting them to those tools is now the responsibility of any librarian who wishes to be involved in digital humanities. For example, a philosophy faculty member set up a consultation with his liaison to discuss a project on which he was working. Initially it appeared he just wanted some tips on what databases to search and the best way to organize what he found. However, as he described his project to the liaison, it became apparent that he was embarking on a major text-analysis project. He mentioned he was working with a doctoral student from computing informatics to create a program to analyze the text of the journal articles. For whatever reason, he was not aware of the host of robust text-analysis applications already available. The liaison shared with him the incredibly useful website DiRT (Digital Research Tools; http://dirtdirectory.org), which is a directory of research tools for scholarly use arranged by function. It listed seventy-eight applications under the heading Analyze Texts. The professor was surprised and said he would share this with his student and see which tool might be the most appropriate for his project. This simple connection may have saved the student from many hours of programming and reinventing the wheel.

The Challenges

At the institutional programmatic level, Atkins Library's efforts to support digital humanities through its Digital Scholarship Lab have been a mixed bag. Professors who have taken advantage of the new services have nothing but praise for the projects and are great ambassadors for the library. However, there are still a great many professors who either have not embraced the principles of digital humanities or do not see how the library can help them. There are still professors within the humanities and social sciences who do not understand the relationship between the library databases and the Internet. They still tell their students they can't use full-text articles from our databases because they think the articles are from the Internet. These same professors are skeptical of any type of digitized resource. On the other hand, there are the professors who feel the library's primary role is to get the resources they need to do their research. Often these professors are so focused on their research they really aren't aware of the most current resources and tools that could enhance their scholarship. And of course, like most people in general, many professors just don't have the time or inclination to change. It's easier to keep doing things the way they have been than to try something new. Every academic institution has professors like these. They are not unique to UNC Charlotte. Although Atkins Library uses a variety of communication tools (e-mail, blogs, Facebook, etc.), professors respond best to personal attention. Connecting with faculty and changing their hearts and minds will be a constant challenge for librarians for ages to come, and unfortunately there doesn't seem to a silver-bullet solution on the horizon. But there is an environment of collaboration growing on campus, which will certainly help in the effort.

Dealing with reluctant faculty is nothing new to librarians. But while trying to develop a positive environment for digital humanities, the library encountered a few challenges that were surprising. Some of the challenges have been overcome, and others are still being addressed. The first was convincing the provost that the library could play a significant role in this area in order to secure funding for the new services. As issues of copyright; scholarly publishing; finding, sharing, and managing large datasets; and open access bubbled up from the rank-and-file faculty, it became clear that a neutral party would be best suited to address the issues. The library is in the unique position of being both a service and an academic unit, which places it in an ideal position to assume responsibility for these issues. The provost agreed with this assumption and has supported the library in the creation of the services. The fact the library chose to build upon services already in place and then implemented the new services incrementally also worked to its advantage in tough economic times. Funding for the digital scholarship initiatives has come from a variety of sources, but primarily from grants, reallocation of current budget, and some one-time monies from the provost's office. The library, however, has also taken advantage of open-source applications and consortial collaboration, which has allowed it to do more with less on a shoestring budget.

One of the more difficult issues the Atkins Library has encountered is its relationship with the university IT unit. Although we have a good collaborative relationship with the Center for Teaching and Learning, a department of the IT unit, the same cannot be said for the unit as a whole. In general, IT is supportive of the library's infrastructure, but its staff do not have a good grasp of the access needs of libraries. Security is of utmost importance to both the library and IT, but exactly what type and how much security is debatable. So there is often a considerable amount of time spent on these issues, which in turn delays the implement of projects and services. And then of course, there is the debate over who should pay for the infrastructure since it benefits the entire campus community. Unfortunately, we have not uncovered any silver bullets to remedy this issue except patience and constantly educating the IT staff about the research and scholarship needs of the students and faculty.

Finally, there has been some resistance, or at least a lack of enthusiasm, on the part of some library staff and librarians. Much like professors, librarians also tend to stay within their comfort zone. Everyone feels there is more and more being expected of them, and they are overwhelmed with the prospect of one more expectation. Although the library administration encourages all the librarians to be proactive in the area of digital humanities and digital scholarship, it does not expect the same level of commitment from everyone. All liaisons are expected to be familiar with the various library programs and projects that support digital humanities, but how involved they get with faculty projects is up to them. The library administration supports those who wish to be more involved in digital humanities projects by providing release time, funding for workshops, and assistance in developing grants.

Keeping Up

Those librarians who choose to be more involved in digital humanities projects employ a variety of practices to stay up-to-date with the field. These practices really aren't that different from what any proactive library liaison or instructional librarian already does, they just focus a little more on issues and practices in the field of digital humanities scholarship and pedagogy. Probably the most challenging of these practices is keeping up with faculty digital humanities projects. It's relatively easy to discover faculty research interests after they have published their findings. It's keeping up with the projects and research they are currently working on that is more of a challenge. If a liaison already has established a personal relationship with a particular professor, the process is much easier. Our liaisons make a concerted effort to meet with every new faculty member to discuss their research and instructional support needs. These meetings lay the foundation for building a collaborative relationship. Attending departmental meetings, or at least reading minutes from the meetings, is of some help, but often those meetings are more administrative in nature. Most of the departments on campus have some type of e-mail distribution list, and many liaisons are members of their department's list. Those tend to be more newsy, announcing new grants and research projects. Many departments and colleges also produce regular newsletters, which also include announcements of grants and awards. Following departments and individual professors on social media is another option. A good number of UNC Charlotte professors use Facebook and Twitter to discuss their research. Of course, not all research is digital humanities research, but once a liaison becomes aware of a project, he or she can begin to develop a strategy for supporting that professor with his or her research.

Keeping up with the field of digital humanities is another matter, but it is relatively easy to accomplish, albeit time-consuming. Again our liaisons use the same practices they use to keep up with trends and issues in any discipline. They follow blogs such as ACRL's *dh + lib* (http://acrl.ala.org/dh), which specially discusses connections between digital humanities scholars and librarians. But discipline-specific digital humanities blogs also exist. ACRL has recently established a Digital Humanities Interest Group on ALA Connect (http://connect.ala.org/node/158885). Other groups that liaisons participate include Zotero's Digital Humanities Group (www.zotero.org/groups/digital_humanities/items) and THATCamp (http://thatcamp.org/about). DHCommons (http://dhcommons.org) and HASTAC (Humanities, Arts, Science, and Technology Alliance and Collaboratory; www.hastac.org) are two additional sites liaisons find extremely helpful. Liaisons find that these sites, along with the Twittersphere, not only provide valuable background information, they are also great places to get ideas for their own research projects.

Since technology is key to digital humanities, it is important for liaisons to be informed about current and emerging technologies. It's not necessary that we know all the technical aspects of these technologies, but we should be able to connect professors with these technical resources. As mentioned earlier in this chapter, liaisons at Atkins Library have found the DiRT directory (http://dirtdirectory.org) an invaluable resource, but we also glean information and resources from a wide variety of sites and blogs. Each liaison has his or her own favorite site for learning about new technologies, and most of them are not specific to digital humanities. The key is identifying new technologies regardless of source and understanding how they might be applied to a digital humanities project.

What Have We Learned?

Although UNC Charlotte is a large institution with a variety of digital humanities projects, it has been pursuing a more STEM-related curriculum and research agenda. Atkins Library has only recently, within the past five years, turned its attention to becoming a major player in the university's digital scholarship activities. The temptation to rush into developing a "digital humanities center" was very inviting because no one else on campus was doing it and they are flashy and trendy right now. Instead, the library chose to take a path best described by a recent OCLC report by Schaffner and Erway.[4] They came to the same realization we did several years earlier, that academic research library are already supporting digital humanities in some way or another.[5] What we decided to do was determine what we were already doing and take those services and expertise and rebrand them in such a way that faculty and students know they can be used to create and implement digital humanities projects in their research or scholarship.

The establishment of the Digital Scholarship Lab is a visible sign of the library's commitment to this endeavor. It's not a center but a lab where students and faculty can explore a variety of resources and experiment with ideas and technologies. And they will find willing collaborators. However, the DLS does not stand alone in this effort; its success depends on the involvement of liaisons and Special Collections librarians. It has been a great catalyst for forming collaborations with other entities on campus and other institutions in the Charlotte region. But the bulk of the work is being done collaboratively with DLS personnel, liaisons, and Special Collections librarians.

In many ways Atkins Library is doing what academic libraries and librarians have been doing for over a century, connecting faculty and students with resources. The difference is now those resources are not just books but include a host of digital resources, with new ones appearing almost daily. The establishment of the DSL has given us the confidence to see ourselves as partners, not just conduits, in the process of all types of digital scholarship, including digital humanities. We are still developing one-on-one relationships with faculty and students, but we are also helping faculty incorporate new digital resources and technologies into their instruction and helping students create dynamic, engaging digital projects. We are also collaborating with faculty on research projects that are adding to the knowledge base of disciplines outside the field of librarianship. It has not necessarily been an easy shift, and there is still a lot of potential for growth, but it has reinvigorated the librarians' sense of professionalism and raised the stature of the library in the eyes of the university community.

Essentially, Atkins Library librarians has taken up Micah Vandegrift's call to action, "Stop asking if the library has a role, or what it is, and start getting involved in digital projects that are already happening."[6] Create a digital humanities–friendly environment!

Notes

1. "ALA's Core Competences of Librarianship," final version, American Library Association, January 27, 2009, www.ala.org/educationcareers/sites/ala.org.educationcareers/files/content/careers/corecomp/corecompetences/finalcorecompstat09.pdf.
2. Micah Vandegrift and Stewart Varner, "Evolving in Common: Creating Mutually Supportive Relationships between Libraries and the Digital Humanities," *Journal of Library Administration* 53, no.1 (2013): 67–78, doi:10.1080/01930826.2013.756699.
3. Chris Alen Sula, "Digital Humanities and Libraries: A Conceptual Model," *Journal of Library Administration* 53 no. 1 (2013) 10–26, doi:10.1080/01930826.2013.756680.
4. Jennifer Schaffner and Ricky Erway, *Does Every Research Library Need a Digital Humanities Center?* (Dublin, OH: OCLC Research, 2014). http://oclc.org/content/dam/research/publications/library/2014/oclcresearch-digital-humanities-center-2014.pdf.
5. Ibid., 14.
6. Micah Vandegrift, "What Is Digital Humanities and What's It Doing in the Library?" *In the Library with the Lead Pipe* (blog), June 27, 2012, www.inthelibrarywiththeleadpipe.org/2012/dhandthelib.

Bibliography

American Library Association. "ALA's Core Competences of Librarianship," final version. January 27, 2009. www.ala.org/educationcareers/sites/ala.org.educationcareers/files/content/careers/corecomp/corecompetences/finalcorecompstat09.pdf.

Schaffner, Jennifer, and Ricky Erway. *Does Every Research Library Need a Digital Humanities Center?* Dublin, OH: OCLC Research, 2014. http://oclc.org/content/dam/research/publications/library/2014/oclcresearch-digital-humanities-center-2014.pdf

Sula, Chris Alen. "Digital Humanities and Libraries: A Conceptual Model." *Journal of Library Administration* 53, no. 1 (2013): 10–26. doi:10.1080/01930826.2013.756680.

Vandegrift, Micah. "What Is Digital Humanities and What's It Doing in the Library?" *In the Library with the Lead Pipe* (blog), June 27, 2012. www.inthelibrarywiththeleadpipe.org/2012/dhandthelib.

Vandegrift, Micah, and Stewart Varner. "Evolving in Common: Creating Mutually Supportive Relationships between Libraries and the Digital Humanities." *Journal of Library Administration* 53, no. 1 (2013): 67–78. doi:10.1080/01930826.2013.756699.

Collaboration and CoTeaching
Librarians Teaching Digital Humanities in the Classroom

Brian Rosenblum, Frances Devlin, Tami Albin, and Wade Garrison

Introduction: Converge, Merge, DH Is the Word

Digital humanities (DH) as an area of engagement with students, staff, and teaching faculty has been rapidly evolving at the University of Kansas Libraries (KU Libraries) over the past several years. As the popularity of DH tools, platforms, and methodologies has increased, so has the demand to support and engage teaching faculty with incorporating DH in their courses and with their own research interests. Many academic libraries, including KU Libraries, are both adjusting to and leading this shift, figuring out ways to support digital scholarship for research and teaching, while at the same time gently delineating our roles, responsibilities, and limitations.

KU Libraries, like many other Research I academic libraries across the United States and Canada, have gone through a significant reorganization.* From 2011 to spring 2013, KU Libraries implemented a process that not only envisioned a new overarching organizational structure, but also created a user-focused model to support faculty research and teaching.[1] The Research and Learning Division created through this process includes four centers based on user groups (Faculty, Graduate, Undergraduate, and Community), populated with librarians and staff to work with those specific constituents across the KU community. The librarians who make up these centers were drawn from previous roles focusing on digital scholarship, instruction services, and traditional liaison roles. Recognizing that the activities of these librarians overlapped in many ways that were not fully being utilized, the new Research and Learning Division has helped to merge these roles. The reorganization has meant that some librarians, placed in new roles, have had a significant learning curve in their new areas of responsibility, but this has also presented opportunities to gain new knowledge and skills and to create new synergies by working with colleagues with whom they had not worked extensively prior to the reorganization.

This chapter will describe three examples of efforts by librarians with subject, instruction, and digital scholarship expertise to provide digital humanities instruction and training to students and faculty and will look at how these efforts relate to our previous and evolving roles within the library. We will also provide concrete examples of in-class assignments, describe what worked well and what could be improved, and discuss some possible ways that we ourselves might develop the knowledge and skills needed to engage in this kind of work. We hope that these examples and observations can serve as models, starting points, or inspiration for subject specialists to both learn more about digital humanities and develop their own courses, assignments, and activities.

---

*   According to the library website, KU Libraries is "one of the top 50 libraries in the Association of Research Libraries" with "more than 4.4 million print volumes" across seven libraries on the Lawrence campus (University of Kansas, "At a Glance," KU Libraries website, accessed September 21, 2014, http://lib.ku.edu/about).

Example 1: An Introductory Digital Humanities Assignment

Our first example is an introductory-level digital humanities lecture and assignment that was delivered as part of an Introduction to Graduate Studies research methods seminar. In Spring 2012, the Director of Graduate Studies and associate professor in the KU French department and the subject librarian for French literature (Devlin, one of the coauthors), radically restructured the department's graduate research methods class. Devlin was embedded as the subject librarian in the class and attended all sessions. Rather than the typical one-off library session, overviews of relevant sources and research strategies were integrated throughout the class at the point of need. Throughout the semester, other librarians were invited into the class to present on topics such as copyright, scholarly communications, and working with special and rare collections. The course included the elements of a traditional bibliography and research methods class but was modified to also focus on developing practical, professionally useful skills and on an introduction to alternative academic careers. These practical skills included how to create a web-based professional portfolio with an academic curriculum vitae or a professional resume; how to write blogs on higher education issues and literary theory; how to produce teaching portfolio materials; and, of particular relevance to this chapter, how to carry out a digital humanities project. While the professor did not have a background in digital humanities, he was cognizant of the importance for humanities students to learn more about this growing area of research. The class was offered a second time in the Fall 2013 semester and was expanded to include graduate students from the Slavic and German departments to increase the class numbers and because many of the topics covered were of common interest to all. By collaborating with these other two language departments, the Introduction to Graduate Studies class can now be offered annually, rather than every two years as it had been in the past.

Two class sessions were allocated in the syllabus to the digital humanities component. One of the coauthors (Rosenblum), who had experience developing and supporting digital projects but not as much experience in classroom DH instruction, was asked to develop an assignment that would be suitable for introductory-level work, that could be described and accomplished within two class sessions, and that would still provide students with an effective, hands-on learning experience. After some preliminary research, he adapted and modified an assignment from Lauren Klein's Digital Humanities class at the Georgia Institute of Technology.[2] The first class session, led by Rosenblum, was devoted to an introductory lecture on digital humanities and included some suggested readings, examples of digital humanities projects, and pointers to resources, tools, publications, and organizations that the graduate students might find useful in learning more about digital humanities. There was also a very brief demonstration of Voyant,[3] an easy-to-use Web-based text-analysis application, and several other tools. The students were then assigned a reading, "The Hermeneutics of Screwing Around; or What You Do with a Million Books" by Stephen Ramsay,[4] and were asked to use a digital tool to apply the methodology of "screwing around" to a text of their choice, write a short blog post to describe their experience, and prepare for a short class presentation. The text of the assignment, adapted from Klein's original, is in appendix 9.1 at the end of this chapter.

Two open sessions were scheduled outside of class time over the next several weeks for students to get individual help with selecting and working with their chosen tool. More than half the students attended one of these open sessions. Rosenblum and the digital humanities librarian (Garrison) provided guidance in thinking about possible uses for the tools, showing more hands-on demos of the tools and introducing basic concepts such as removing stop words and the difference between text editors and word processors. The intent of the sessions was to simply give the students some ideas and enough knowledge to get started but not determine their research question for them. Rather, the assignment was intended to spur on learning by doing through a combination of trial and error and critical thinking, in the manner that much digital humanities work gets done.

Most of the students selected Voyant to explore a literary text, probably because it was the application shown most extensively in class and it includes a number of different types of visualizations and tools within the application. Other tools used by students included Juxta, Scalar, and Poem Viewer.[5]

One student, already proficient in programming and text analysis, developed his own Python scripts to support his analysis of the use of diminutives in Russian and other Slavic languages. The students wrote about their findings on their class blog, and during the second digital humanities class session later in the semester they gave a three-minute presentation on their findings to the rest of the class. The blogs were thoughtful and presentations were successfully delivered in a fun and engaging class session. The professor leading the class was impressed with the enthusiasm and engagement of the students in exploring a new digital tool.

The students used the tools for a variety of explorations, from looking at word frequencies and usage patterns (there were many word clouds) to looking at character relationships and networks. One student used Scalar to begin work on a scholarly, multimedia edition of a nineteenth-century novel. There were several instances of more than one student using the same tool and the same text. In these cases it was interesting to see the very different thought processes they used, the different questions they asked about the texts, and the different results they obtained. Mostly the assignment was a chance for the students to get some hands-on experience working with text and to get used to the idea of experimenting with tools that are often in a constant state of development. The students in the class liked the assignment and provided positive feedback at the end of the course. Some expressed a desire for even more digital humanities!

The development and incorporation of a digital humanities assignment into the Introduction to Graduate Studies class not only introduced these students to research in the digital humanities, but also engaged them by encouraging them to "play around" with a new tool. Additionally, it was a successful collaboration between a faculty member, a subject librarian, and a digital humanities specialist that supported faculty and graduate students in new ways of learning in the classroom and expanded their knowledge of humanistic research. The class also resulted in a new opportunity for the student noted above who was proficient in Python. This student later became the graduate student representative on the advisory board of KU's

Institute for Digital Research in the Humanities (IDRH, described below) and taught an introduction to text mining workshop at IDRH's workshop series the semester following the class. This opportunity and connection probably would have gone unrealized if this collaborative effort at bringing digital humanities into the classroom had not happened. As librarians' traditional roles in teaching continue to evolve, these kinds of partnerships will be essential to leveraging librarians' expertise to offer new services and work collaboratively with faculty to integrate digital humanities into the classroom. The Introduction to Graduate Studies class, including the same digital humanities assignment, will be offered again in the Fall 2014 semester.

Example 2: A Semester-Long Collaborative Digital Project

The Center for Faculty/Staff Initiatives and Engagement came together as a unit in May 2013, comprising staff with digital scholarship, instruction, and liaison expertise. In June 2013, three librarians from this center (Rosenblum, Garrison, and Albin) began a collaboration with a religious studies professor on a semester-long assignment for his graduate-level course on the archaeological site of the mystical cult Megaloi Theoi, located on the island of Samothrace in the Aegean Sea. Rosenblum and Garrison had previous DH experience and knowledge of various tools, while Albin, who had minimal DH knowledge, had expertise in pedagogy and research instruction. As in the first example above, the professor did not have any DH experience. He had an extensive collection of personal photos from Samothrace that he wanted to incorporate into his upcoming fall seminar.

The first step in this potential collaboration was to have a couple of very casual, noncommittal, low-stress conversations with the professor about what he might be envisioning for his upcoming course. In these conversations, librarians discussed the 818 photos, what to teach, how to teach, learning outcomes, level of librarian involvement, and what DH tools or platform to use. Each meeting was exploratory and somewhat awkward and involved a considerable amount of brainstorming. The unfocused nature of the conversations was to be expected. Librarians were working with a faculty member who was new to digital humanities, they were all in a newly formed faculty center and had to figure out how we worked together, and lastly, they were still negotiating how to define new roles and responsibilities. However, even with the conversations going in multiple directions, it was important to separately and then collaboratively envision a range of possibilities for the course. It was agreed fairly early on that this collaboration needed to be flexible and open, yet at the same time still have some structure built in for hands-on, librarian-led instruction sessions. Since this was a very early attempt by librarians in the faculty center to introduce and instruct graduate students and faculty in a digital project over a semester, it was imperative that adaptations were made as needed.

The librarians established that Omeka would be an appropriate platform to use.[6] It is designed to accommodate a range of items including photographs, is user-friendly and well-suited for collaborative work, and is free. Selecting a platform brought to light the potential time and labor involved in preparing, modifying, and maintaining the software. Rosenblum and Garrison had experience with Omeka, but Albin, who would be designing and teaching Omeka to the students, didn't even know how to properly pronounce the name of the platform.

When they contacted KU Information Technology about server space, the librarians discovered that IT didn't have a server environment with the correct specifications to run Omeka, so it was installed on an external server; the Institute for Research in the Digital Humanities (IDRH) paid a minimal monthly fee to house it there. An Omeka site was set up for the course and the entire collection of images, which had no associated metadata other than the image filename, was imported into the system. A sandbox site was also created allowing Albin to learn how Omeka worked, how to import images, how to create metadata using Dublin Core, how to display images via themes and exhibits, how to use plugins, and on occasion, how to break Omeka, which Rosenblum would then fix. Through experimenting and breaking the sandbox, Albin was able to conceptualize the types of handouts the students might need to understand, navigate, and build online open-access exhibits.

Meetings with the professor progressed over the summer. He decided that his students would use the photographs as an archive through which to theorize the role and significance of the archeological site. Each student would select a building and create an exhibit based on the photos and original text. Then as a class, they would collaboratively write an introductory page introducing the project and the exhibits. It was decided that a minimum of three hands-on training sessions during class time (2½ hours each) would be spread out over the semester, with the possibility of a fourth session closer to the end of the semester. The librarians would also meet with students one-on-one as needed.

The first two instruction sessions were designed to introduce students to Omeka, including creating collections and exhibits, the Semantic Web, and simple Dublin Core. While it was not a goal to turn the students into mini metadata librarians, the librarians felt that it was important that students grasp the significance and differences between tagging and more controlled vocabularies. Since the students were working on an archaeological site together, they needed to consider their potential audiences and whether or not they needed to include any discipline-specific language. To get their brains thinking about terms, words, descriptors, and tagging versus metadata, they were given the assignment of looking at photos on Flickr, specifically photos of Star Wars action figures with chipmunks and buildings from the 1983 World's Columbian Exposition,[†] individually creating tags and metadata for specific photos based only on the images and then together as a class discussing the terms they chose for tagging and the terms they chose for metadata.

In the third instruction session, students began building their collections from the 818 items, creating rudimentary layouts for exhibits, and

---

† Images used for assignment: Chris McVeigh, "Space Cowboy," photograph taken September 21, 2008Chris McVeigh, Chipmunk Adventures Album on Flickr, https://www.flickr.com/photos/powerpig/2878681351; "South Portal of Art Building," photograph, from *The Columbian Gallery: A Portfolio of Photographs from the World's Fair* (Chicago: Werner Company, 1894), in World's Columbian Exposition Collection at The Field Museum, GN90799d_CG_071w, posted to The Field Museum Library's Flickr photostream July 26, 2005, https://www.flickr.com/photos/field_museum_library/3410234992/in/set-72157616234589478.

brainstorming on metadata. The only metadata imported with the images when they were uploaded were the file names created by the professor. After the third session, librarians worked with students one-on-one as needed. They kept in touch with the professor and toward the end of the semester held a fourth and final session. Questions were sent ahead of time, allowing the librarians to do research in preparation for the class. This time around the students' questions were much more connected to the overall aesthetic of the project website, with requests to modify the layout and look and feel of the Omeka theme. The professor, not fully understanding the expense of customization of a corporate site, also asked to consider creating a theme that resembled the Waldorf Astoria's Omeka site. (The heavily customized theme the professor was referring to has since changed.) However, because only Rosenblum has some basic knowledge of the PHP and CSS necessary to modify themes and templates in Omeka, and because making such modifications creates challenges for the long-term maintenance of sites, the librarians could not accommodate those requests, especially for what was a pilot project for a class. That meeting and two subsequent meetings with the professor and his teaching assistant (TA) were to some degree frustrating for all parties.

During the final two meetings, the professor and his TA, who was very proficient with WordPress, suggested that the librarians create a WordPress site for the class and transfer all of the content from the Omeka site. There was a discussion about the pros and cons of using WordPress, with much of the conversation revolving around whether the professor and TA wanted to emphasize the final text and content of the exhibitions that the students created or whether they wanted to think of the project as an ongoing curation of a collection of several hundred individual images. (It turned out to be the former.) Mostly, however, the conversation centered on the issues of labor, commitment, and sustainability. For example, if the students and professor wanted to use WordPress as a platform, largely because of the graduate student's familiarity with the software, they would need to think about how to maintain the site in the future after the student has graduated and moved on. The libraries would not be able to support a WordPress site, not for technical reasons, but because of time and resources.

How the project concluded at the end of the semester was not necessarily a big surprise. Even though there may have been some frustration and disappointment, all parties involved, whether or not they recognize it, gained a considerable amount of knowledge about developing and implementing a digital project. What started off as a smallish undertaking—guiding students and the professor in the creation of collections and exhibits for possible public use—morphed into graduate students recognizing that their work, if it went public, would be used by people all over the world. In that sense, it's understandable that their concerns surrounding the aesthetics of the project site would increase towards the end of the semester and get pushed to the forefront. During their initial introduction to Omeka, the Semantic Web, and Dublin Core, they were not as invested as to how the site looked. Everybody was using a different theme for their exhibit, but by the end of the semester they saw the need for an overall cohesive representation of the site and had a desire for a bit more flashiness than what the default Omeka themes or the librarians could offer. Regardless of the issue of flash or fancy, Omeka still proved to be an excellent tool for teaching students about the practical and theoretical issues involved in creating digital projects.

For the librarians, the experience of working with a faculty member and the students on assignments and courses with a DH focus was extremely beneficial. It has given us a better understanding for working and negotiating in future collaborations on campus. It taught us that parameters and common understandings of roles and responsibilities need to be negotiated and constantly reiterated, regardless of the assignment, project, or course redesign. Collaborating and partnering with faculty ensures that both the professor and students understand the complexity of DH (pros and cons, benefits, and struggles.)

Example 3: Teaching the Teacher: Course Development Grants and Workshops

Our final example involves librarians not directly involved in the classroom, but helping build digital humanities capacity at the university through an incentive program designed to encourage professors to add digital humanities material to their courses. As we have seen in the examples described above, faculty often don't have the expertise to teach digital humanities to their students, even as they recognize the importance of introducing DH concepts and topics into their classroom. In addition, as we have also seen, it can be time-consuming for librarians to take on this role, especially when we are still developing our own expertise in this area. Librarians doing in-class DH instruction in this way would not be scalable if the demand significantly increases. In the long run, we may be able to better leverage our limited resources by sharing and repurposing our work and experiences in digital humanities pedagogy and by spreading DH knowledge and capacity more widely among others. The course development grant initiative administered by KU's Institute for Digital Research in the Humanities (IDRH) is one example of a small effort in this direction, and it is increasingly involving librarian expertise.[‡]

IDRH was founded in 2010 to provide resources and training in the practices and tools of the digital humanities for the KU community and is itself an example of a strong collaborative initiative between the libraries and the campus community. The institute is supported through a partnership between the KU Libraries, the Hall Center for the Humanities, and the College of Liberal Arts and Sciences (CLAS) and is administered jointly by a CLAS faculty codirector (Dwyer) and a KU Libraries codirector (Rosenblum). IDRH's primary programs include a digital humanities conference held every September, a monthly seminar series held at the Hall Center for the Humanities, a digital humanities seed grant program intended to help faculty pilot new digital projects, and a regular series of hands-on

---

[‡] For more information, please see the Institute for Digital Research in the Humanities website, accessed September 21, 2014, http://idrh.ku.edu.

workshops on digital tools and methods. In developing programs to support digital humanities research at KU, IDRH realized that education and training was a major factor in generating viable project proposals, and we have begun to explore ways to increase DH expertise among both faculty and students on campus. The Course Development Grant program is one effort towards this end.

The Course Development Grant program is intended to help develop an interdisciplinary palette of courses in digital humanities at KU.[§] IDRH offers a $1,000 stipend to tenured and tenure-track faculty who develop a new course in the digital humanities. The guidelines state that the course may be in any humanities or closely related discipline and may cover specific topics within a discipline (e.g., nineteenth-century English literature), as long as at least 50 percent of the course content covers DH skills, methods, and tools. The program can be used to develop undergraduate or graduate courses and favors proposals that attract students from a variety of departments and disciplines and that use open-source, nonproprietary, cross-platform tools. All proposed courses must be taught on the Lawrence or Edwards campus within three semesters of receiving funding, and participants are asked to submit a syllabus of the new course after it is offered.

Applicants submit a short two-to-three-page proposal in late spring outlining the proposed course, potential assignments, the frequency with which it will be offered, target student audience, and "the potential impact you expect the course to have on KU's digital humanities profile." Faculty from all humanities and related disciplines are invited to submit proposals. The submissions are reviewed by a small committee of librarians and faculty from IDRH community, including grant recipients from previous years. (See appendix 9.2 for a copy of the grant guidelines.)

While it was hoped that the program would lead to the development of a university-wide general introduction to DH course, that has not happened yet (in large part because there is not a clear departmental home for such a course, which would be highly interdisciplinary in both content and

---

§   Information on the Course Development Program can be found at "Course Development Grants," Institute for Digital Research in the Humanities website, accessed February 5, 2015, http://idrh.ku.edu/course-development-grants.

participants). Nevertheless, in three years the program has helped develop or revise seven courses across a range of disciplines:

- Introduction to Graduate Studies (French and Italian, Slavic, German combined), awarded 2014

- American Literature I (English), awarded 2014

- The Digital World of Louise Erdrich (English), awarded 2013

- Advanced German I (German), awarded 2013

- Manzoni in the Digital Age (French and Italian), awarded 2012

- Infomania (Journalism), awarded 2012

- The Digital Shakespeare (English), awarded 2012

The courses incorporate a range of digital humanities material and assignments, from the "screwing around" assignment discussed above, to introductory mapping and visualization exercises, to more in-depth analysis and critique of digital humanities projects and tools. The Introduction to Graduate Studies course discussed as example 2 above is one of our latest grant recipients, and that course is set to expand its digital humanities content in the coming years. (We plan to collect the syllabi from these courses from the instructors when they are available and make the available online and eventually make them available online.)

Grant recipients participate in a sixty-to-ninety-minute workshop session in late spring with IDRH staff, previous course development grant recipients, and, increasingly, librarians. So far, over the course of the three years the program has been in place, we have had three former subject liaisons participate in the workshop sessions. The grantees discuss intended learning outcomes and assignments for each course, and other participants, including the librarians, offer suggestions and share experiences from previous work in the classroom. These workshop sessions, while short, have proven to be stimulating and productive and a useful way for both instructors and librarians to become familiar with new pedagogical ideas and to improve and guide their course planning.

It is too soon to say how successful the Course Development Grant program has been in developing a palette of courses with significant DH content. The courses take time to develop and get into the university's course catalog. A couple of the courses have already been offered once, and others are still in development and will be offered for the first time in 2014 or 2015. While the expectation is that instructors will continue to develop and improve the DH aspects of the classes over time, there is no guarantee that this will happen. So the long-term outcomes of this program remain to be seen.

However, there have been several clear and immediate short-term benefits. The program has been effective in tapping into the existing interest in digital humanities instruction on the part of faculty and generating new interest. It is bringing faculty without DH experience into the conversation and providing a small forum for discussing, planning, and generating assignments that can be tested out in classroom. It provides some guidance for faculty new to digital humanities. And, through the vehicle of including previous year's recipients in the workshop sessions, it has begun to generate a small community of instructors and librarians to communicate and share ideas, providing another forum for librarians and faculty to partner. In short, for a relatively low cost, it has provided a way to start and maintain conversations with faculty about digital humanities instruction, resulting in some concrete activities and instruction in the classroom.

The next steps for IDRH include getting richer feedback from instructors after they have taught their new courses and gathering course materials and outcomes (syllabi, assignments, student work, and feedback) in order to create a repository of materials that can be shared and repurposed for other instructors at KU and beyond. IDRH also intends to work with other campus units, such as KU's Center for Teaching Excellence and the Honors Program, to continue to develop and expand such efforts. Finally, there is an opportunity to include a wider range of library staff in the program, especially in helping faculty craft instruction proposals, in reviewing proposals, and in participating in the workshop sessions.

Conclusion

Digital humanities is an area of scholarship that provides rich opportunities for engagement between librarians, faculty, and students. In the examples described above, all parties involved (the students, the faculty, and the various librarians with different areas of specialization) learned new skills and gained new DH knowledge that will inform and improve the way librarians engage with future faculty and student partnerships and with each other. Each party brings their own expertise and values together, ensuring stronger partnerships, more trust in collaborations, and a willingness to stretch their understanding of digital humanities. Librarians played a key role in conceiving, developing, and carrying out the in-class sessions and other initiatives described above.

In fact, librarians are essential to digital humanities development in the classroom for several reasons and are better positioned than many in the university to collaborate and lead the way in digital humanities instruction and engagement. The interdisciplinary nature of DH, with its focus on emerging tools and methodologies that span disciplines, means that DH expertise can't reside within a single department or school. Librarians are well situated to step in here with their own interdisciplinary expertise and connections across campus. In addition, DH's use of digital collections (whether a researcher's own private collection or materials provided by cultural heritage institutions) and the data-driven nature of DH—its engagement with issues such publishing and dissemination of knowledge, copyright and intellectual property, file formats, metadata and preservation, and managing and structuring data—are a natural alignment with the goals, activities, and professional expertise of librarians. In addition, while librarians may still be somewhat uncomfortable with our own knowledge of DH skills and methods, research faculty, as we have seen in our examples above, often have even less experience in digital scholarship and welcome guidance from librarians.

The examples in this chapter show additional reasons that librarians should not be seen as just service providers, but recognized as partners in aiding students and faculty with skill development as well as project development. Digital projects are complex endeavors that require all parties to have a mutual understanding of desired outcomes and each party's roles and responsibilities and to know what can be reasonably accomplished in any given circumstance. Even in smaller-scale initiatives, it is usually not a matter of a librarian providing a one-off class session to meet a request for a presentation or assignment in DH. Instead, librarians can start and keep alive ongoing conversation about tools, methods, learning outcomes, and collaborations that are at the heart of digital scholarship.

At KU Libraries, we hope to further develop our own expertise by implementing an internal professional development program to develop expertise in several "tracks" such as digital scholarship, teaching and learning, data, and scholarly communication. Our newly created Research and Learning Division, with its merging of traditional librarian roles, provides an opportunity for cross-training and professional development by having staff share their expertise with each other in a coordinated internal training program. The intent of this program is to give librarians with subject and instruction experience an opportunity to strengthen their knowledge of digital humanities and for digital scholarship and data librarians to learn about creating effective learning outcomes and the learning styles of different communities. Also, training our staff to train each other and to work on collaborative digital projects will enhance our own skills and expertise and enable us to be better teachers and collaborators with faculty and students. At the same time, we want to take heed of Trevor Muñoz's framing of digital humanities in libraries: "Digital humanities in libraries isn't a service and libraries will be more successful at generating engagement with digital humanities if they focus on helping librarians lead their own DH initiatives and projects."[7] Towards that end, we plan to explore project-based programs that bring together small groups of librarians from around the library to collaborate on a small digital projects, providing an opportunity for deeper learning than can be provided in a workshop.

There are many indications that digital humanities is becoming an important area of knowledge for campus educators and one that librarians will need to be familiar with and integrate with the ACRL Framework[8] and other literacies in our work to develop assignments of varying lengths for both undergraduate and graduate students. KU Libraries have had increasing conversations with individual faculty, as well as with department heads and teaching and research units across campus—such as the Center for Teaching Excellence, the undergraduate honors program, and the Center for Undergraduate Research—about integrating digital humanities into their activities. Finally, there is a growing volume of literature devoted to digital humanities pedagogy in a variety of venues ranging from published monographs (such as this volume) and journals, to conference presentations, to blog posts and online forums. We are monitoring these sources and looking at ways to bring their knowledge into our conversations with campus partners, into the classroom, and into our own instruction and research activities.[9]

Through the multiple approaches to developing digital humanities knowledge, we are preparing ourselves to meet the evolving requirements of effective, engaged library service.

Notes

1. Erin Ellis et al., "Positioning Academic Libraries For the Future: A Process and Strategy for Organizational Transformation" (paper presented at 35th International Association of Scientific and Technological University Libraries Conference, Aalto University, Espoo, Finland, June 2–5, 2014), http://hdl.handle.net/1808/14141; see also Janice M. Jaguszewski and Karen Williams, *New Roles for New Times: Transforming Liaison Roles in Research Libraries* (Washington, DC: Association of Research Libraries, August 2013), http://www.arl.org/storage/documents/publications/nrnt-liaison-roles-revised.pdf
2. Lauren Klein, "LCC 3843: Digital Humanities—Fourth Online Assignment: Sherlock Holmes Text Analysis," 2012, http://lkleincourses.lmc.gatech.edu/dh12/files/2011/12/oa4.pdf.
3. Stéfan Sinclair and Geoffrey Rockwell, Voyant Tools website, accessed September 21, 2014, http://voyant-tools.org.
4. Stephen Ramsay, "The Hermeneutics of Screwing Around; or What You Do with a Million Books," in *Pastplay: Teaching and Learning History with Technology*, ed. Kevin Kee (Ann Arbor, MI: University of Michigan Press, 2014), http://quod.lib.umich.edu/d/dh/12544152.0001.001/1:5/—pastplay-teaching-and-learning-history-with-technology?g=dculture;rgn=div1;view=fulltext;xc=1#5.1.
5. University of Virginia, Juxta Commons website, accessed September 21, 2014, www.juxtacommons.org; Alliance for Networking Visual Culture, Scalar website, accessed September 21, 2014, http://scalar.usc.edu; Oxford e-Research Centre, University of Oxford, "About" page, Poem Viewer website, accessed September 21, 2014, http://ovii.oerc.ox.ac.uk/PoemVis/about.html.

6. Roy Rosenzweig Center for History and New Media, Omeka website, George Mason University, accessed September 21, 2014, http://omeka.org.
7. Trevor Muñoz, "Digital Humanities in the Library Isn't a Service," *Trevor Muñoz* (blog), August 19, 2012, http://trevormunoz.com/notebook/2012/08/19/doing-dh-in-the-library.html.
8. Association of College and Research Libraries Standards Committee, "Framework for Information Literacy for Higher Education," version ACRL MW15 Doc 4.1, accessed February 3, 2015, http://acrl.ala.org/ilstandards/wp-content/uploads/2015/01/Framework-MW15-Board-Docs.pdf. Pending approval of the ACRL Board of Directors.
9. Please see the following sources: Association for Computers in the Humanities, "How Do We Introduce Undergraduates to the Digital Humanities?" Digital Humanities Questions and Answers Thread, accessed September 23, 2014, http://digitalhumanities.org/answers/topic/how-do-we-introduce-undergraduates-to-the-digital-humanities; Brett D. Hirsch, ed., *Digital Humanities Pedagogy: Practices, Principles and Politics* (Cambridge: Open Book Publishers, December 2012), www.openbookpublishers.com/product/161/digital-humanities-pedagogy—practices—principles-and-politics; Christopher Blackwell and Thomas Martin, "Technology, Collaboration, and Undergraduate Research," *Digital Humanities Quarterly* 3, no. 1 (2009), www.digitalhumanities.org/dhq/vol/3/1/000024/000024.html; College English Association, "Digital Humanities Pedagogy," special issue, *CEA Critic* 76, no. 2 (July 2014), http://muse.jhu.edu/journals/cea_critic/toc/cea.76.2.html.

Bibliography

Alliance for Networking Visual Culture. Scalar website. Accessed September 21, 2014. http://scalar.usc.edu.

Association for Computers in the Humanities. "How Do We Introduce Undergraduates to the Digital Humanities?" Digital Humanities Questions and Answers Thread. Accessed September 23, 2014. http://digitalhumanities.org/answers/topic/how-do-we-introduce-undergraduates-to-the-digital-humanities

Association of College and Research Libraries Standards Committee, "Framework for Information Literacy for Higher Education," version ACRL MW15 Doc 4.1. Accessed February 3, 2015. Pending approval of the ACRL Board of Directors. http://acrl.ala.org/ilstandards/wp-content/uploads/2015/01/Framework-MW15-Board-Docs.pdf.

Blackwell, Christopher, and Thomas Martin. "Technology, Collaboration, and Undergraduate Research." *Digital Humanities Quarterly* 3, no. 1 (2009). www.digitalhumanities.org/dhq/vol/3/1/000024/000024.html.

College English Association. "Digital Humanities Pedagogy." Special issue, *CEA Critic* 76, no. 2 (July 2014). http://muse.jhu.edu/journals/cea_critic/toc/cea.76.2.html.

Ellis, Erin L., Brian Rosenblum, John M. Stratton, and Kathleen Ames-Stratton. "Positioning Academic Libraries for the Future: A Process and Strategy for Organizational Transformation." Paper presented at the 35th International Association of Scientific and Technological University Libraries Conference, Aalto University, Espoo, Finland, June 2–5, 2014. http://hdl.handle.net/1808/14141.

Hirsch, Brett D., ed. *Digital Humanities Pedagogy: Practices, Principles and Politics.* Cambridge: Open Book Publishers, December 2012. www.openbookpublishers. com/product/161/digital-humanities-pedagogy—practices—principles-and-politics.

Institute for Digital Research in the Humanities. "Course Development Grants." Institute for Digital Research in the Humanities website. Accessed February 5, 2015. http:// idrh.ku.edu/course-development-grants.

Institute for Digital Research in the Humanities website. Accessed September 21, 2014. http://idrh.ku.edu.

Jaguszewski, Janice M., and Karen Williams. *New Roles for New Times: Transforming Liaison Roles in Research Libraries.* Washington, DC: Association of Research Libraries, August 2013. http://www.arl.org/storage/documents/publications/nrnt-liaison-roles-revised.pdf.

Klein, Lauren. "LCC 3843: Digital Humanities—Fourth Online Assignment: Sherlock Holmes Text Analysis." 2012. http://lkleincourses.lmc.gatech.edu/dh12/files/2011/12/oa4.pdf.

Muñoz, Trevor. "Digital Humanities in the Library Isn't a Service." *Trevor Muñoz* (blog), August 19, 2012. http://trevormunoz.com/notebook/2012/08/19/doing-dh-in-the-library.html.

Oxford e-Research Centre. "About" page. Poem Viewer website. University of Oxford. Accessed September 21, 2014. http://ovii.oerc.ox.ac.uk/PoemVis/about.html.

Ramsay, Stephen. "The Hermeneutics of Screwing Around; or What You Do with a Million Books." In Pastplay: *Teaching and Learning History with Technology*, edited by Kevin Kee, 111-172. Ann Arbor, MI: University of Michigan Press, 2014. http://quod.lib.umich.edu/d/dh/12544152.0001.001/1:5/—pastplay-teaching-and-learning-history-with-technology?g=dculture;rgn=div1;view=fulltext;xc=1#5.1.

Roy Rosenzweig Center for History and New Media. Omeka website. George Mason University. Accessed September 21, 2014. http://omeka.org.

Sinclair, Stéfan, and Geoffrey Rockwell. Voyant Tools website. Accessed September 21, 2014. http://voyant-tools.org.

University of Kansas. "At a Glance." KU Libraries website. Accessed September 21, 2014. http://lib.ku.edu/about.

University of Virginia. Juxta Commons website. Accessed September 21, 2014. www.juxtacommons.org.

Appendix 9.1: Digital Humanities Assignment

Digital Humanities Assignment
Introduction to Graduate Studies
Fall 2014

This assignment adapted from Lauren Klein, Georgia Tech University: http://lkleincourses.lmc.gatech.edu/dh12/assignments/

(1) Please read "The Hermeneutics of Screwing Around; or What You Do with a Million Books" by Stephen Ramsay: http://www.playingwithhistory. com/wp-content/uploads/2010/04/hermeneutics.pdf

In "The Hermeneutics of Screwing Around; or What You Do with a Million Books" Stephen Ramsay contrasts the controlled, ordered nature of conventional search, like Google, with a research methodology characterized by "surfing and stumbling," otherwise known as "screwing around." The result of such a research methodology, he says, can be revelatory. He asks: "Could we imagine a world in which 'Here is an ordered list of the books you should read,' gives way to, 'Here is what I found. What did you find?'"

Inspired by Ramsay's provocation, your assignment is to do just that—to use one of the tools below to apply the methodology of "screwing around" to a text of your choice. After "surfing and stumbling" through the tools and texts, you should **(2) craft a blog post** that includes:

- (a) A screen capture of the best (or most interesting) instance(s) of what it was that you found; and

- (b) A short account of 300–500 words that explains what it was that you found, why you think it's the best (or the most interesting), and what other questions you have that remain. You may also include a critical assessment of your experience learning and using the tool. For example, what were the challenges (technical and/or intellectual) of using it; how might this tool be beneficial (or not) to your research; would a close reading approach be better for this question?

- *Note: it is also okay if you find nothing significant. That is often the case, especially when learning a new tool. You can still make it "interesting" by including both (a) and (b) above in the blog post, addressing the challenges or difficulties you encountered, and explaining why you think you found nothing significant.*

Tools

Choose one of the following tools, read through the documentation, upload a text (or multiple texts), and see what you find.

VOYANT: http://voyant-tools.org/documentation: http://docs.voyant-tools.org/ full list of Voyant tools: http://docs.voyant-tools.org/tools/

LEXOS: http://lexos.wheatoncollege.edu/documentation: http://wheaton college.edu/lexomics/

JUXTA:http://juxtacommons.org/(youwillneedtoregisterforafreeaccount) documentation: http://juxtacommons.org/guide

PAPER MACHINES (ZOTERO PLUGIN): http://papermachines.org/ documentation: http://papermachines.org/?page_id=30

POEM VIEWER: http://ovii.oerc.ox.ac.uk/PoemVis/

CORPUS.BYU.EDU: http://corpus.byu.edu/

BOOKWORM: http://bookworm.culturomics.org/ (you will need to register)

NAMED ENTITY RECOGNIZER (NER): http://nlp.stanford.edu:8080/ ner or http://cogcomp.cs.illinois.edu/page/software_view/4 (you will need to download and install the application)

TEMPORAL TAGGER (SUTime): http://nlp.stanford.edu:8080/sutime (you will need to download and install software)

Texts

You can obtain full-text versions of many of the novels you are reading in class at http://gutenberg.org or http://archive.org (Note, due to copyright restrictions, translations may be older, different versions than the version you are reading for class.)

With the permission of the class professors, you may choose another text or set of texts for analysis.

*Note: If you are not already familiar with the differences between a **text editor** (e.g. TextWrangler) and a **word processor** (e.g. Microsoft Word) please see:* http://chronicle.com/blogs/profhacker/writing-power-tools-text-editors/38940

A text editor is far better tool for preparing and manipulating texts for further analysis.

Appendix 9.2

Course Development Grants

http://idrh.ku.edu/course-development-grants

As part of an effort to develop an interdisciplinary palette of courses in digital humanities at KU, the Institute for Digital Research in the Humanities is offering a $1000 stipend to tenured and tenure-track faculty who develop a new course in the digital humanities.

Priority will be assigned to proposals that meet following criteria and topical foci:

- Undergraduate courses, or Undergraduate/Graduate courses
- Courses attracting students from a variety of departments and disciplines
- Courses that use open-source, non-proprietary, cross-platform tools
- Methods that can be applied to a variety of humanities disciplines

Suggested Topics:

- A (general) introduction to the Digital Humanities (high priority)
- Scripting and coding
- Markup languages for humanists (XML, TEI)
- Visual representation of data
- The creation of corpora and/or use of existing corpora
- Analyzing and presenting audiovisual sources
- The ethics of data access and privacy

- Social impacts of new media

- Visual and textual models of epistemology

- Cyberinfrastructure and the humanities

- Collaborative research methods in the humanities

The course may be in any humanities or closely-related discipline, and may cover specific topics within a discipline (e.g. 19th c. English literature), as long as at least 50% of the course content covers DH skills, methods, and tools. All proposed courses must be taught on the Lawrence or Edwards campus within 3 semesters of receiving funding. We expect to make up to three awards.

All applicants who are selected for the program will be asked to participate in a one hour Digital Humanities curriculum workshop in late April or early May (TBA).

How to Apply: Interested participants are invited to submit a short proposal (two to three pages, double-spaced) that includes: (1) a narrative description of the new course, including a list of; (2) the course title and a (possible) course number; and, (3) a discussion of the potential impact you expect the course to have on KU's digital humanities profile. The proposal should indicate whether or not the course is undergraduate or graduate, the expected enrollment, whether or not it is intended as a principal course, and the frequency with which it will be offered. It is expected that the course will be offered sometime during the next three semesters and that it will be offered at least three times within the next six-year period. Faculty from all humanities and related disciplines are invited to submit proposals.

Additional Guidelines

- **The deadline for proposals is Monday, April 28, 2014. All proposals should be submitted to ———— no later than 5:00 p.m. Central Time on that day.**

- The department chair and/or dean, as appropriate, must endorse all proposals.

- Successful applicants will be notified on or before Friday, May 9.

- The workshop for program participants will be scheduled for May, 2014. Date and time to be announced. Attendance by participants in the full program of the workshop is required in order to receive the summer stipend.

- Participants will be asked to submit to IDRH a syllabus of the new course after it is offered.

- For more information, please contact Arienne Dwyer or Brian Rosenblum, co-directors, IDRH, ——————— or ——@———————.

CHAPTER TEN

Spaces, Skills, and Synthesis

Anu Vedantham and Dot Porter

Introduction

The term digital humanities is not universally embraced. Faculty, students, and librarians generally greet it with nonplussed expressions. What does it mean? Is there such a thing as "analog humanities"? What is included? What is excluded? Who is a digital humanist? Who is not?[1]

We face similarly confused reactions when librarians venture into new territory—fancy study spaces, makerspaces, embedded librarianship, and so on. When a library opens a loud study space, the campus reacts with "But the space has no books. Why is this space in the library? What makes this space a library anyway?" Our miles of bookcases also receive confusing feedback. Some faculty members state with pride that they never enter the library. Others become incredibly upset when books are moved to off-site storage. As we change our perceptions of physical books, we are forced to confront our definitions of how we manage our academic work.

In contrast, consider trends in industries such as banking or real estate. One expects banks and realtors to have functioning, attractive websites and to use technology to their advantage. We do not use terms such as *digital banking* or *digital real estate*. There are parallels within the university. Faculty and students in the sciences have integrated coding and technology into their work without facing terms such as *digital physics* or *digital biology*. Investing in appropriate technologies is a requirement in all fields, and the humanities are no exception.

In this chapter, we describe three learning spaces at Penn Libraries in terms of planning history, physical layout, technology capabilities, staffing, and programmatic decisions. We describe how support for "digital humanities" (DH) has grown deeper, more varied, better funded, and more effectively coordinated across units.

The work we describe is much greater than the efforts of the two authors. It reflects the dedication and creativity of scores of humanities scholars, librarians, instructional design staff, and administrators. We present our experiences and ideas in the larger context of Penn Libraries, attempting to distill concepts that may resonate in your campus context.

We write this chapter in our own voices. One of us works on the first floor of our main library in a busy area where scores of people pass by her office daily on campus tours. One of us works on the sixth floor of the same building with a city skyline view, a gallery, and quiet surroundings. The spaces we inhabit as individuals color our own academic work as well as the relationships we build within and beyond campus.

University Context

The University of Pennsylvania (Penn) is an Ivy League university in an urban location. Penn has twelve schools and is consistently ranked among the top ten universities in the United States. The university's responsibility-centered budgeting structure contributes to a highly decentralized campus environment. Innovations happen continuously all over campus, but sharing of ideas across units can be a challenge.

The School of Arts and Sciences houses all the humanities disciplines. The school has twenty-seven academic departments and offers fifty-four majors for over 6,300 undergraduate students as well as thirty-three doctoral and ten master's programs for more than 2,100 graduate students.[2]

Penn Libraries is seen as a neutral place that does not favor one discipline over another (we hear the phrase "The library is like Switzerland"). We are recognized as the provider of comfortable, nurturing spaces, and strong technology infrastructure; in particular, our management of the campus-wide Canvas courseware system helps us engage with teaching and learning across campus.

Librarians at Penn have staff ranking, not faculty positions, a situation that reflects and contributes to perceptions of librarians as supporters of research, rather than as full collaborators or independent researchers. In recent years, we have developed staff-led research projects to engage staff with library work and collections and to support them in personally experiencing how it feels to do research. It is a slow but worthwhile process, and we believe it could strengthen the relationship between librarians and faculty.

DH projects are conducted at Penn in a variety of contexts, within academic departments as well as in the libraries. We offer a few examples. PennSound, supported by the School of Arts and Sciences, records poetry readings and makes those recordings available for download. The Schoenberg Institute for Manuscript Studies (SIMS) focuses on DH projects in the context of medieval manuscript collections. The Penn Humanities Forum has launched a Digital Humanities Forum (DHF),[3] which, in collaboration with Penn Libraries, has held several large symposia each year, bringing to campus internationally known DH leaders. A faculty committee is exploring the DH landscape on campus as part of strategic planning in the School of Arts and Sciences. Library conversations with this committee have helped us articulate our own capabilities, resulting in a crowdsourcing project to catalog library expertise to answer the question "Who to ask for what?"[4]

We structure this chapter in three segments to reflect the title—spaces, skills, and synthesis—beginning with our physical spaces.

Spaces

Libraries are associated primarily with a sense of place. We "go to the library," a physical building that contains resources to help us think, read, find materials, and conduct research. The appearance and functionality of the library can affect our research productivity as well as our metacognition— our perception of our own productivity. Spaces designed to encourage brainstorming and discussion need to look, feel, and function differently from those designed to support deep reading, note taking, writing, or presentation practice.

As documented by the Learning Spaces Collaboratory *Guide*, creative combinations of space and technology can catalyze scholarship.[5] Colocation of library expertise near collaboration spaces can help faculty and students draw connections between traditional library capabilities (collections, subject specialists, bibliographers, catalogers) and newer capabilities (scanning, digitization, data analysis and visualization, new media creation, web/blog design, audio/video editing). Effective space management through provision of reliable technology infrastructure can impart confidence to faculty and students taking on DH projects.

When a library space works well, it becomes a coveted destination.[6] We observe people "voting with their feet." During final exams one semester at the Weigle Information Commons, a young woman looked around and, finding no open tables, pulled up her chair to a recycling bin and used it as a table for her laptop. She preferred to write her research paper there in the crowded open area rather than move to empty seats one floor above. When a space "feels right" for a particular purpose, people choose it again and again even when it is overflowing. Over 2,000 groups of students on average reserved space in the Weigle Information Commons each month during 2013.[7]

The Importance of Learning Space Design

Think about your local mall. If it included a long row of identical coffee shops, would you still want coffee? How do endless stacks of books affect you? Recently Penn Libraries hosted a qualitative research exhibit created by a graduate nursing class on the topic of stress.[8] Graduate students described their concerns through photographs. One graduate student reflected on the Sisyphean pessimism created by a photo of endless rows of book stacks on our fourth floor. When presented in creative ways, collections can instead inspire optimism and curiosity in learners. Bookstores, for example, choose artistic setups over book stacks, specializing in cozy corners, topical exhibits, and displays. Library spaces must prioritize the sense of place, an atmosphere that invites you to walk around and find a corner for your needs. We describe three spaces in the Penn Libraries that differ in layout, function, staffing, and programming—to support specific types of academic work.

Space Planning History

In 2006, Penn Libraries opened the Weigle Information Commons (WIC) after a five-year planning process with committees representing faculty, students, and staff. A joint funding model with the School of Arts and Sciences created a renewing connection between Penn Libraries and the humanities departments. Formal "program partner" relationships with campus organizations including the writing center, academic support services (including support for students with disabilities), public speaking center, undergraduate research opportunities center, and career services help maintain the momentum built during planning. The space aims to support small-group collaboration by undergraduate students, with a one-stop-shop approach to academic support services.

In 2013, Penn Libraries opened the Kislak Center for Special Collections, Rare Books and Manuscripts after a seven-year planning effort. The large-scale renovation of two floors created spaces for presentations, discussions, and teaching as well as spaces for storing, cataloging, displaying, and working with library-owned materials. The space aims to encourage broad and creative use of physical materials and to serve as a state-of-the-art gathering place for campus.

In 2014, Penn Libraries opened the Collaborative Classroom after a two-year planning effort that included active collaboration with an undergraduate student group, the Student Committee on Undergraduate Education (SCUE), and visits to other universities. The project complements a campus initiative funded by a 2013 grant from the Association of American Universities (AAU).[9] The space aims to support campus interest in new pedagogical methods including "flipped classroom" instruction.

Facilities, Furniture, and Technology

Weigle Information Commons (WIC)

The WIC has 6,600 square feet of space on the first floor of the main library building. It includes twelve Data Diner Booths that look and function just like their restaurant counterparts with the addition of computers. Each seats six people, and the benches are long and wide to accommodate the occasional nap. The high bench backs create a conversational buzz while limiting eavesdropping. Mixed in with the booths are ten study rooms for private conversations and two open alcoves for large-group brainstorming. The space includes a thirty-five-seat seminar room with built-in videoconferencing and the Vitale Digital Media Lab for self-service media creation. The variety of spaces in close proximity enables powerful synthesis activities.[10] Humanities classes will start with lecture or large-group discussion in the seminar room, break up for small-group conversations in the booths, and reconvene to share conclusions.

Several rooms allow self-service high-definition video recording and videoconferencing (Skype, Google Hangouts, etc.), role playing, and live interviews. The Vitale Digital Media Lab supports self-service media creation with a variety of gadgets including a vinyl record digitizer, a slide scanner, and a large-format printer. Faculty and students can borrow video cameras, audio recorders, and portable scanners for offsite use.

Kislak Center for Special Collections, Rare Books and Manuscripts

The Kislak Center occupies the two top floors of the same library building. Renovations have made collections of rare materials dramatically more interesting and accessible. The Class of 1978 Pavilion is a glamorous space with built-in videoconferencing and video-recording capability that can accommodate 140 people for lectures or be rearranged for smaller discussions. Nearby is a row of three 20-person seminar rooms that can be combined by removable partitions.

The center includes the Vitale Media Lab (Vitale II), which focuses DH programming on cultural heritage and special collections materials. The room can be reconfigured easily for groups of up to twenty people and includes a high-definition ceiling-mounted camera for enlarging manuscripts on large monitors and sharing via videoconference. Closely related to Vitale II is the Schoenberg Institute for Manuscript Studies (SIMS), which focuses on research around medieval manuscripts, both physical and digital.

Down the hall, the Rare Book Reading Room provides a central space with small pullout rooms for researchers to handle materials. The Kislak Center also includes the Goldstein Exhibit Hall, the historically important Lea Library with its collection of eighteenth-century manuscripts, the Moelis Terrace for informal study, and a balcony with a splendid view of the Philadelphia skyline.

Collaborative Classroom

The Collaborative Classroom is an active learning space that includes a thirty-seat classroom for formal instruction set into a wide "porch" area where students can work informally in small groups. The classroom is located on the first floor next to WIC and a rare books exhibit area. Created in a room that formerly housed government documents, all the walls are writable surfaces. Designed for problem-solving activities, the space contains five round tables (with power and Internet wired into the centers) and one instructor station, each with a projection screen. Technology and furniture choices were made to explicitly support "flipped classroom" pedagogies.[11] An elaborate audiovisual system gives faculty members one-touch power to take or cede control over the six display screens.

Common Aspects and a Neighborhood

Common technology capabilities across the three spaces include movable furniture, ability to display from personal laptops, access to MacBook laptops and iPads, and an extensive inventory of educational software.

All three spaces are in the Van Pelt-Dietrich Library Center, a half-century-old building with a twenty-four-hour café on the lowest level.

Together they create a powerful "neighborhood." Faculty and students can accomplish different tasks on different floors—touch a manuscript in the reading room, take photos of a few pages in Vitale II, create a video of their conversation about the photos in a WIC study room, or annotate the photos on the writable walls in the Collaborative Classroom. Helping patrons explore, understand, and feel ownership over the capabilities available in our neighborhood of spaces is the challenge we face as librarians.

Skills

In support of learning spaces, Penn Libraries has invested in expanding skill sets of library staff through professional development of current staff and recruitment of individuals with specialized skill sets, partially through postdoctoral DH fellowships. Reflections on DH support have required a reexamination of what it means to be a librarian and who is needed on deck in a modern library. We discuss three specific roles we perceive in the relationships librarians have developed with DH researchers.

Librarian as Concierge

Successful DH projects require thoughtful planning. Eliciting the initial vision for a project requires careful conversations similar to the traditional reference interview. What do you want to accomplish? How will you recognize success? What obstacles do you perceive? How will you organize your project effectively? What skills are needed for the project to be successful? Who has those skills? It is worth mentioning that this is true whether the project instigator is student, faculty, or librarian, new to DH or seasoned.*

Subject specialists who are themselves new to or nervous with technology tools may hesitate to guide faculty choices, defaulting to a "But that's not my role" response. Having instructional design and information technology experts on staff and pairing them with subject specialists can improve library contributions in the initial stages of a DH project. Creating collaborative relationships between IT experts and subject specialists

---

* We use the term *project instigator* to refer to the person who is leading a project, whether faculty, student, or librarian.

also has positive side effects as described later in the context of our Digital Scholarship Workshop series.

A few tensions arise that are worth tackling head-on. Sometimes librarians are seen as insiders, and sometimes as outsiders. The librarian can stay outside the departmental politics, helping all members of a department and not distinguishing across hierarchies of tenured/untenured, standing/ad-hoc, faculty/graduate student/staff, and so on. The outsider role can be especially helpful in sharing successes and challenges across departments. If one department or research group faces difficulties with implementing a particular software program, the librarian can help share that information (while maintaining strict privacy guards) with another department that is considering a similar project. Successes can be shared through the library website and blogs, where we showcase good projects and abstract out from project details to the general functionality, helping with replication across campus.[12] Facilitating peer-to-peer sharing for faculty, such as our annual Engaging Students through Technology symposia, be highly effective.[13]

Librarians can benefit from insider knowledge if they have personal experience conducting research so that they come to the project understanding how difficult it can be to achieve productive research results. A librarian with strong relationships (think "embedded librarianship") within a department can develop intuition that helps when new DH projects emerge.

Librarian as IT Expert

To support or lead DH projects, libraries need staff with both wide and deep expertise, A project instigator may want to first look at a range of options before picking a tool set. (Should I start with a website or a multimedia-friendly database? Would a podcast work for me, or is video needed?) At this stage, assistance from the library needs to be perceived as unbiased and impartial. Project instigators do not want to be "convinced into" a particular tool, platform, or software choice, particularly if it seems like that the librarian is reverting to his or her own personal expertise ("If you have a hammer, everything looks like a nail").

During this initial stage of tool selection, we need to acknowledge that exploring a new tool can be surprisingly stressful. An interface that feels natural to a regular user can look arcane and intimidating to a newcomer. When librarians take time to prepare extensive demonstration materials in a disciplinary context, faculty are more easily able to look past user interface limitations and glimpse the capabilities of a DH tool.

Once the project instigator has chosen the tools, deep knowledge is in demand. The project instigator needs to be paired up with a librarian who knows those tools well, can point out pitfalls ahead of time, and can effectively liaise with other library staff as needed. Every DH tool has its strengths and weaknesses, and knowing details early can reduce frustration.

We have worked toward providing a "geek squad" of sorts by making the expertise of our staff more transparent for faculty and students. We have used simple tools—a publicly editable Google Doc tied to a Springshare LibGuide—to collect data from our librarians about their own expertise with DH tools. The crowdsourcing project took about four weeks. Librarians added in their names next to tools they were comfortable with. The results provide an easy place to find out whom to ask about what, and a useful listing of DH tools building on the DIRT Directory framework.[14]

Librarian as Researcher

We face ambivalence from faculty members and students on the perception of librarians as researchers. As faculty and students use more online resources, subscription databases as well as materials available openly through the Internet, librarians need to develop new skills and approaches. One approach taken at Penn Libraries is to support library staff in some departments to be DH researchers in their own right in addition to supporting faculty and student research.[15] We see advantages for librarians to stay active in personal research activities—to continue their own learning and to remain connected to the difficulties of being a learner.

We have successfully used blogging as a way to expose the scholarship activities within the library to the broader campus community. We have several blogs highlighting the work of different units, including the

Schoenberg Institute blog, the DH tag on the general *PennWIC* blog, and the *Unique at Penn* blog.[16]

Staffing Details

Providing support for the three types of roles defined above requires library staffing that is varied and flexible. Our spaces are supported by traditionally educated librarians, instructional designers, and software geeks. In addition to permanent staff, we take advantage of multiyear fellowships, year-long graduate internships, short-term visiting scholars, and ad hoc consultants.

WIC includes three full-time and two half-time staff and up to a dozen graduate and undergraduate students. Staff expertise includes video editing (Final Cut Pro, Premiere, iMovie), graphic design (Photoshop, InDesign, Illustrator), web design (WordPress, CSS), instructional design (lesson planning, assignment design), data analysis (Excel, Microsoft Access), and so on.

The Kislak Center has many full-time and part-time staff, including curators to collect and interpret collections, catalogers to describe materials, and staff to manage the reading rooms. SIMS has a separate research agenda, undertaken primarily by librarians and library staff. It is not a support unit for faculty and students, although faculty and students collaborate on SIMS projects. Directly involved with DH support are five full-time staff: two curators for Digital Research Services, a digital content programmer, a project manager for the Schoenberg Database of Manuscripts,[17] and a web developer. Staff expertise includes software development using programming languages, web server management, data mining, text mining, data visualization, TEI encoding, and Omeka.

The Collaborative Classroom is supported by several full-time librarians (including subject specialists and social science research specialists) and graduate students in the Research and Instructional Services department with assistance from WIC. A Teaching and Learning Fellow with a doctorate in education supports faculty who teach in the space.

Communication among the groups of staff has been crucial and an ongoing challenge. One effective mechanism is *The Thread*, a library-facing blog where staff share updates informally.[18] Another is the Public Services

Forum, a monthly library-wide meeting for librarians to share accomplishments and challenges. A recent Digital Scholarship Workshop series has successfully engaged librarians and the campus community by exploring DH topics through joint presentations that include tool demonstrations as well as conversation about effective liaison librarianship.[19]

Program Support Models

Our three spaces and their staff configurations support different approaches to DH work. Collaborations in WIC typically begin with a faculty request for support for a course-related assignment. We meet with the faculty member to understand goals, course design, and expectations. We design and conduct training sessions for the students, as well as for teaching assistants.[20] We assist with setup of shared spaces (physical and online) and workflows. We hold open work sessions for students shortly before assignment deadlines to help manage last-minute stresses. We create showcases of exemplary student work.[21] Demand for course-level assistance has been steady for several years,[22] and we provide custom training on web design (WordPress, Tumblr, Google Sites), graphic design (Photoshop, PowerPoint, Instagram), and video (iMovie, Final Cut Pro, iPhoto, Canvas).

We explore new technologies, purchase sample gadgets for lending, help people feel more comfortable with new technologies, and showcase examples that might fuel replication. We provide iPads and laptops to support ad hoc use, such as a class project involving iPads and rare books.[23] We organize workshops for general audiences and provide ad hoc consultations. In 2013, WIC conducted over 220 open workshops for over 1,700 attendees and about 80 workshops by request for 1,000 attendees.[24]

Once a semester, we hold a Gadget Day for people from around campus to share their favorite new toys. We provide access to Lynda.com for self-paced skill improvement, especially with the Adobe Creative Suite of software. Once a year, we hold an Engaging Students through Technology Symposium, which attracted over 150 faculty and graduate students last year. Our faculty advisory group helped us build a faculty development module on Nurturing Student Creativity through Video Projects.[25] We run an annual Mashup Video contest to recognize student creativity.

Collaborations in the Kislak Center often include working with special collections materials, in addition to technical training. Programming offered through Vitale II tends to be ongoing and aimed at specific audiences, rather than through repeat sessions of discrete workshops. Much programming centers on what we call Focused Labs, set times each week for faculty, students, and librarians to meet and work through specific tools and techniques. The Focused Labs for 2013–2014 included Code Academy courses in Python and HTML/CSS[26] and an Omeka users group. Although all started off strong, by the end of the spring semester attendance had decreased. We are exploring ways to strengthen Vitale II programming, encouraging librarians in other departments to hold sessions in the space. We have organized several DH-focused events including three unconferences—PhillyDH@Penn 2013 and 2014, and THATCamp Penn 2012.[27]

Since opening in February 2014, the Collaborative Classroom has hosted several full-semester courses, brainstorming sessions for academic departments, outreach events, and workshops on DH topics including social media and mind mapping. In one presentation for the Digital Humanities Forum, a faculty member presented an extensive DH project that focuses on Philadelphia history and includes mapping, GIS, video, and animation technologies.[28]

Synthesis

In this section, we explore examples of synthesizing spaces and skills. An important component of DH work is to assist librarians and staff with IT expertise in learning to articulate how what they know (creating a searchable web catalog) is helpful for a DH project (create a searchable catalog of student-selected items from the Penn Museum). Staff with significant IT expertise may not always understand the nervousness of faculty and students who are just getting started. Subject librarians can help bridge gaps and translate jargon.

Examples

The examples below are actual projects, though some details have been stylized.

- A professor of Persian history visited the Vitale Digital Media Lab in WIC carrying an oversize battered book. She wanted to create an English translation of the book, which contained several hundred pages of Arabic text and color illustrations. We guided her through scanning and photography options available across different departments. After she had created a project plan, we trained her undergraduate students to scan and resize the original illustrations and lay out the pages with English text replacing the Arabic text. Over several weeks, her project grew to include scanning, optical character recognition, color management, graphic design, file and scan management, workflow planning, and backup procedures. She reflected that our guidance on the complexity of the process was especially helpful because she could assess feasibility and costs in terms of her time and her students' time.

- A professor of South Asian studies came to WIC with ideas for her eighty-person introductory undergraduate class. Students were preparing simplistic presentations and class time watching group presentations was minimally engaging. We explored a variety of technology options, including screen video creation (Canvas, Jing, PowerPoint), forms and polls (Google Forms, online voting systems), video editing (Final Cut Pro, iMovie, Windows Movie Maker) and video sharing (YouTube, Canvas, Blackboard). We conducted training for the professor and her four teaching assistants on how to manage the new course assignment: five-minute videos by each student that would be watched and voted on by the full class, with the winners shown at an end-of-term celebration. The process of creating an effective assignment included iterative analysis of the tools available in active conversation with the course TAs, demos in the classroom, and "tech office hours" for the students shortly before each deadline. The results are included in a class showcase page.[29] After watching the professor present at our annual symposium,[30] several faculty members around campus decided to incorporate this simple voice-over–PowerPoint technology solution in their courses.

- Several librarians expressed concern about their own knowledge regarding popular digital tools and techniques. They created a Digital Scholarship series to bring together librarians, faculty, students, and staff for workshops primarily led by librarians. Topics included choosing the right online exhibit software, qualitative research, choosing a citation manager, working with archival materials, and an Omeka overview. The series has provided short lunchtime workshops to explain what each tool does and why it is useful so that librarians can make informed decisions about which tools they want to learn.

- The Director of the Kislak Center and an English professor co-taught a freshman seminar The World of Manuscripts (ENGL 016.304), which introduced students in the class to a wide range of manuscript and manuscript-like materials (including cuneiform tablets and letters of Mary Shelley). As their final project, the students undertook a study of Penn's Wycliffite New Testament, Ms. Codex 201,[31] each student taking responsibility for a different aspect of the book. That study culminated in a short video, made with the assistance of library staff and using the ceiling camera available in Vitale II.[32] The video is public on the SIMS YouTube channel and showcases the contributions of the students and librarians.[33]

- Not all collaborations unfold as intended. A history of art professor came to the Kislak Center interested in a website to combine artifacts and archival documents relating to the Beth Shean archaeological dig held by the Penn Museum. The semester-long project included a small grant from the Digital Humanities Forum. Library staff conducted Omeka training, and students were responsible for selecting, curating, scanning, and loading materials into Omeka. However, the students found Omeka clunky and the exhibit-building function difficult. The hosted nature of the service limited our ability to customize the experience using server back-end functionality. The students chose to move the project to Squarespace, a commercial website hosting platform, without input from library staff. Although the Squarespace website is beautiful, the cataloging and reuse capabilities possible with Omeka were lost. We are now exploring ways to possibly combine an Omeka back end with a Squarespace front end.[34]

- WIC's iPads in the Classroom program has worked well in conjunction with rare books and our stacks.[35] One English class used our iPads to explore rare materials with interactive research into authors and provenance. The professor reflected on her experiences, saying, "While I've given students similar assignments for several years, this is the first year that they've done the depth of research that I expected."[36]

These examples emphasize the importance of choosing between tools and surveying the universe of available tools. Faculty appreciate a safe space to play in, a sandbox of sorts, where trying out a new tool has a low level of risk. Once a professor has identified a tool that is a good fit, the need for hands-on training can be met in many ways, including using online tutorials from vendors. The librarian need not feel compelled to have expertise in all tools of potential interest, but the librarian does need to stay up-to-date on name recognition of the universe of currently popular tools.

Repercussions for New Media Literacies

In addition to raising standards for librarian expertise, the importance of effective synthesis of DH tools leads to higher expectations for students and faculty. Alan Dix has written about the popular YouTube video "Middle Ages Tech Support" to explain how a familiar technology, such as the book, may have stumped scholars in previous centuries.[37] Today, our expectations for technology skills increase steadily. Mastery of skills in video creation, blogging, social media use, web design, text mining, and data analysis has become an expectation rather than an aspiration. Both faculty and students can face pressures to ramp up their own digital skills,[38] sometimes on short notice. The Technology Acceptance Model (TAM) may help us anticipate areas of difficulty.[39] For example, perceptions of difficulty of use and perceptions of usefulness impact how some students acquire video-creation skills.[40] We may want to consider identity-related obstacles to the process of gaining digital skills. Explicit consideration of digital literacies and obstacles to their acquisition can help us organize how we support DH projects.

Conclusion

In this chapter, we have reflected on the evolution of three spaces at the University of Pennsylvania Libraries. We end with a few philosophical comments.

All three spaces discussed here were created after extensive visits to other campuses and in coordination with national organizations considering learning-space design. Reviewing concrete examples from other contexts has helped us make informed choices when meeting with contractors and architects. Our staffing and programming decisions have also benefited from conversations with colleagues in other institutions.

How we manage our spaces after the ribbon cutting has been an important choice. We have taken the "better broken than dusty" attitude towards our shiny new spaces, taking care to make all of campus feel welcome and comfortable. It can be tricky to maintain high-tech spaces when they are packed with patrons who won't always behave as expected. When we hosted the forty-eight-hour Penn Apps hackathon, every bit of floor space in the Kislak Center was filled with sleep-deprived undergraduates. Opening up spaces deliberately requires taking risks, and support for risk taking (with a sense of humor) from the highest levels of library administration has been essential.

Skill sets come in and out of fashion. The human connections we make with faculty and students are as important, if not more, than the specific technical skill we bring to a consultation. The push and pull between librarian-as-support-staff and librarian-as-researcher is a real one, and each librarian finds his or her own comfortable spot. Through writing this chapter together, we explored our own perceptions of this continuum.

Writing this chapter together has also been an example of successfully crossing organizational boundaries. As we struggle through our own writing and research projects, it increases our ability to empathize with faculty and students embarking on their research efforts.

Acknowledgments

This article has benefited from the assistance of Kim Eke, Jim English, Vickie Karasic, Will Noel, Nick Okrent, Rebecca Stuhr, and many other colleagues from the University of Pennsylvania.

Notes

1. Melissa Terras, Julianne Nyhan, and Edward Vanhoutte, eds., *Defining Digital Humanities: A Reader* (Farnham, UK: Ashgate Publishing, 2013), www.ashgate.com/isbn/9781409469636.
2. University of Pennsylvania, "Penn Facts," accessed February 7, 2015, www.upenn.edu/about/facts.php.
3. University of Pennsylvania, Penn Digital Humanities Forum website, accessed February 7, 2015, http://humanities.sas.upenn.edu/dhf.shtml.
4. See the DH Tools list at Penn Libraries, "Tools and Library Experts, in Alphabetical Order," Guides: Digital Humanities, last updated October 17, 2014, http://guides.library.upenn.edu/toolexpertise.
5. See Jeanne L. Narum, ed., *A Guide for Planning for Assessing 21st Century Spaces for 21st Century Learners* (Washington, DC: Learning Spaces Collaboratory, November 2013), www.pkallsc.org/basic-page/lsc-guide-planning-assessing-21st-century-spaces-21st-century-learners.
6. See Joan K. Lippincott, "Information Commons: Meeting Millennials' Needs," *Journal of Library Administration* 50, no. 1 (2010): 27–37.
7. See WIC annual reports at Weigle Information Commons, "Reports and Publications," Penn Libraries, University of Pennsylvania, accessed February 7, 2015, http://commons.library.upenn.edu/reports-and-publications.
8. See Anu Vedantham, "Pressure Release," *PennWIC* (blog), May 2, 2014, http://pennwic.wordpress.com/2014/05/02/pressure-release.
9. Grant press release article available at University of Pennsylvania, "Penn to Implement AAU Undergraduate STEM Education Initiative," news release, June 25, 2013, www.upenn.edu/pennnews/news/penn-implement-aau-undergraduate-stem-education-initiative.
10. Details are available at Anu Vedantham, "Learning Space Design," *PennWIC* (blog), July 3, 2014, http://pennwic.wordpress.com/2014/07/03/learning-space-design.
11. A photo gallery of teaching examples is available at Weigle Information Commons, "Collaborative Classroom," Flickr album, accessed February 7, 2015, https://www.flickr.com/photos/pennwic/sets/72157645502444793.
12. See, for example, our success stories category at "Success Stories," *PennWIC* (blog), last updated December 10, 2014, http://pennwic.wordpress.com/category/success-stories.

13. See details from several years at Weigle Information Commons, "Engaging Students through Technology Symposium," Penn Libraries, University of Pennsylvania, 2014, http://commons.library.upenn.edu/engaging-students-through-technology-symposium.

14. Penn Libraries, "Tools and Library Experts"; see DiRT Directory (formerly part of Project Bamboo) at DiRT: Digital Research Tools, accessed February 7, 2015, http://dirtdirectory.org.

15. See Dot Porter, "What If We Do, in Fact, Know Best? A Response to the OCLC Report on DH and Research Libraries," *dh + lib* (blog), February 12, 2014, http://acrl.ala.org/dh/2014/02/12/what-if-we-do-in-fact-know-best-a-response-to-the-oclc-report-on-dh-and-research-libraries.

16. See *Schoenberg Institute for Manuscript Studies*, Penn Libraries blogs, University of Pennsylvania, accessed February 7, 2015, http://schoenberginstitute.org; *PennWIC* (blog), posts tagged "digital humanities," accessed February 7, 2015, http://pennwic.wordpress.com/tag/digital-humanities; *Unique at Penn*, Penn Libraries blogs, University of Pennsylvania, accessed February 7, 2015, http://uniqueatpenn.wordpress.com.

17. Schoenberg Database of Manuscripts, Penn Libraries website, accessed February 7, 2015, http://dla.library.upenn.edu/dla/schoenberg.

18. Penn Libraries' staff blog is at *The Thread*, Penn Libraries blogs, University of Pennsylvania, accessed February 7, 2015, http://libthread.wordpress.com.

19. See *PennWIC* (blog), posts tagged "digital scholarship," accessed February 7, 2015, http://pennwic.wordpress.com/?s=digital+scholarship.

20. See training materials at Penn Libraries, Guides: Tutorials and Tech Guides, last updated November 14, 2014, http://guides.library.upenn.edu/tutorials.

21. See Weigle Information Commons, "Student Work Showcase," accessed February 7, 2015 http://commons.library.upenn.edu/student-work-showcase.

22. See course listing at Weigle Information Commons, "Course Usage of the Weigle Information Commons," Penn Libraries, accessed February 7, 2015, http://commons.library.upenn.edu/course-usage.

23. See Cathy Turner, "Using iPads in the Rare Book Room," *PennWIC* (blog), January 5, 2013, http://pennwic.wordpress.com/2013/01/05/using-ipads-in-the-rare-book-room.

24. See Weigle Information Commons, "Reports and Publications."

25. See Weigle Information Commons, "ELIXR MERLOT Faculty Development Initiative," Penn Libraries, University of Pennsylvania, accessed February 7, 2015, http://elixr.merlot.org/case-stories/teaching-strategies/nurturing-student-creativity-with-video-projects/ funded through ELIXR MERLOT.

26. CodeAcademy, "Recommended for You," accessed February 7, 2015, www.codecademy.com/learn?choice=language.

27. See PhillyDH@Penn 2013 website, last updated June 27, 2013, http://penn2013.phillydh.org; PhillyDH@Penn 2014 website, last updated June 20, 2014, http://penn2014.phillydh.org; THATCamp@Penn: The Humanities and Technology Camp website, last updated May 3, 2012, http://penn2012.thatcamp.org.

28. See Amy Hillier, Mapping Du Bois, *The Philadelphia Negro* website, accessed February 7, 2015, www.mappingdubois.org.

29. Lisa Mitchell's Course Showcase at Weigle Information Commons, "PowerPoint Videos—Showcase 2012," accessed February 7, 2015, http://commons.library. upenn.edu/showcase-mitchell-sast-2012

30. See Lisa Mitchell, "Screen Videos as Student Projects: Engaging Students through Technology 2011," YouTube Video, 12:59, posted by pennlibraries November 30, 2011, https://www.youtube.com/watch?v=titDzisK5FE.

31. See Penn Libraries, "Ms. Codex 201—New Testament in the Translation of John Wycliffe," Penn in Hand: Selected Manuscripts, accessed February 7, 2015, http:// hdl.library.upenn.edu/1017/d/medren/1551783.

32. simsmss, "Penn Ms. Codes 201, Presented by Students in the World of Manuscripts Freshman Seminar (ENGL 016.304)," *Schoenberg Institute for Manuscript Studies* (blog), Penn Libraries blogs, January 22, 2014, http://schoenberginstitute. org/2014/01/22/penn-ms-codex-201-presented-by-students-in-the-world-of-manuscripts-freshman-seminar-engl-016-304.

33. Alexandra Pierson et al., "University of Pennsylvania Library's Ms Codex 201," YouTube video, 9:04, posted by SchoenbergInstitute December 18, 2013, https:// www.youtube.com/watch?v=oOkJ5bm-jZ8.

34. Beth Shean: After Antiquity website, accessed February 7, 2015, http://beth-shean. squarespace.com.

35. See Weigle Information Commons Guides, "iPads in the Classroom," last updated October 13, 2014, http://guides.library.upenn.edu/ipad.

36. Turner, "Using iPads in the Rare Book Room."

37. Alan Dix, "Physicality and Middle Ages Tech Support," *Alan Dix* (blog), December 13, 2007, http://alandix.com/blog/2007/12/13/physicality-and-middle-ages-tech-support.

38. See, for example, a discussion of video literacy at Anu Vedantham and Marjorie Hassen, "New Media: Engaging and Educating the YouTube Generation," *Journal of Learning Spaces* 1, no. 1 (2011).

39. See initial proposal for the TAM model at Fred D. Davis, "Perceived Usefulness, Perceived Ease of Use, and User Acceptance of Information Technology," *MIS Quarterly* 13, no. 3 (September 1989): 319–40.

40. See, for example, research on gender-related issues in video creation skills in Anu Vedantham, "Making YouTube and Facebook Videos: Gender Differences in Online Video Creation among First-Year Undergraduate Students Attending a Highly Selective Research University" (EdD diss., University of Pennsylvania, 2011).

Bibliography

Beth Shean: After Antiquity website. Accessed February 7, 2015. http://beth-shean. squarespace.com.

CodeAcademy. "Recommended for You." Accessed February 7, 2015 www.codecademy. com/learn?choice=language.

Davis, Fred D. "Perceived Usefulness, Perceived Ease of Use, and User Acceptance of Information Technology." *MIS Quarterly* 13, no. 3 (September 1989): 319–40.

DiRT: Digital Research Tools website. Accessed February 7, 2015. http://dirtdirectory.org.

Dix, Alan. "Physicality and Middle Ages Tech Support." *Alan Dix* (blog), December 13, 2007. http://alandix.com/blog/2007/12/13/physicality-and-middle-ages-tech-support.

Hillier, Amy. Mapping Du Bois. *The Philadelphia Negro* website. Accessed February 7, 2015. www.mappingdubois.org.

Lippincott, Joan K. "Information Commons: Meeting Millennials' Needs." *Journal of Library Administration* 50, no. 1 (2010): 27–37.

Mitchell, Lisa. "Screen Videos as Student Projects: Engaging Students through Technology 2011." YouTube video, 12:59. Posted by pennlibraries November 30, 2011. https://www.youtube.com/watch?v=titDzisK5FE.

Narum, Jeanne L., ed. *A Guide for Planning for Assessing 21st Century Spaces for 21st Century Learners*. Washington, DC: Learning Spaces Collaboratory, November 2013. www.pkallsc.org/basic-page/lsc-guide-planning-assessing-21st-century-spaces-21st-century-learners.

Penn Libraries. "Digital Humanities." Guides, Penn Libraries, University of Pennsylvania. Last updated October 17, 2014. http://guides.library.upenn.edu/toolexpertise.

———. "Ms. Codex 201—New Testament in the Translation of John Wycliffe." Penn in Hand: Selected Manuscripts, Penn Libraries, University of Pennsylvania. Accessed February 7, 2015, http://hdl.library.upenn.edu/1017/d/medren/1551783.

———. Schoenberg Database of Manuscripts. Penn Libraries, University of Pennsylvania. Accessed February 7, 2015. http://dla.library.upenn.edu/dla/schoenberg.

———. "Tutorial and Tech Guides." Penn Libraries, University of Pennsylvania, last updated November 14, 2014, http://guides.library.upenn.edu/tutorials.

PennWIC (blog). Accessed February 7, 2015. http://pennwic.wordpress.com.

PhillyDH@Penn 2013 website. Last updated June 27, 2013. http://penn2013.phillydh.org.

PhillyDH@Penn 2014 website. Last updated June 20, 2014. http://penn2014.phillydh.org.

Pierson, Alexandra, James Bessolo, Linda Valadez, and Patricia Kamwela. "University of Pennsylvania Library's Ms Codex 201." YouTube video, 9:04. Posted by SchoenbergInstitute December 18, 2013. https://www.youtube.com/watch?v=oOkJ5bm-jZ8.

Porter, Dot. "What If We Do, in Fact, Know Best? A Response to the OCLC Report on DH and Research Libraries." *dh + lib* (blog), February 12, 2014. http://acrl.ala.org/dh/2014/02/12/what-if-we-do-in-fact-know-best-a-response-to-the-oclc-report-on-dh-and-research-libraries.

Schoenberg Institute for Manuscript Studies. Penn Libraries blogs, University of Pennsylvania. Accessed February 7, 2015. http://schoenberginstitute.org.

simsmss. "Penn Ms. Codes 201, Presented by Students in the World of Manuscripts Freshman Seminar (ENGL 016.304)." *Schoenberg Institute for Manuscript Studies*, Penn Libraries blogs, University of Pennsylvania, January 22, 2014. http://schoenberginstitute.org/2014/01/22/penn-ms-codex-201-presented-by-students-in-the-world-of-manuscripts-freshman-seminar-engl-016-304.

Terras, Melissa, Julianne Nyhan, and Edward Vanhoutte, eds. *Defining Digital Humanities: A Reader*. Farnham, UK: Ashgate Publishing, 2013. www.ashgate.com/isbn/9781409469636.

THATCamp@Penn: The Humanities and Technology Camp website. Last updated May 3, 2012. http://penn2012.thatcamp.org.

The Thread. Penn Libraries blogs, University of Pennsylvania. Accessed February 7, 2015. http://libthread.wordpress.com.

Turner, Cathy. "Using iPads in the Rare Book Room." *PennWIC* (blog), January 5, 2013. http://pennwic.wordpress.com/2013/01/05/using-ipads-in-the-rare-book-room.

Unique at Penn. Penn Libraries blogs, University of Pennsylvania. Accessed February 7, 2015. http://uniqueatpenn.wordpress.com.

———. Penn Digital Humanities Forum website. Accessed February 7, 2015. http://humanities.sas.upenn.edu/dhf.shtml.

———. "Penn Facts." Accessed February 7, 2015. www.upenn.edu/about/facts.php.

———. "Penn to Implement AAU Undergraduate STEM Education Initiative." News release, June 25, 2013. www.upenn.edu/pennnews/news/penn-implement-aau-undergraduate-stem-education-initiative.

Vedantham, Anu. "Learning Space Design." *PennWIC* (blog), July 3, 2014. http://pennwic.wordpress.com/2014/07/03/learning-space-design.

———. "Making YouTube and Facebook Videos: Gender Differences in Online Video Creation among First-Year Undergraduate Students Attending a Highly Selective Research University." EdD diss., University of Pennsylvania, 2011.

———. "Pressure Release." *PennWIC* (blog), May 2, 2014. http://pennwic.wordpress.com/2014/05/02/pressure-release.

Vedantham, Anu, and Marjorie Hassen. "New Media: Engaging and Educating the YouTube Generation." *Journal of Learning Spaces* 1, no. 1 (2011).

———. "Collaborative Classroom." Flickr album. Accessed February 7, 2015. https://www.flickr.com/photos/pennwic/sets/72157645502444793.

———. "Course Usage of the Weigle Information Commons." Penn Libraries, University of Pennsylvania. Accessed February 7, 2015. http://commons.library.upenn.edu/course-usage.

———. "ELIXR MERLOT Faculty Development Initiative." Penn Libraries, University of Pennsylvania. Accessed February 7, 2015. http://elixr.merlot.org/case-stories/teaching-strategies/nurturing-student-creativity-with-video-projects/.

———. "Engaging Students through Technology Symposium." Penn Libraries, University of Pennsylvania, 2014. http://commons.library.upenn.edu/engaging-students-through-technology-symposium.

———. "PowerPoint Videos—Showcase 2012." Penn Libraries, University of Pennsylvania. Accessed February 7, 2015. http://commons.library.upenn.edu/showcase-mitchell-sast-2012.

———. "Reports and Publications." Penn Libraries, University of Pennsylvania. Accessed February 7, 2015. http://commons.library.upenn.edu/reports-and-publications.

———. "Student Work Showcase." Penn Libraries, University of Pennsylvania. Accessed February 7, 2015. http://commons.library.upenn.edu/student-work-showcase.

Weigle Information Commons Guides. "iPads in the Classroom." Penn Libraries, University of Pennsylvania. Last updated October 13, 2014. http://guides.library.upenn.edu/ipad.

Digital *Humanities* IN THE LIBRARY:

PART 4

Projects in Focus: From Conception to Completion and Beyond

CHAPTER ELEVEN

A Digital Adventure
From Theory to Practice

Valla McLean and Sean Atkins

Introduction

"Do you know anyone who knows anything about digital storytelling?" When this straightforward question arrived by e-mail from a history faculty member, coauthor Sean Atkins, I did a quick Internet search, which yielded the following definition from EDUCAUSE: "digital storytelling is the practice of combining narrative with digital content, including images, sound, and video, to create a short movie."[1] The origins of digital storytelling were in the early 1990s, when a group of artists and designers from San Francisco came together to see how "digital media tools could be used to empower personal storytelling."[2] Educational applications of digital storytelling can be found at all levels, from elementary to graduate school, and in disciplines from the sciences to the humanities to health and community studies.* Common genres of digital storytelling include deeply

---

* For examples of digital storytelling in the classroom, see the University of Houston's website Educational Uses of Digital Storytelling, accessed June 8, 2014, http://digitalstorytelling.coe.uh.edu), and the June 2008 special issue of the journal *Arts and Humanities in Higher Education* 7, no. 2.

personal narratives as well as historical documentaries and informational or instructional stories. Interest in digital storytelling in higher education continues to grow with seminars and a master's program currently dedicated to digital storytelling.[3]

With limited time before the beginning of a new semester, Sean and I sat down to discuss how to design a digital storytelling project (DSP) for undergraduate students. In our early endeavors, the focus was on the basics of designing an effective assignment and establishing technology support for the students. Upon reflection and after creating numerous iterations of the assignment, we found that other questions, larger issues, and philosophical discussions demanded our attention, anchored our thoughts, and provided direction for the DSP. In this chapter we will explore, based on our experiences in an introductory, first-year undergraduate history class, the relationship between digital humanities (DH) and digital storytelling, the correlation between technology and pedagogy, the intrinsic and instrumental value of digital storytelling in an undergraduate humanities curriculum, and the intersection between digital storytelling and information literacy.

Digital Humanities and Digital Storytelling

What are the digital humanities? One only has to look at over 500 responses collected between 2009 and 2012 at the Day in the Life of the Digital Humanities (Day of DH), an open, online community project where DH scholars share what they do in the field on one particular day each year to see that defining what is meant by DH is problematic. When asked to define digital humanities, one participant stated, "Digital humanities is a field of study characterized by critical analysis of the relationship between the produced surfaces of digital media and the information structures and cultural structures that produce them; alternatively (or additionally) it is characterized by a critical interest in how humanities scholarship is produced, consumed, and transformed in and through digital media."[4] Another participant offered the simple definition "research and teaching relating to digital resources in Humanities."[5]

An emphasis on the research and scholarly activities of faculty at large research-focused institutions currently dominates the DH literature. The work of these academics and the resulting projects can be complex, requiring a specialized technological skill set and digital tools that allow for data visualization, text mining, editing and analysis, and transcription. Is there a place for DH at an undergraduate institution with an emphasis on teaching and learning? We believe there is and argue, as do others, that "pedagogically, undergraduate forays into the digital humanities need not be as complete or ambitious as building formal archives and discovery tools from scratch.... The point is to spur students to 'think critically and differently' about digital gateways and to 'encourage new forms of close reading, knowledge production and interpretation' in the context of the modern information landscape."[6] Digital storytelling is situated within this inclusive concept of DH. Core traits of both DH and digital storytelling strengthen this argument, with both requiring the use of digital tools, creativity, consumption of information, production of digital artifacts, and reliance on collaboration.

Pedagogy and Digital Storytelling

In 2010, Robert Clarke and Andrea Adam examined digital storytelling as a pedagogical tool in higher education. During interviews with academics in Australia working in media and communication, they found that "participants identified certain learning outcomes and student experiences as being possible with digital storytelling—such as multimodal communication and collaboration—that could not necessarily be achieved through the writing of standard essays."[7] An argument can also be made for providing students with the opportunity to contextualize a topic within a broader discipline through nontraditional learning and assessment. Michael Coventry argues that digital stories have "proven to be a powerful medium for students to represent a theoretically informed understanding of texts and contexts in a form other than 'traditional' writing."[8] In our case, students engage with a topic in history not by producing a written text but by creating a digital artifact. The idea that history can be more than words on paper may inspire students to think differently about the discipline. Moreover, it addresses the many competencies students bring to their courses, instead of just their writing skills.

Today's students leaving high school and entering university came of age in a time of great technological advances. For them, the Internet has always existed; communicating through e-mail, text messaging, and social media is seamlessly integrated into their daily life. They are likely accustomed to posting images on Instagram or Flickr and view videos regularly on YouTube. Suzanne M. Miller argues, Generation Y, children born after 1981, which is "immersed in popular and online culture, thinks of messages and meanings multimodally not just in terms of printed words, but also in terms of images and music."[9] As a result, students interact with and think differently about technology than earlier generations and arrive in the undergraduate classroom with experience in multimodal literacy, the "meaning-making that occurs through the reading, viewing, understanding, responding to and producing and interacting with multimedia and digital texts."[10]

Digital storytelling and its capacity for student engagement is a common theme in the literature on digital storytelling. Helen C. Barrett ascribes value to digital storytelling because it potentially "facilitates the convergence of four student-centered learning strategies: student engagement, reflection for deep learning, project-based learning and the effective integration of technology into instruction."[11] Although Clarke and Adam drew from a relatively small sample of participants, their findings are worthy of consideration when integrating new technologies into the curriculum, specifically in regard to what they call constructive alignment and resource and support services.[12] The use of technology in the classroom, even as a tool to enhance a lecture, requires careful thought by the faculty member as to how it aligns with the intended learning outcomes. Clarke and Adam maintain that "academics believe strongly in using the medium thoughtfully and reflexively to determine where and how it can best elicit and support appropriate student learning and development."[13]

Assigning a DSP requires consideration be paid to both material and human resources and planning requirements. What type of software is required for digital storytelling? Is the software commercially available, or is it freeware? Are there computers on campus with the required software so students are not required to have their own computer and purchase software? Patrick Lowenthal claims one of the most important issues of digital storytelling is access. Educators should not assume students have access to computers at home to complete a digital storytelling project.[14] There are many technological challenges to using digital storytelling in the classroom. It is important to make sure staff are available to help students who may have questions about how to use the digital tools. Clarke and Adam also conclude in their research that, in order to benefit from the process, "students needed to be supported with software, resources and guidance, to achieve a quality of output they would not be able to achieve on their own."[15]

Part of the planning process for this type of assignment should also include a decision on whether the digital storytelling projects will be private or public. If the privacy of students is not a concern, projects can be posted on a site that hosts videos such as YouTube. An alternative to posting online is the option to save the project on a CD or USB key. It is also important to determine what form of assessment will be used for the DSP. Many institutions have posted rubrics to evaluate digital storytelling projects, and with attribution, these can be a helpful starting point.[16] Jason Ohler, professor of media psychology, provides a master list of digital story assessment traits.[17] Any rubric for evaluating a DSP will want to account for several points, including content, assignment objectives, planning, scripts and storyboards, mechanics, story structure, story coherence, and use of technology.

Information Literacy and Digital Storytelling

Information literacy is not sufficient for addressing the competencies required to use multimedia and visual images effectively in a digital storytelling project. Multiple literacies are at play in this type of project, including digital literacy, the ability to "read and interpret media (text, sound, images) to reproduce data and images through digital manipulation, and to evaluate and apply new knowledge gained from digital environments,"[18] and visual literacy, the ability to derive meaning "from images of everything that we see—to read and write visual language."[19] The proposed revisions to the Association of College and Research Libraries (ACRL) Information Literacy Competency Standards for Higher Education, adopted in 2000, in particular the centrality of the concept of "metaliteracy," offer one possible solution to the limitations of the current definition of information literacy.[20] Metaliteracy challenges "traditional skills-based approaches to information literacy by recognizing related literacy types and incorporating emerging technologies" with a "particular emphasis on producing and sharing information in participatory digital environments."[21]

The shared goal of information, digital, and visual literacies is the ability to access, evaluate, incorporate, use, and understand information, albeit in different formats. Mackey and Jacobson argue while information literacy "prepares individuals to access, evaluate and analyze information, metaliteracy prepares individuals to actively produce and share content through social media communities. This requires an understanding of new media tools and original digital information which is necessary for media literacy, digital literacy and ICT literacy. The ability to evaluate and use visual information is also supported by metaliteracy, not only for the appreciation of visual images but for the development of new visuals as well."[22]

Mackey and Jacobson identify seven elements of metaliteracy, of which three have a direct relationship to digital storytelling in an educational setting: students should first, understand format type; second, produce original content in multiple media formats; and third, understand personal privacy, information ethics, and intellectual property issues.[†] Understanding format type requires students to expand their critical-thinking abilities to address the changing nature of how information is made available. Students may be asked to avoid using blogs, wikis, and other formats of information in an academic setting when each may have initial value to the research process.[23] In a digital storytelling project, students are asked to

---

† From Trudi E. Jacobson and Thomas P. Mackey, "Proposing a Metaliteracy Model to Redefine Information Literacy," *Communications in Information Literacy* 7, no. 2 (2013): 87. The seven elements are understand format type and delivery mode; evaluate user feedback as active researcher; create a context for user-generated information; evaluate dynamic content critically; produce original content in multiple media formats; understand personal privacy, information ethics, and intellectual property issues; and share information in participatory environments.

move beyond traditional scholarly sources and incorporate visual images as well as audio and video. Producing original content in multiple media formats relates to the ability of individuals to express an original idea and create unique content using social media.[24] Students use digital tools such as iMovie or Movie Maker to create and share content as creators of a digital story. Understanding the related issues of personal privacy, information ethics, and intellectual property is addressed in digital storytelling, as students need to know how to ethically repurpose content.[25]

The Digital Storytelling Project

In order to illustrate one means of combining pedagogy and technology, we would like to share observations and experiences based on our work in a university introductory Canadian history class. MacEwan University is an undergraduate institution in Edmonton, Alberta, Canada, with approximately 14,000 full-time students. The university's educational philosophy is one that places a priority on teaching and learning and student engagement.

Survey-level undergraduate history courses are often fairly prescriptive in terms of thematic content, assigned material—textual and otherwise—and methods of assessment. These structural impositions can be a challenge for alternative methods of teaching and learning. There are three considerations that must be addressed before bringing a DSP into the classroom. First, as we address earlier, is the question of resources—both human and material, and inside and outside of class. Second, there is the question of how to convey the relevancy and instrumental (as well as intrinsic) value of the DSP to the class. Finally, one must conceptualize the ways in which DSP contributes to "doing history" in the twenty-first century.

True to the humanities' spirit, the DSP idea came about largely as an attempt to address how to establish and implement a digital component in the course without excising other valuable assessment tools. The instructor must avoid giving the students the impression that the DSP is merely an appendage to the material, an instructor's flight of fancy, or an alternative to the term paper. Consequently, the DSP idea slowly took shape over the better part of a semester in anticipation of its implementation the next term. A collaborative approach between librarians and humanities faculty is indispensable to preparing for the DSP project. To fully understand what students were being asked to do in creating a digital story, we set out to create our own story. We found this activity to be invaluable because, as we worked through the steps of the assignment, we came to understand the time commitment involved as well as some of the technical skills the project. This firsthand experience allowed us to both locate and develop resources to increase the students' chances of success. We have found that each class we work with is made up of students with varying degrees of technological skills. Digital geniuses, although they exist, do not by any means dominate the composition of the class. Mature and traditional-age students alike have expressed anxiety around this project. It is important to clearly identify a person who is available to help students with their technology questions.

Further, access to a well-funded and well-resourced technological support service that is closely aligned with the library is another practical reality when considering a DSP. In addition, taking stock of what hardware and software materials students have ready access to is another important consideration. Finally, access to open media software such as Audacity and to computers with iMovie and the Windows-based equivalent (such as Movie Maker) is essential for students on tight budgets. Putting student laptops and iPads to good research use becomes a positive by-product of the process.

It is no small irony that students who may have little hesitation using various technological tools in their personal lives may become quite reticent when directed to apply technology toward academic goals. Consequently there is a mind-set that the instructor must anticipate and the student must conquer. One of the ways in which to prevail over this potential quandary is to demonstrate the *intrinsic and instrumental value* of the DSP. The internal sense of accomplishment in delivering an original digital media product helps to establish creative confidence that extends well beyond the immediate gratification of a good grade. Student development and personal growth are not mutually exclusive from developing basic learning skills. Either one may serve as the foundation for the other, but experience suggests that establishing the former from the outset serves as a facilitator for the latter in due time.

Approaching the project as an artistic endeavor positions the DSP as an expression of identity, one that may become a source of pride. Students may not enter the project with a clear sense of what they will do, but, as they work through their projects and with the materials at hand, they begin to take ownership over their stories. At the same time, we want our students to look critically at their topics. The narrative being crafted is not limited to the descriptive. We encourage our students to approach the topic with an historian's eye, using the various tools, both material and mental, that professional historians use. Indeed, we remind our students that the past is amorphous, out of time, and hence difficult to shape—that is what history is for. The line between the imaginative and the critical is sometimes blurred.

The practical, real-time worth of the DSP is the other half of the value equation. The DSP is an important assessment tool; its share of the final grade is 15 percent. In regard to the DSP's instrumental value, students also become aware of the technical skills acquired or further developed in the process. In addition, those choosing an interview-based DSP have an opportunity to not only enlarge the project to include participants outside the class but have a chance to "give something back" in return. Interviewees are generally enthusiastic to provide their time and are empowered knowing that their views and words are valued.

The Preview: Introducing the Digital Story (The First Week)

Approaching the DSP as an ongoing process is key to a successful conclusion. Students are keen to try new learning methods but want to see for themselves what the project is about. We have learned that referencing the project in the course outline is not sufficient. Consequently, the very first items students are introduced to on the first day of class are examples of student projects from earlier terms. These examples come with just enough explanation to immerse the students' minds in the project. Students view the two major strands of the DSP—the *interview-based* and *thematic story* approaches in the *first week* of class. Little is conveyed by way of mention of the stories (beyond the stories themselves) other than the course themes or topics, which they will choose from a predetermined list. Experience suggests that students become comfortable with the project when they see their colleagues' productions.

The Setting and the Characters: Aligning Themes with Course Lectures (The Second Week)

Gauging student understanding of and responses to the DSP requirements from the outset can be difficult. We have found that students will demonstrate a marked level of ambivalence and will rarely approach the instructor in the first two weeks about any assignment. Nevertheless, in the *second week* students become more cognizant of the immediacy of conceptualizing their project through an alignment of the various topics or themes that match the course lecture. At this point, they can see not only the relevancy of the project to the course syllabus but also the added importance of thinking about their chosen topic. We encourage students to approach faculty for topic-related questions and the librarian for technology-related concerns shortly thereafter so they can start thinking about their projects. Often students will either know little to nothing of the topic or wonder if there is sufficient material going forward. Conveying enthusiasm goes a long way to assuaging anxieties.

The Plot: The Interview Option, Swap Board, and Storyboard

The *third week* of the course sees the students weigh in on their topics with respect to the interview option. Additionally, they have the opportunity to switch topics with a colleague through the online "swapboard" in the university's LMS, Blackboard. This is also the week where the librarian introduces the students to the resource materials and the software by way of a one-hour tutorial in the library. Anecdotal evidence suggests that this session is vital to allaying student anxieties concerning the mechanics of digital media as well as an opportunity for students to use both the librarian and the instructor as sounding boards for their project thoughts. This session is also the moment when the digital story assignment handout is discussed (see appendix 11.1). Students must be given clear direction in terms of the tasks they are entrusted to complete. This assignment is not simply a discursive narration.

The Library Tutorial

A one-hour tutorial during class time is scheduled in the library in a forty-seat computer lab. The lecture part of the class is limited to thirty minutes, with the remaining of class time given to students for asking questions of both the librarian and the instructor and beginning to locate sources for the assignment. Using an online course guide, the librarian directs students to valuable resources needed to complete the digital storytelling project.[‡]

The class begins with a quick overview of the requirements of the digital storytelling project. Students view a number of storytelling examples to provide ideas for their own work. Moving from a general understanding of the assignment and what digital storytelling looks like, the librarian discusses the key steps for producing a digital story. The librarian reminds students of the importance of developing an effective research strategy for locating resources for the project before they engage with the software and master the mechanics of designing a digital story. Students spend time in class brainstorming with both the faculty member and the librarian on ways to narrow their broad topics. As this assignment requires the use of both primary and secondary sources, the librarian reviews how to locate and evaluate both types of sources. Since students are encouraged to find primary sources using library resources and those found freely on the Web,

---

‡   The online guide includes information on how to create a digital story, and storyboards, digital storytelling examples, tools or software for digital storytelling (iMovie and Movie Maker), finding media (images, audio and video) as well as information on copyright and citing. MacEwan University Library, "Digital Storytelling," accessed June 9, 2014, http://libguides.macewan.ca/digitalstorytelling.

the librarian places special emphasis on evaluating images and multimedia for use in academic papers. Bernard R. Robin and Sara G. McNeil emphasize, as do we, the importance of writing a script and storyboarding before trying to master one of the digital storytelling tools. No matter how much "expertise a student has with technology; a poorly written story will not be improved by fancy transitions and other digital effects."[26] We provide a storyboard template in MS Word, but students can draw one by hand, or as recommended by Robin and McNeil, create a storyboard in Excel or PowerPoint, or use Celtx storyboard and scriptwriting software.[27] Many nonprofessional filmmakers engage in digital storytelling, so we instruct students to try to find a balance between the content of the stories and their technical aspects.

Our project asks students to use iMovie or the Windows-based equivalent Movie Maker to create a digital story. We reassure the students that the digital tools are user-friendly. Students who are apprehensive are encouraged to attend one of the drop-in Learning Commons workshops or to contact the librarian for one-on-one support. Students are expected to provide citations for their sources, so we also discuss information on the use of copyrighted material in a multimedia assignment.

One of our initial concerns about this project was that students would have difficulty using iMovie or Movie Maker. To address and skill deficit, a class was scheduled in the library on how to use iMovie and Movie Maker. A worksheet was designed by the librarian to help develop the skills associated with the project, such as how to start a project and how to download and save images. We found that students have a wide range of capabilities when it comes to using the software, so it proved impossible to structure a class that was both accessible enough for students with limited skills and challenging enough for students familiar with and confident using the tools. We would recommend not dedicating class time to learning how to use the digital tools. Instead, students should be encouraged attend drop-in workshops or meet with the subject librarian.

The Development

The *interval weeks (4–9)* give way to the other course requirements (i.e., midterm; term paper; weekly reading and writing tasks), but we give intermittent reminders, largely through storyboard writing tasks and additional viewings to keep the digital project in mind. Those students who feel they lack the confidence or skills to work in digital media are encouraged to make appointments with the librarian so as to have an improved handling of the material. It is also important at this time to identify those students doing an interview-based project in order to prepare them for the proper protocol and methodology of interviewing. These students must also have the relevant release forms in hand in order to meet the ethical requirements.[§] Generally, only one quarter to one third of the class chooses the interview option.

We have no illusions that the students will have the digital story first and foremost on their minds for the duration of the course. Indeed, students often weigh the other term tasks and, in conjunction with the timelines, determine that the digital storytelling project "can wait." Although we find their procrastination frustrating, we believe that forcing the digital storytelling project on the students leading up to the final couple weeks is counterproductive and threatens the contemplative considerations of the project.

The Climax: Viewing Day

Throughout the term, we encourage the students to explore their topics as they see fit within the context of the central ("BIG") questions and rubric. One of the common questions students ask is whether they will be

---

§   MacEwan University to date does not have its own internally generated documents. We use documents from Concordia University's Centre for Oral History and Digital Storytelling modified to meet the requirements of MacEwan University. For more on Concordia University's Centre for Oral History and Digital Storytelling as well as ethical requirements and related documents consult the Centre's website (Centre for Oral History and Digital Storytelling, "Toolbox," Concordia University, accessed July 11, 2014, http://storytelling.concordia.ca/toolbox).

required to show their work to the class and, if so, in what venue. Corollary to that query is whether they will be required to discuss their work with the class and if they are being assessed at that time. We believe students' work replaces the traditional "show and tell" where the telling sometimes overshadows the showing. The digital project speaks and shows. Further, the environment for their presentations should be collegial and casual (it is the last day of class after all!). Consequently, students are informed earlier in the term that their work will not be assessed on viewing day so they must either bring a copy of their project on a CD or flash drive or send it electronically to the instructor the evening before viewing. The class is split into two or three groups, where one group (or groups) is free to circulate and view other projects for a set period of time.

We encourage students to present their work to their colleagues for both individual and collective reasons. First, students gain a measure of confidence, not to mention a sense of closure, when they present this way. Second, when students understand that they are expected to show their work to their peers, the number of late submissions declines. A small measure of peer pressure seems to have some effect on meeting the deadline.

Epilogue: EAT and Assessing the Product

Despite the equal attention by both librarian and instructor to delivering a successful digital story, student expectations and concerns about consistency determine that only the course instructor should be engaged in assessment. Furthermore, digital stories are best delivered in relatively smaller classes, with maximum capacities of forty students.

Both critical thinking and imaginative efforts are considered in the assessment. In the interest of transparency, the rubric is distributed in the first quarter of the semester. Use of the rubric is vital to maintaining accuracy and equity, which are requirements in all methods of assessment In the interests of transparency, the rubric is distributed in the first quarter of the semester which allows for which, like all methods of assessment, is vital to maintaining accuracy and equity. Still, marking a digital story is both structurally similar to and procedurally different from grading a paper. A few points are helpful in the triangular matters of *equity, accuracy, and transparency (EAT).*

Equity: The instructor faces the prospect of viewing several dozen films in a relatively narrow space of time that must include term paper assessment and final exam preparation. A sense of eager anticipation and excitement never lacks in the lead-up to the submissions. These notions are quickly put to the test when the stories arrive en masse. Instructors must be prepared to put aside an equal amount of time for each project, regardless of the number of submissions, time constraints, and other grading requirements. In the interests of equity, the instructor views each digital presentation once. The instructor may choose to pause the presentation any number of times for matters of clarity or note taking, but assessment follows once the film is viewed in its entirety. We believe that, for now, the instructor should be the sole assessor given that she spends the balance of the time with the student through the term and is the individual who originally goes over the rubric with the class. We do believe, however, that instructor/librarian collaboration is essential to the original construction of the rubric. Consequently, we do not rule out the possibility of future reforms to the assessment process (e.g., librarian-only marking or librarian/instructor marking) but this arrangement must be explicitly conveyed to the students at the outset of the term.

Accuracy: Experience suggests that the best framework for assessment is the rubric method. The rubric must be worded in a straightforward and precise manner. We have found that no more than six criteria should be used, and within each, the comments must be clearly stated and distinguishable from levels both below and above.

Transparency: Three items ensure clarity. First, the rubric is distributed in advance. Second, rubric criteria are discussed as a group at that time. We emphasize at this time that demonstrating proficiency with digital medial tools alone is limited as part of the assessment method.. This measure works constructively at dissuading students from paying for (or otherwise acquiring) professional services—an example of academic fraud. Finally, the corresponding levels of assessment that intersect with the criteria are aligned with the university's grading scale where *Satisfactory, Good/Very Good*, and *Excellent* are matched with a grade and point value. We do not include *Insufficient/Fail* as part of the grading scheme unless there is evidence of academic fraud.

Invariably there will be a handful of presentations that we are unable to view, usually due to software incompatibilities or, more rarely, corrupted files. We use these inevitabilities as a way of encouraging our students to try their best to avoid these problems by giving enough advance preparation time. Still, some projects will be unwatchable the first time around. We do not deduct points for these projects but recognize that students are ultimately responsible for submitting a complete project. At the same time, the responsibility for addressing these issues as soon as possible lies with the instructor, especially given the pressures associated with the end-of-term push. Viewing the digital projects as soon as they are submitted goes a long way towards alleviating these contingencies.

Conclusion

Digital storytelling presents librarians with both challenges and opportunities in the digital humanities. It can be a challenge to understand the complexity of DH projects and their value in the undergraduate humanities curriculum. It can also be a difficult task for librarians to determine how they should collaborate with teaching faculty to support student success. Yet within this complexity is the opportunity for librarians to expand their knowledge about the relationship between technology and pedagogy and make sound decisions based on that knowledge. This can involve embracing the development of both human and material resources, such as designing drop-in technology workshops and online course guides for digital storytelling projects. The challenge of addressing the various literacies at play in a digital storytelling project also provides the chance for librarians to consider the objectives of metaliteracy as a possible means to steering students towards success in an ever-changing digital environment.

Notes

1. Educause Learning Initiative, *7 Things You Should Know about Digital Storytelling* (Louisville, CO: Educause, January 15, 2007), 1, http://net.educause.edu/ir/library/pdf/ELI7021.pdf.
2. Center for Digital Storytelling, "How It All Began," accessed May 21, 2014, http://storycenter.org/history.

3. See Ball State University, "Master of Arts in Telecommunication (Digital Storytelling)," accessed May 30, 2014, http://cms.bsu.edu/academics/collegesanddepartments/telecommunications/academicsandadmissions/programsofstudy/mastersdegree; University of Mary Washington, "DS106," accessed May 30, 2014, http://ds106.us.

4. Julia Flanders, from summary of responses to Day of Digital Humanities from 2009 to 2012, What Is Digital Humanities website, accessed June 8, 2014, http://whatisdigitalhumanities.com.

5. Cate MacKay, from summary of responses to Day of Digital Humanities from 2009 to 2012, What Is Digital Humanities website, accessed June 8, 2014, http://whatisdigitalhumanities.com.

6. Steve Kolowich, "Behind the Digital Curtain," *Inside Higher Ed*, January 27, 2012, para. 12, https://www.insidehighered.com/news/2012/01/27/could-digital-humanities-undergraduates-could-boost-information-literacy.

7. Robert Clarke and Andrea Adam, "Digital Storytelling in Australia: Academic Perspectives and Reflections," *Arts and Humanities in Higher Education* 11, no.1–2 (2010): 168. doi:10.1177/1474022210374223.

8. Michael Coventry. "Cross-Currents of Pedagogy and Technology: A Forum on Digital Storytelling and Cultural Critique," *Arts and Humanities in Higher Education* 7, no. 2 (2008): 166, doi:10.1177/1474022208088646.

9. Suzanne M. Miller, "English Teacher Learning for New Times: Digital Video Composing as Multimodal Literacy Practice," *English Education* 40, no. 1 (October 2007): 62.

10. Maureen Walsh, "Multimodal Literacy: What Does It Mean for Classroom Practice?" *Australian Journal of Language and Literacy* 33, no. 3 (2010): 213.

11. Helen C. Barrett, "Researching and Evaluating Digital Storytelling as a Deep Learning Tool," in *Proceedings of Society for Information Technology and Teacher Education International Conference*, ed. Caroline M. Crawford et al. (Chesapeake, VA: AACE, 2006): 647.

12. Clarke and Adam, "Digital Storytelling in Australia," 167–68.

13. Ibid., 169.

14. Patrick Lowenthal, "Digital Storytelling in Education: An Emerging Institutional Technology?" in *Story Circle: Digital Storytelling around the World*, ed. John Hartley and Kelly McWilliam (Hoboken, NJ: Wiley-Blackwell, 2009), 258.

15. Clarke and Adam, "Digital Storytelling in Australia," 170.

16. See University of Houston, "Educational Materials, Evaluation and Assessment," Educational Uses of Digital Storytelling website, accessed July 15, 2014, http://digitalstorytelling.coe.uh.edu/page.cfm?id=24&cid=24&sublinkid=43 and University of Maryland, Baltimore County, "Grading Rubrics," Digital Stories @ UMBC website, accessed July 11, 2015, http://stories.umbc.edu/rubrics.php.

17. Jason Ohler, *Digital Storytelling in the Classroom* (Thousand Oaks, CA: Corwin Press, 2008), 68.

18. Barbara R. Jones-Kavalier and Suzanne L. Flannigan, Connecting the Digital Dots: Literacy of the 21st Century," *Educause Quarterly* 29, no. 2 (2006): 9 https://net.educause.edu/ir/library/pdf/EQM0621.pdf.

19. "What Is Visual Literacy? Centre for Visual Literacy website, accessed July 15, 2014, www.vislit.org/visual-literacy.

20. For more information see ACRL, "Framework for Information Literacy for Higher Education," Draft 2. Chicago: ACRL, June 2014, http://acrl.ala.org/ilstandards/wp-content/uploads/2014/02/Framework-for-IL-for-HE-Draft-2.pdf.
21. Thomas P. Mackey and Trudi E. Jacobson, "Reframing Information Literacy as a Metaliteracy," *College and Research Libraries* 72, no. 1 (2011): 62.
22. Ibid., 76.
23. Trudi E. Jacobson and Thomas P. Mackey, "Proposing a Metaliteracy Model to Redefine Information Literacy," *Communications in Information Literacy* 7, no. 2 (2013): 87.
24. Ibid., 89.
25. Ibid.
26. Bernard R. Robin and Sara G. McNeil, "What Educators Should Know about Teaching Digital Storytelling," *Digital Education Review*, no. 22 (December 2012): 41 http://greav.ub.edu/eng/news/nuevo-numero-de-digital-edu.html .
27. Ibid., 42.

Bibliography

ACRL (Association of College and Research Libraries). "Framework for Information Literacy for Higher Education," Draft 2. Chicago: ACRL, June 2014. http://acrl.ala.org/ilstandards/wp-content/uploads/2014/02/Framework-for-IL-for-HE-Draft-2.pdf.

Arts and Humanities in Higher Education 7, no. 2 (June 2008). Special issue.

Ball State University. "Master of Arts in Telecommunication (Digital Storytelling)." Accessed May 30, 2014. http://cms.bsu.edu/academics/collegesanddepartments/telecommunications/academicsandadmissions/programsofstudy/mastersdegree.

Barrett, Helen C. "Researching and Evaluating Digital Storytelling as a Deep Learning Tool." In *Proceedings of Society for Information Technology and Teacher Education International Conference*, edited by Caroline M. Crawford, Roger Carlsen, Karen McFerrin, Jerry Price, Roberta Weber, and Dee Anna Willis (Chesapeake, VA: AACE, 2006): 647–54.

Center for Digital Storytelling. "How It All Began." Accessed May 21, 2014. http://storycenter.org/history.

Centre for Visual Literacy. "What Is Visual Literacy? Centre for Visual Literacy website, accessed July 15, 2014, www.vislit.org/visual-literacy.

Clarke, Robert, and Andrea Adam. "Digital Storytelling in Australia: Academic Perspectives and Reflections." *Arts and Humanities in Higher Education* 11, no. 1–2 (2010): 157–176. doi:10.1177/1474022210374223.

Concordia University. "Toolbox." Centre for Oral History and Digital Storytelling website. Accessed July 11, 2014. http://storytelling.concordia.ca/toolbox

Coventry, Michael. "Cross-Currents of Pedagogy and Technology: A Forum on Digital Storytelling and Cultural Critique." *Arts and Humanities in Higher Education* 7, no. 2 (2008): 165–70. doi:10.1177/1474022208088646.

Educause Learning Initiative. *7 Things You Should Know about Digital Storytelling.* Louisville, CO: Educause, January 15, 2007. http://net.educause.edu/ir/library/pdf/ELI7021.pdf.

Heppler, Jason. What Is Digital Humanities? website. Database of quotations from participants in the Day of DH between 2009 and 2012. Accessed June 8, 2014. http://whatisdigitalhumanities.com.

Jacobson, Trudi E., and Thomas P. Mackey. "Proposing a Metaliteracy Model to Redefine Information Literacy." *Communications in Information Literacy* 7, no. 2 (2013): 84–91.

Jones-Kavalier, Barbara R., and Suzanne L. Flannigan. "Connecting the Digital Dots: Literacy of the 21st Century." *Educause Quarterly* 29, no. 2 (2006): 8–10. https://net.educause.edu/ir/library/pdf/EQM0621.pdf.

Kolowich, Steve. "Behind the Digital Curtain." *Inside Higher Ed*, January 27, 2012. https://www.insidehighered.com/news/2012/01/27/could-digital-humanities-undergraduates-could-boost-information-literacy.

Lowenthal, Patrick. "Digital Storytelling in Education: An Emerging Institutional Technology?" In *Story Circle: Digital Storytelling around the World*, edited by John Hartley and Kelly McWilliam, 252–59. (Hoboken, NJ: Wiley-Blackwell, 2009).

MacEwan University Library. "Digital Storytelling." Course guide. Accessed June 9, 2014. http://libguides.macewan.ca/digitalstorytelling.

Mackey, Thomas P., and Trudi E. Jacobson. "Reframing Information Literacy as a Metaliteracy." *College and Research Libraries* 72, no. 1 (2011): 62–78.

Miller, Suzanne M. "English Teacher Learning for New Times: Digital Video Composing as Multimodal Literacy Practice." *English Education* 40, no. 1 (October 2007): 61–83.

Ohler, Jason. *Digital Storytelling in the Classroom: New Media Pathways to Literacy, Learning and Creativity*. Thousand Oaks, CA: Corwin Press, 2008.

Robin, Bernard R., and Sara G. McNeil. "What Educators Should Know about Teaching Digital Storytelling." *Digital Education Review*, no. 22 (December 2012): 37–51 http://greav.ub.edu/eng/news/nuevo-numero-de-digital-edu.html.

University of Houston. The Educational Uses of Digital Storytelling website. Accessed June 8, 2014. http://digitalstorytelling.coe.uh.edu.

———. "Educational Materials: Evaluation and Assessment." Educational Uses of Digital Storytelling website. Accessed July 15, 2014. http://digitalstorytelling.coe.uh.edu/page.cfm?id=24&cid=24&sublinkid=43.

University of Maryland, Baltimore County. "Grading Rubrics." Digital Stories @ UMBC website. Accessed July 11, 2014. http://stories.umbc.edu/rubrics.php

University of Mary Washington. "DS106." Accessed May 30, 2014. http://ds106.us.

Walsh, Maureen. "Multimodal Literacy: What Does It Mean for Classroom Practice?" *Australian Journal of Language and Literacy* 33, no. 3 (2010): 211–39.

Appendix 11.1: Digital Story Assignment Handout

THE 2014 POST-CONFEDERATION CANADIAN HISTORY DIGITAL STORYTELLING PROJECT

The Stories That Are Told, The Stories That Are Not

I. Introduction

The art and practice of storytelling is as old as humanity. Through time we have embraced storytelling as a way of making sense of our place in the world. The motivations for telling stories vary but certain universal concepts such as imagination, legitimacy, meaning, learning and entertaining are at the heart of the process. We tell stories not only because we like to but because we *have* to.

Author Julian Barnes addresses TWO fundamental issues concerning the meaning of history in his 2011 award winning novel, *The Sense of an Ending.** The first question concerns *history's obsession with winners and losers:*

> History isn't the lies of the victors... [or the self-delusions of the losers], as I once glibly assured [my history teacher] Old Joe Hunt; I know that now. It's more the memories of the survivors, most of whom are neither victorious nor defeated.

Barnes also struggles with history's fondness for marking the *rise and fall of societies, civilizations, nations and peoples*:

> Someone once said that his favourite times in history were when things were collapsing because that meant something new was being born. Does this make any sense if we apply it to our individual lives? To die when something is being born—even if that some-

---

*   Julian Barnes, *The Sense of an Ending* (Toronto: Random House, 2011). All subsequent excerpts are from the e-book version.

thing new is our very own self? Because just as all political and historical change sooner or later disappoints, so does adulthood.

Barnes can't accept history's obsessions with the stories of winners and losers, rising and falling—yet our history texts and lectures spend a lot of time discussing these themes. What are your thoughts?

II.   *The Big Question*

You may address either of the following for your digital story project

1. ***What is missed or glossed over when we tell these kinds of stories, of winners and losers/rising and falling? What essentials should be there?***

2. ***What are the kinds of post-Confederation Canadian stories you want to tell—and be told?***

III.   *The Project: A Brief Synopsis*

This digital project gives **you** the opportunity to apply the imaginative process through the story telling process. Furthermore, **your** thoughts are what matters! You may choose to apply the questions above into your project any way you (and your partner where applicable) see fit. Your final product should be a 3-5 minute multimedia presentation that addresses these ideas with an accompanying brief one-page reflection paper (Weekly Journal #5).

Guidelines & Explanations

The accompanying rubric will address those issues directly concerning assessment. There are some other considerations, however, that should be dealt with from the outset:

1. ***How is this project related to the course?*** Beyond the obvious—you are dealing with an aspect of Canadian history—you could try aligning your presentation with your chosen term paper topic. It may be far-fetched to argue that one will inform the other but at the very least you will have an opportunity to enrich your own learning by getting into greater depth.

2. *Is this project History or something else?* This project is rooted in history but enriched through some of the other subjects you may be studying (or have already finished). Since the use of one or two primary sources of any kind is required, however, this is predominantly a history project. Indeed, your presentation should ideally centre on your chosen source(s). Some questions to consider include: How does this object speak to me? What does it mean in a more universal sense?

3. *How do I address the two questions discussed above? Should I include both?* Please feel free to consider them any way you see fit. In fact, you may want to **argue that Barnes rejection of traditional history—winners and losers, rising and falling—IS what history is all about** Whatever you decide consider using some (or all) of the "10 Cs" to help shape your presentation. See lecture #1 on Blackboard if you need additional guidance.

4. *Is this project an oral history?* Time constraints ensure that interviews[†] are not mandatory but consider its place in your story. There is a methodology to the interview process, however, so it is best to decide from the outset if you will be engaged in the interview process. If so, please see me as soon as the decision is made and consult the "Digital Storytelling" folder on Blackboard for more information on the interview process.

5. *Am I free to create my own story?* You **are** creating a story by default—whether you wish to tell "a story of stories" through interviewing[†] or create your own. Brainstorming and scripting are highly recommended. The use of a storyboard is also highly recommended (see below). A visual aid of this kind allows you to "map out" your story and is indispensable in addressing the binaries discussed above. Storyboards do not have to be impressive physical displays (they will not be part of the final assessment)—just enough to give you direction as a reference.

---

† Interviews may require a consent form. Please see me for more information.

6. *How many forms of media (i.e. still images, sliding images, memes, moving images, sound, sound mashups, etc.) should I use and which ones should take priority? Should the final product take the form of a 'stand-alone' web site?* In a nutshell—the choices of media and shape are yours and should conform to your comfort zone. Still, sometimes less can be more....remember that your story also contains a message—one that should come through in the end.

7. *What about the required reflection part of the project?* Don't fret it. Keeping a journal is an important part of the imaginative process but not mandatory. The journal does not comprise any part of the final assessment mark and does not have to be submitted. Nevertheless, since each presentation—whether singular or in pairs—requires a one page reflection at the time of presentation, you could draw upon your journal comments when crafting your written brief at the end. Remember: the reflection piece IS a requirement.

8. *How about feedback?* There will be an assignment drop-box or discussion board on Blackboard so you can upload storyboards, script drafts, and proposed images for instructor and/or peer feedback.

IV. The Process

Here is a brief breakdown of the steps:

THE OTHER BIG QUESTION(S): Do I want to work alone? Am I prepared to work collaboratively?

- Brainstorming: You will have an opportunity to share your ideas with others in the class (sometimes called a "story circle"). This is the time when you can help each other refine your ideas and find a partner (when applicable).

- Scripting: You will author a 200-300 word script that will become the audio for your stories. Peers and the instructor can ask questions and provide feedback on the script as well.

- Storyboarding (Hand Out): Consider using a comic strip format to show how the words in your script will synch up with the images you plan to use in your story. Time permitting this can be another opportunity for feedback.

- Recording and Editing: This is where the piece comes together.

- Fine Tuning and Titling: Add transitions, titles, and credits. It's important for this to come last, as transitions can change the timing of a piece.

- Burning & Uploading: Export your project and burn them to CD or DVD—at least one copy for you and another for the teacher.

Digital Storytelling Projects Will Be Viewed in the Library on…

V. *A one page reflection on your digital storytelling experience will be submitted as part of the weekly journal exercise for this class*

CHAPTER TWELVE

"And There Was a Large Number of People"

The Occom Circle Project at the Dartmouth College Library

Laura R. Braunstein, Peter Carini, and Hazel-Dawn Dumpert

> ". . . ther I preachd began about 2 and there was a large Numb^r of People and I Spoke from the Words I have a mesage &c and there was an affectionate attention amongst the People...."
>
> —Samson Occom, Journal, 3 June 1788

SAMSON OCCOM (1723–1792) was a Mohegan Indian and one of the earliest (if not the first) Native American students of Eleazar Wheelock, the founder of Dartmouth College. As an itinerant preacher, Occom ministered to Native and white communities throughout the northeast. After breaking with Wheelock for several reasons, Occom went on to found an independent Indian community in upstate New York. The Dartmouth College Library's Occom Circle Project, led by English professor Ivy Schweitzer and funded by a grant from the National Endowment for the Humanities, is producing a scholarly digital edition of Occom's papers, including journals, letters, sermons, herbals, and accounts.[1] In addition to Occom's papers, the project also includes documents that discuss Occom by others in his "circle," including Eleazar Wheelock, Nathaniel Whitaker, Joseph Johnson, David Fowler, and George Whitefield. Upon completion, the collection will be fully searchable, with person, organization, place, and event indexes. These documents, all of which are held in the archives of the Dartmouth College Library, are a foundational collection of primary sources in Native American studies, colonial history, and American religious history.[*]

Digitizing Occom's papers has been an organization-wide endeavor for the Dartmouth College Library, involving staff from many departments, including Special Collections, Preservation, Cataloging and Metadata Services, and Reference. A half-time project manager directs the transcription and markup process, which involves library staff, faculty, undergraduate students, and the English subject librarian. This chapter will describe the development of our project management process, which has been accomplished almost entirely within the existing organizational culture of the library. The library does not at the time of this writing have a separate digital humanities department, program, or center, but it has a long tradition of producing digital projects. It is still in the early stages of developing staff dedicated to leading and supporting large-scale, ongoing digital humanities projects. The Occom Circle Project provides a case study in organizational change and an example of how subject specialists and department liaisons can work within their libraries' existing cultures to develop new skills and connections to support and foster the digital humanities.

Samson Occom, 1723-1792

"I was Born a Heathen and Brought up in Heathenism"—so opens Samson Occom's 1768 autobiography.[2] Occom was, in fact, born a Mohegan Indian in eastern Connecticut in 1723. In his teenage years, he had two experiences that shaped the rest of his life: the first was a religious awakening that first

---

*   The authors wish to thank Ivy Schweitzer and Jay Satterfield for their feedback in revising this chapter.

made him fear for his soul and then brought him to Christianity. The second was watching deliberations related to the infamous Mason case, a controversy over indigenous land rights that turned on the Connecticut colony's exploitation of Indian illiteracy.† These two experiences—one spiritual and one political—led him to seek a Christian education with the New Light minister Eleazar Wheelock in 1743. Occom and Wheelock had a complicated relationship. On the one hand, Wheelock provided Occom with a classical education (including Latin, Greek, and Hebrew) not offered even to most white students at the time. On the other, Wheelock kept Occom beholden to him for support, both financial and moral.

Occom was ordained in 1759 after serving as a lay minister and teacher for many years at Montauk on Long Island. He always struggled financially and was well aware that he was supported much less extravagantly than English ministers doing similar work. In 1764, he and his family moved back to Mohegan. He soon ran afoul of local clergy because he was drawing Native parishioners away from their services. He also became embroiled in the Mason land case in an attempt to protect the Mohegans from financial ruin. It wasn't long before accusations of misconduct were leveled against Occom. Wheelock, disgusted by these accusations, convened a synod that acquitted Occom of all charges save those related to the Mason controversy. Fearing Occom's further involvement in local issues, Wheelock sent him to England in 1766 in the company of local minister Nathaniel Whitaker to raise money for Wheelock's Moor's Indian Charity School. In England, Occom and Whitaker, who was something of a hustler, traveled the country; Occom preached while Whitaker took up collections. Their tour raised an astounding £12,000—equivalent to approximately $2.4 million today.

On his return to the colonies in 1768, Occom found himself without means of support. Wheelock had neglected Occom's family and, for various reasons, turned his attention from his former pupil in order to pursue the founding of a college on the New Hampshire frontier. Occom and Wheelock fell out over the use of the funds raised in England, which Wheelock

---

†   For background on the Mason case, see Michael Oberg, *Uncas: First of the Mohicans* (Ithaca: Cornell University Press, 2003), 207–13.

used to establish the institution that became Dartmouth College. Occom never set foot on campus nor saw his former mentor in person again. This was a turning point in Occom's life and his first step toward spiritual and intellectual independence.

In 1772, a Mohegan Indian named Moses Paul was convicted of murdering a white man while under the influence of alcohol. He was sentenced to death and asked Occom to preach his execution sermon. Occom spoke to a large, mixed-race crowd on the subject of temperance, an issue of deep concern to the English establishment in its relationship to Indian communities. At the urging of others, Occom had the sermon printed, and it went through nineteen editions (including a Welsh translation), making Occom the sixth-most published American author of the 1770s. The sermon launched him on a new path of celebrity.[3]

Over the next fifteen years, Occom became increasingly disenchanted with white culture, while at the same time he deepened his connection to his Christian faith. In 1787, he wrote a sermon titled "Thou Shalt Love Thy Neighbor as Thyself" in which he declared that those who held slaves—which included almost all white men of station at the time—were not Christian. Even in an environment where several states had moved to outlaw slavery, this was a radical statement. Frustrated by his own circumstances and by those of his Christian brethren across a number of tribes, he and several other graduates of Moor's School set up a Christian Indian settlement called Brothertown in Oneida territory in upstate New York. Occom moved back and forth between Oneida and Mohegan for many years and finally died in Brothertown in 1792.

While there are many things about Occom that made him unique among his peers—his education, his experience in England, his international acclaim and recognition, his straddling of two cultures—he stands out most prominently today in that he is the foremost colonial Native American to have left behind a published body of written work. It is this body of work, along with the opinions and perceptions of his Anglo-American colleagues, that makes Occom of particular and compelling interest to modern scholars of eighteenth-century history, literature, and culture.

The largest body of Occom's papers is held by Rauner Special Collections Library at Dartmouth College.

The Occom Circle Project

Rauner Library is committed to integrating its collections into the intellectual life of Dartmouth College. In most academic years, around one hundred classes hold sessions in Rauner, using materials from the rare book, manuscript, and archival collections. Ivy Schweitzer, Professor of English and Women's and Gender Studies, has regularly brought her Early American Literature class in to use Rauner's collections. Her teaching collaboration with College Archivist Peter Carini led to an invitation to present and discuss Samson Occom's papers as part of Dartmouth's annual Pow-Wow, an event celebrating Native American culture held annually since the college refocused attention on supporting Native American education in the early 1970s.[4] Their presentation during the May 2007 Pow-Wow was attended by members of the Mohegan tribe. During the session with Schweitzer and Carini, a member of the Mohegan Tribal Council asked why, if Occom was such an integral and important part of the founding of the college, was he not more visible at Dartmouth—at the time, the only space in Hanover named for Occom was a large pond on the periphery of campus. This question sparked a lively discussion and inspired the idea for the Occom Circle Project.

Over the next few months, Schweitzer and Carini had several discussions about the possibility of digitizing Occom's writings. At the crux of the discussion was the recent publication of Joanna Brooks's book *The Collected Writings of Samson Occom, Mohegan: Leadership and Literature in Eighteenth-Century Native America,*[5] a critical edition of Occom's written work that included a number of documents that were not part of Dartmouth's holdings. Rather than simply repeat Brooks's work in digital form, Schweitzer decided that a digital scholarly edition of Occom's writings at Dartmouth, combined with documents from his contemporaries (particularly regarding their perception of Occom), would provide a new and interesting angle, while at the same time facilitating her curricular use of the documents.

Schweitzer, in consultation with Carini and David Seaman, Associate Librarian for Information Management, applied for a grant from the National Endowment for the Humanities and was awarded $250,000 to create a scholarly digital edition of approximately 530 eighteenth-century documents, comprising letters, accounts, journals, sermons, and other documents by, about, and related to Samson Occom.[6] The grant proposed to digitize the documents, transcribe them, and mark up the transcriptions using the Text Encoding Initiative (TEI) XML schema. The markup would allow scholars to search and sort the documents in ways that a simple plain-text transcription would not allow. It would also make it possible to present the documents in both a scholarly diplomatic version and a modernized version that would regularize variations in spelling and handwriting common to eighteenth-century documents, making the material more accessible to undergraduates as well as to K–12 students and general readers.

To date, the Occom Circle Project, funded in part by the National Endowment for the Humanities and supplemented by the Dartmouth College Library, has resulted in 586 scanned documents either by or about Occom, plus a number of other documents pertaining to other Native American students taught by Eleazar Wheelock at Moor's Indian Charity School in Connecticut. These scanned documents amount to 3,098 images (or pages), each of which has been cataloged, transcribed, and marked up using TEI. The final product presents the transcriptions side-by-side with the scanned documents to allow scholars and students to judge and interpret the documents and transcriptions for themselves.

The Project and the Process

The Occom Circle Project is one of the Dartmouth College Library's most complex projects to date. The initial project team was led by primary investigators Schweitzer and Carini, with five additional members from library departments including Library Leadership, Cataloging and Metadata Services, the Digital Library Technologies Group, and Preservation Services. Hazel-Dawn Dumpert was hired from outside the library as project manager, and members of Dartmouth College's Web Design and

Development team served as consultants. So far, the project has involved at least forty individuals from the library, Computing Services, and the grant team. It has also employed a number of Dartmouth undergraduates and graduate students and postdoctoral fellows from Dartmouth and other institutions.

Not initially included among the team members were department liaisons from the disciplines most relevant to the project: English, history, and Native American studies. This was neither a deliberate exclusion nor an oversight, but rather a function of the way new digital projects had been initiated within the current organizational structure of the library. Project leaders within the library—in this case, Carini, the subject specialist for college history—made proposals to a cross-departmental, cross-functional committee, which then decided how to move forward in accommodating new projects. Department liaisons often initiated new projects in the library's digital program, on their own or in collaboration with faculty, but their roles once projects were underway had not been defined. The process of developing and carrying out the Occom Circle Project served to reveal both the strengths and the challenges of the current organizational structure and to suggest additional ways of involving department liaisons in digital projects in order to improve both library services and the projects themselves.

While the project was defined to a certain extent by the grant, a number of specifics needed clarification. To ensure that all parties were clear about the expectations and outcomes from the project, the project team drew up a success statement. The success statement included a narrative that laid out in broad strokes the technical expectations for the final product as well as the expected behaviors of the Occom Circle website, such as "The encoding will allow linking to contextualizing information about people, events, places, and organizations mentioned in the letters as well as facilitating research related to textual elements within the documents." This was followed by an itemized list of actions that spelled out in more detail the expectations for each step in the process. This document has been important both for keeping the project on track and for managing expectations, as well as being a reminder of commitments made by various library departments. The project team began by setting out a timeline and identifying milestones. For the first two years, the team met on a monthly basis to report progress, sort out details of work, and discuss technical problems.

The first step in launching the Occom Circle Project relied on the College Archivist's expertise in identifying all of the relevant documents. Carini, assisted by an undergraduate student, identified all of the documents written by Samson Occom in Dartmouth's manuscript holdings and then made a first review to determine other documents in the collection that discussed Occom. Ivy Schweitzer then identified additional materials, including documents by other Native American students of Eleazar Wheelock. Each of the relevant documents was examined and verified to make sure its content was consistent with catalog records. During the 1950s and 1960s, photocopies of documents not owned by Dartmouth had been added to the collection, so potential documents had to be checked to ascertain that they were in fact eighteenth-century manuscripts and not modern copies. A very basic condition check was also conducted at this time. Once the documents were inventoried and verified, they were sent to Preservation Services for assessment and treatment. Treatments included minor repair and stabilization and, occasionally, more extensive treatment. Several documents had pressure tape on them and had to be sent to the Northeast Document Conservation Center in Andover, Massachusetts, to have the tape and residue removed. Once the documents were treated, they went to the library's Digital Production Unit for scanning. The documents were scanned at 600 dpi. The decision was made to scan all of the pages, including blank pages, so that scholars using the digital collection could be sure they were seeing the entire document.

As the documents were scanned, the transcription team began the laborious process of transcribing the contents. This was by far the slowest and most painstaking part of the process. Not only did the transcription involve deciphering eighteenth-century handwriting, it meant puzzling out the hands of multiple writers, each with their own idiosyncrasies. These included an original version of shorthand and a wide variety of abbreviations. The final step in the process was marking up the documents using the standards of the Text Encoding Initiative. Transcribers provided a simplified initial markup at the beginning of the process, but the final markup and the development of TEI headers that in turn facilitated the creation of Encoded Archival Description and MARC records for each document was performed by members of the text encoding team from Cataloging and Metadata Services. The final results are documents for which specific elements have been consistently noted by the team to facilitate searching and to improve access to and comprehension of the documents. For example, TEI allows us to regularize variant spellings in the collection so that if someone searches for *Occom*, he or she will find all the documents where Occom is mentioned, even if the spelling is "Occum." The markup also provides clarification of unique abbreviations or strike-throughs, such as "Chh", that the team determined stood for *church*.

Managing the Occom Circle Project

The grant for the Occom Circle Project provided for a half-time project manager, Hazel-Dawn Dumpert, who was hired from outside the Dartmouth College Library. The ultimate aim of the project manager (PM) should be the establishment of a smooth and steady workflow and the facilitation of an easy interchange of labor between departments and team members. In the case of the Occom Circle Project, which was a ground-up effort, the PM began with the very basic task of meeting individually with each team member to get a feel for his or her duties, goals, and ideas and thus to envision a preliminary network of how each member's distinct tasks fit into the project as a whole.

From there, the PM's next big duty was to assist the project director in hiring student assistants. As anyone who has employed student workers knows, this can be a hit-or-miss endeavor. To help refine the search for reliable assistants, the Occom Circle PM gave promising candidates a short presentation to relate what their duties would entail, encouraging them to give the work serious thought before joining up. The development early on of an easily repeatable training program ensured consistency and a steady learning curve. Likewise, the PM learned to quickly identify, and gently but firmly dismiss, those students whose performance or work habits did not show promise or improvement. While this was not the most enjoyable aspect of the project, it was crucial in terms of minimizing time wasted on training those who were not a good fit.

One of the PM's trickier endeavors was deciding which tasks to delegate, and to whom. While having an overview of a project's processes is not only helpful but necessary, a PM can risk becoming the sole keeper of that overview. For example, a particularly resourceful student worker was promoted from the transcription of letters to the researching of the names, places, and organizations contained in the documents. This student soon became invaluable to both the project and the PM, building a narrative of the players and events involved in the Occom documents. Although other research assistants were also recruited, they did not prove to be as effective, so the PM, satisfied with the work of this particular student, did not assiduously pursue new assistants. Thus, when the student graduated, the PM was left as the only team member with a thorough knowledge of the project overview and, more important, of how this wider perspective affected everything from the proofreading and markup of the documents; to the indexing of people, places, and organizations; to the implementation of website display options and beyond. If, for whatever reason, the PM were suddenly to no longer be involved in the project, the absence would have been difficult for other team members to overcome. In hindsight, it likely would have proved beneficial to the project *and* the PM to be more proactive about delegating some long-term duties to other permanent team members, thereby distributing project information more evenly and increasing the exposure of project documents to those who could help to ensure accuracy and consistency.

Connecting with Department Liaisons

What were the roles of department liaisons in the Occom Circle Project? The library's existing organizational structure assigned one lead contact for digital projects—in the case of the Occom Circle, the College Archivist, who is the subject specialist for college history—to coordinate the project both inside and outside of the library. Laura Braunstein, department liaison to English (one of the appointments of principal investigator Ivy Schweitzer), had heard about the project from library and faculty colleagues and from the PM (Dumpert), and was looking to learn more about the digital humanities—both as a field in general and in terms of learning skills and competencies that she (Braunstein) would need to support faculty, students, and researchers doing new work in this area.

Braunstein approached the PM in the summer of 2013 and asked to contribute in any way useful—not necessarily using her disciplinary expertise as a department liaison, but by learning the project from the ground up. She negotiated with her manager to contribute five hours per week to the project and began with the same training program used for the student assistants. She learned eighteenth-century paleography and transcribed letters, journals, and accounts using the simple markup developed for the project. She worked with student assistants, the PM, and principal investigator Schweitzer to proofread document transcriptions. Later, she learned the Text Encoding Initiative markup language in order to complete the headers and markup for individual documents. This part of the process had heretofore been accomplished solely by the PM and by staff on the text markup team in the library's Cataloging and Metadata Services department. While Braunstein could have asked to join the text markup team, joining the project as if she were a student assistant offered additional opportunities to view the project as a whole from the perspective of the PM. Learning TEI through participating in the Occom Circle Project was a challenging process, but was enormously helpful in demonstrating the sheer scale of work and army of collaborators involved in producing a digital edition of this size. Understanding a project from the inside helps department liaisons advise other faculty and researchers who are interested in initiating new digital projects and provides valuable experience for librarians working within their libraries' existing cultures to build digital humanities programs.

Lessons Learned

The Dartmouth College Library has a long history of involvement in producing digital editions,[‡] but none have approached the scale of the Occom Circle Project. The road has not always been smooth, but we are lucky to have been able to draw upon the expertise and experience of our staff, who met technical and organizational challenges as they arose. When producing a large digital edition, defining the scope of the project and having a detailed understanding of the actions and expected outcomes are extremely important. Having the success statement as a reference point and guide kept the project on track as individual documents moved through the process. Having a set of milestones and a carefully thought-through workflow helped assure that the "large number of people" involved knew where their tasks fit into the whole.

Even with these planning and reference tools in place, the project—like most endeavors of its kind—ran into several technical problems. Some of these problems were minor, while others had a significant impact on the project. An example of a relatively minor problem was the discovery that several separate letters were often written on a single document. Special Collections had cataloged each letter at the item level without regard to whether it was originally written on a separate piece of paper. Since the eighteenth-century authors did not give any thought to future digital projects when they were writing—and paper was expensive!—these letters often ended or began on the same page as an earlier letter by another author. This situation complicated the process of relating individual transcriptions to specific images within the database.

A similar issue that had a much larger impact on the project was also related to scanning. When the collection was originally scanned, some

---

‡   The search interface for the Dartmouth Dante Project was co-designed in the early 1980s by the library's Digital Library Technologies Group. See Robert Hollander, Steven Campbell, and Simone Marchesi, eds., Dartmouth Dante Project website, Dartmouth College, accessed August 1, 2014, http://dante.dartmouth.edu, and the Dante Project's successor, Dante Lab, accessed <date of access>, http://dantelab.dartmouth.edu. For more recent examples, see the Dartmouth Digital Library Program, accessed <date of access>, www.dartmouth.edu/~library/digital.

larger documents—generally folio sheets—were scanned a single page at a time, while smaller documents—such as multi-page quarto-sized journals—were scanned open so that two pages appeared in one image. This presented some problems in making a one-to-one match between page images and transcriptions, with the end result that several large sets of double images had to be split apart digitally.

From the project management perspective, digital projects such as the Occom Circle Project can often be an education in lessons learned the hard way. Scrupulous record-keeping can help minimize back-to-the-drawing-board delays. Indeed, if we were to offer only one piece of advice to a project manager, it would be to keep track of everything. Information is easier to let go of than to gather together, and the Occom Circle PM soon learned that something that appeared to be inconsequential at the beginning of the project—for instance, building a list of each and every manuscript number related to each individual mentioned in the documents—would be of great importance further down the road. A detailed daily work journal, as well as a spreadsheet to keep track of all of the project's various lists, proved to be of enormous benefit in corralling all the various aspects of the project.

Another aspect of the project that came to light only after a great deal of time had passed was the fact that the markup of certain documents would differ significantly from others. Although the transcription of letters—which comprised the majority of the project documents, and so were tackled first—was often difficult in terms of deciphering handwriting, their TEI encoding was a fairly straightforward and even pleasant task. When it came time for journals and accounts, however, team members were somewhat dismayed to find themselves faced with a whole new set of unforeseen problems, including but not limited to the difficulties of transcribing ledgers in ways that would ultimately display correctly on the published site and the sheer volume of person and place names contained in the journals (some of which ran longer than forty pages, contained nearly one hundred names, and entailed exacting specifications in their TEI markup). Only in hindsight did the PM realize that a healthy sampling of each type of document at the outset would have helped to sketch out timelines and prevent "coding fatigue" later in the project.

Our advice for department liaisons who want to support and foster new digital humanities projects at their libraries would be to pay close attention to what processes the organization already has in place for initiating, organizing, and operating existing projects, from the smallest to the largest. It would be unnecessarily complex, not to mention nearly impossible, to include every relevant library staff member on every project, and doing so should certainly not be a goal for even the most ambitious team. Yet given that much of department liaison work is outreach to and information sharing with faculty, students, and community members, there is always room to improve project communication. This can be an avenue for the departmental liaison to take positive action. Ask questions of anyone who will answer; spend time "informational interviewing" colleagues; don't assume that digital humanities projects will function in the same way as other cross-departmental initiatives; and get comfortable with the possibility that channels of communication may occasionally have some static. If the project does not appear to have a place for the traditional contributions of a department liaison, consider it an opportunity to learn something new. Is there a process to which you can contribute? Is there a technical skill that you can learn? At the very least, commit to understanding what it would take for the library to support and foster new projects that your faculty might want to propose. Faculty members, students, and other scholars often hear about opportunities for collaboration from their colleagues; they might not comprehend the scale, technical resources, and staff time involved in producing many digital humanities projects.

Samson Occom worked tirelessly until his death to speak to and for his people. His journal entries over many years describe his itinerant preaching to Native and white communities throughout the northeast. A detail that he noted at nearly every stop on his travels was that "a large Number of People" had gathered to listen to him. A large number of people at Dartmouth College have worked to produce a scholarly digital edition of Occom's writings to bring his voice to new readers and to honor Native American intellectual traditions. Part of the project's funding from comes the National Endowment for the Humanities' We the People initiative, which specifically supports public humanities scholarship to enhance civic life.[7]

Through our edition of his works, Occom speaks to an even larger number of people in audiences he could have never anticipated. The Occom Circle Project testifies to the transformative potential of the digital humanities as a field of community-based knowledge and scholarship.

Notes

1. Ivy Schweitzer, ed., The Occom Circle Project website, Dartmouth College Library, accessed August 1, 2014, https://www.dartmouth.edu/~occom/.
2. Samson Occom, "Autobiographical Narrative, Second Draft (September 17, 1768)," in *The Collected Writings of Samson Occom, Mohegan: Leadership and Literature in Eighteenth-Century Native America*, ed. Joanna Brooks (Oxford: Oxford University Press, 2006), 52.
3. Samson Occom, *A Sermon, Preached at the Execution of Moses Paul, an Indian* (New London, CT: T. Green, 1772).
4. See Dartmouth Native American Program, "History of the Dartmouth Pow-Wow," Dartmouth College, accessed August 1, 2014, www.dartmouth.edu/~nap/powwow/history.html.
5. Samson Occom, *The Collected Writings of Samson Occom, Mohegan: Leadership and Literature in Eighteenth-Century Native America*, ed. Joanna Brooks (New York: Oxford University Press, 2006.
6. Bonnie Barber, "Schweitzer Awarded National Endowment for the Humanities Grant to Digitize Occom Papers." *Dartmouth Now* (blog), Dartmouth College, July 24, 2010, http://now.dartmouth.edu/2010/07/schweitzer-awarded-national-endowment-for-the-humanities-grant-to-digitize-occom-papers.
7. See NEH, We the People website, accessed August 1, 2014, http://wethepeople.gov/index.html.

Bibliography

Barber, Bonnie. "Schweitzer Awarded National Endowment for the Humanities Grant to Digitize Occom Papers." *Dartmouth Now* (blog), Dartmouth College, July 24, 2010. http://now.dartmouth.edu/2010/07/schweitzer-awarded-national-endowment-for-the-humanities-grant-to-digitize-occom-papers.

Dartmouth College. Dante Lab website. Accessed August 1, 2014. http://dantelab.dartmouth.edu.

———. Dartmouth Digital Library Program website. Accessed August 1, 2014. www.dartmouth.edu/~library/digital.

Dartmouth Native American Program "History of the Dartmouth Pow-Wow." Dartmouth College. Accessed August 1, 2014. www.dartmouth.edu/~nap/powwow/history.html.

Hollander, Robert, Steven Campbell, and Simone Marchesi, eds. Dartmouth Dante Project website. Dartmouth College. Accessed August 1, 2014, http://dante.dartmouth.edu

NEH (National Endowment for the Humanities). We the People website. Accessed
    September 23, 2014. http://wethepeople.gov/index.html.
Oberg, Michael. *Uncas: First of the Mohicans* (Ithaca: Cornell University Press, 2003).
Occom, Samson. "Autobiographical Narrative, Second Draft (September 17, 1768)." In
    *The Collected Writings of Samson Occom, Mohegan: Leadership and Literature in
    Eighteenth-Century Native America*, ed. Joanna Brooks, 52–59. Oxford: Oxford
    University Press, 2006.
———. *The Collected Writings of Samson Occom, Mohegan: Leadership and Literature in
    Eighteenth-Century Native America*, edited by Joanna Brooks. New York: Oxford
    University Press, 2006.
———. *A Sermon, Preached at the Execution of Moses Paul, an Indian*. New London, CT:
    T. Green, 1772.
Schweitzer, Ivy, ed. The Occom Circle Project website. Dartmouth College Library.
    Accessed August 1, 2014. https://www.dartmouth.edu/~occom/.

CHAPTER THIRTEEN

Dipping a Toe into the DH Waters
A Librarian's Experience

Liorah Golomb

DESPITE HAVING attended numerous events and workshops on the topic of digital humanities (DH), my grasp of the practice remained tenuous. Theory and quick workshops could take me only so far; in order to improve my knowledge of the digital humanities (and thus my skills as a subject librarian), I felt I needed to engage in an actual project. By doing so I hoped to be better prepared to work with faculty in liaison departments in their DH ventures.

In my work as Humanities Librarian at the University of Oklahoma, I have not yet been asked to participate in a digital humanities project. We are a large Tier 1 institution, but the library has only recently emphasized digital resources and services. A digital scholarship lab now resides in the library but at the time of this writing had not yet been established or staffed; therefore, no special equipment or expertise was available to me for DH scholarship. Of necessity, any DH experimentation I wished to conduct would have to be of the sort that does not require storage of large datasets, digitization of materials, or an online exhibit space.

Most DH projects discussed in this book concern digitizing primary source materials such as rare books, manuscripts, letters, diaries, photographs, and three-dimensional objects. The creators then add useful metadata and scholarly context, and often their institutions make the material available at no cost to the public over the Internet. But there is another aspect of DH in which computing tools are used to analyze or compare texts. Computers have been used to create concordances and assist in analysis of literary texts since the late 1950s.[1] In 1965, *The Shakespeare Newsletter* published a special issue on computer studies, including an extensive list of projects scholars might wish to take on, ranging from metrical analysis and orthographic standardization to "Ferreting out, where and if possible, trends of Shakespeare's thought, how his mind worked, etc."[2]

In contrast to language-saturated gold mines like Shakespeare's plays, writing done for the camera relies heavily on nonverbal cues to tell a story, even more so than contemporary work written for the stage. The stage is limited in how effectively it can direct a viewer's gaze, how quickly it can move between one set and another, and how much an actor can convey with small gestures. Methods of transcribing visual elements into a form that can be analyzed by machine have been developed by linguists;[3] I, however, am not a linguist, and applying multimodal transcription to a visual medium is far, far beyond my capabilities.

Lengthy fight scenes, solitary drinking, changes in location, character entrances and exits, the absence of conversation—these examples of nonverbal elements of a film or television script convey crucial information to the viewer. Clearly, an analysis of just the dialogue of a television program would give a very incomplete picture, yet I set about to do just that. This chapter documents my attempts to mine the dialogue from the American television show *Supernatural* (2005–present) with the goal of acquiring the skills necessary to analyze results in a meaningful way. Patterns and frequencies of word usage might be used to identify key themes of the show, as well as plot and character arc shifts over the course of the show's nine (and counting) year run. I describe my process, including finding (and in two cases, creating) episode transcripts and making them usable for text mining; locating, testing, and selecting tools; the challenges of examining text in a medium that also relies on visual information; what was learned from the experience; and what might be done with the information garnered.

This is an account of an experiment filled with missteps and mistakes arising from the limitations of my prior knowledge of text mining. Nonetheless, I consider it a success because I did learn quite a lot about computer-assisted textual analysis, and I now have a much better idea of how to go about doing the project I have in mind. It is my hope that this experiment will encourage subject librarians who are unsure of their practical abilities vis-à-vis digital humanities to learn from my mistakes, make some of their own, and test the waters themselves. Once we feel comfortable with at least some aspects of digital humanities research, we will be better equipped to help the researchers we serve.

Background

The germ of my idea to text-mine the dialogue of the series *Supernatural* began to sprout around the summer of 2012. Very little about *Supernatural* resembles other television shows, and I suspected that it could be demonstrated that the show's dialogue is as unconventional as its other components: more original, less dependent on catchphrases, and better at using language to differentiate characters than other shows.

By way of background, *Supernatural* is a weekly, hour-long horror genre program produced by the CW Network. Created by Eric Kripke, it follows the story of Sam and Dean Winchester (played by Jared Padalecki and Jensen Ackles, respectively), two brothers raised as hunters of ghosts, demons, werewolves, forgotten gods, and numerous other creatures believed by most of us to be urban legends or mythological. It has received attention from the media and scholars of both the show and, because of its loyal, vocal, and creative viewership, fandom studies. Academic work includes studies of *Supernatural*'s fans and fan-created work,[4] analytical examinations of the show in relation to religion and philosophy[5] and to sexuality and gender representation,[6] and topics as diverse as the show's use of time and its attitude towards marijuana use.[7] A huge bibliography could be created citing media recognition of *Supernatural*, particularly by entertainment sites, but two of the recent mainstream sources to notice the show are the *New York Times* and National Public Radio's *All Things Considered*.[8]

Supernatural focuses as much on the relationship between the brothers as it does on monster hunting. In general, older brother Dean is characterized as being a good soldier, overly protective of his brother, and dedicated to the "family business" of "saving people, hunting things."[9] Younger brother Sam, on full scholarship at Stanford in the series's pilot, tries and fails to escape the hunting life and is seen as being selfish and disobedient. These roles are fluid; what remains constant is the brothers' codependence, which drives much of the action. As Kripke noted in the commentary to a fifth-season episode, "the boys are… kind of chained together and one moves ahead and drags the other one with him and then they reverse and… it's the epic love story of Sam and Dean."[10]

Among the ways in which *Supernatural* diverges from most shows on television are its lack of fixed sets, the small size of its regular cast, and the absence of romantic entanglements. Until the eighth season, Sam and Dean had no fixed address, travelling instead from hunt to hunt in a 1967 Chevy Impala and paying for motel rooms with fake credit cards and pool-hustled cash. The regular cast consisted of only Padalecki and Ackles for five of the series's ten produced or in-production seasons; a third actor, Misha Collins (Castiel), is credited as a series regular for four nonconsecutive seasons, and a fourth, Mark Sheppard (Crowley), joined the regular cast for season 10. Few women have appeared in more than one episode, and love scenes are typically of the one-night-stand variety.

The plot of *Supernatural* rarely takes a conventional route, either. The good guys don't always win; for that matter, there is a lot of gray area between "good" and "evil." While there is as much blood and gore as network television lets the show get away with, and a particular ominous look that *Supernatural* generally sports, several episodes have broken the pattern, including one in which the Winchester brothers find themselves in an alternate universe, on the set of a television show called *Supernatural*, where they are mistaken for the actors Jared Padalecki and Jensen Ackles. Subject matter as grand as destiny and apocalypse have been explored, along with themes as commonplace as addiction, betrayal, loss, lack of self-worth, and failure. Sam and Dean have shared fried pickles with Death himself.

The original question I posed to myself was whether I could prove *Supernatural*'s exceptionalism objectively by comparing its dialogue to that of other contemporary genre shows, for example *Teen Wolf* (MTV, 2011–present) or *The Vampire Diaries* (the CW Network, 2009–present). Interesting as that idea may be, I quickly discarded it as requiring considerably more time than I can invest. My next idea was to mine all of the dialogue from all nine aired seasons of *Supernatural* and look for changes in language that might inform the shifts in tone, emphasis, and relationships over the course of the series. For example, if I searched for frequency of the word *family*, would I find it more heavily used in the earlier seasons, before the show took some very dark turns? What conclusions might I draw if I found that Dean used the word *brother* significantly more often than Sam did?

Preparing the Data

The first step in doing any mining of *Supernatural* scripts was to make them ready to be organized into corpora. One reason why I felt that this project was feasible was because the transcripts of every aired episode are available on the Supernatural Wiki, a fan-created and -maintained site.[11] Also known as the Super-wiki, the site has been in existence since 2006, contains over 2,700 pages, has more than 33,500 users, and boasts over 300,000 hits worldwide per month.[12]

Super-wiki administrator Jules Wilkinson informed me by e-mail on December 25, 2013, that Warner Brothers, the copyright holder of *Supernatural* scripts, does not provide them to the Super-wiki. Fans produce transcripts in one of two ways: by transcribing straight from a recording of an episode or by using subtitle files as a starting point. Subtitle files are available on the Internet; the one Wilkinson mentioned is TVsubtitles.net (www.tvsubtitles.net). Wilkinson described the process from there:

> Once the subtitle file is downloaded it can be saved as a text file. It includes timestamps and each line of dialogue—although not who is saying what. The fan transcribing needs to remove the time-

stamps, put in who says what and add act/scene breaks and stage directions. At a minimum I ask fans transcribing to add act breaks, and enough stage directions to give context…. Of course then the transcript needs to be posted on and formatted for the Wiki. It probably takes around 3 hours minimum to do a transcript.

I can attest to the time it takes to produce a transcript. Two episodes in season 9 had not been transcribed, so I took on the task myself, using the subtitle files as a base. One of the episodes I transcribed, 9.20, "Bloodlines," had an unusual amount of cross-cutting. In addition, the episode was serving a dual purpose as a pilot for a *Supernatural* spin-off (ultimately unsuccessful) and was populated almost entirely with new characters, some of whom were difficult to distinguish from one another. A particular portion of the episode that took up no more than five minutes of screen time took upwards of an hour to transcribe.

Laura Quilter, another fan who has done some *Supernatural* episode transcribing, begins with the subtitle files, but does not rely upon them. She described her process:

I watch the show, and pause & replay to clear up inaudible dialog, or to add things in that were missed, or to make corrections. I add in visual cues that I think help the reader to make sense. My goal is to capture the viewer's experience as they watch the show—not to capture the script, but to capture the transcript—the script as acted / produced / edited. (e-mail, December 21, 2013)

Had I known at the outset that subtitle files were available, I might have used them as my raw data. However, since I did not know, I used a different method to get the transcripts into a plain-text format that could be processed by machine. (There are analysis tools able to process HTML; however, since I wanted to remove the fan-contributed embellishments, plain text seemed like a better option.) Using the transcripts on the Super-wiki, I selected the Printable Version option available on each transcript's page, copied and pasted everything into a text editor, and saved each transcript in an individual file in UTF-8 format. Then I stripped out everything except the dialogue and the speakers. And here arose my first hurdle. Very little about the Super-wiki transcript pages is standardized. A description of the anatomy of a typical *Supernatural* episode will help explain how that lack of standardization affected my work:

1. The episode begins with a recap, usually scenes culled from several different episodes, captioned either "THEN" or, after a hiatus, "THE ROAD SO FAR."

2. This is followed by a "NOW" caption, and the episode proper begins. This segment is known as the "teaser."

3. The "SUPERNATURAL" title card flashes.

4. Act 1 begins. The opening credits appear over the action during this segment. It takes several minutes for all the credits to be shown.

5. The first commercial break comes about fifteen or twenty minutes into the episode and divides Acts 1 and 2. The next commercial break comes between Acts 2 and 3, and so on, for five acts.

6. The episode ends and is followed by rolling end credits and the various logos of the production and distributor entities.

The only information requested on the template for creating a new transcript page for the Super-wiki is the episode number and title, the writer(s), the director, and the original air date. Beyond that, transcribers differ greatly in how much information they include and how they format it. While some begin with a table of contents linking to the various parts of the broadcast, others do not. With regard to the first item, some fans transcribe the recap with references to the episodes from which the recap scenes were taken, meticulously credited and hyperlinked. See figure 13.1.

THEN [edit]

From 5.01 Sympathy for the Devil, DEAN talks to SAM.

DEAN
You chose a demon over your own brother, and look what happened.

From 4.22 Lucifer Rising, DEAN and SAM watch light burst out of the sigil drawn by LILITH's blood.

SAM (voiceover from 5.01 Sympathy for the Devil)
I did it. I started the apocalypse, and I set Lucifer free.

From 5.01 Sympathy for the Devil, SAM covers his ears against LUCIFER's voice.

From 5.03 Free to Be You and Me, LUCIFER as JESSICA becomes LUCIFER as NICK.

From 5.01 Sympathy for the Devil, SAM talks to DEAN.

SAM
I'm sorry. I would give anything—

From 4.21 When the Levee Breaks, SAM throws DEAN into a mirror.

SAM (voiceover from 5.01 Sympathy for the Devil)
Anything—to take it all back.

From 5.01 Sympathy for the Devil, DEAN talks to SAM.

DEAN
I know you would.

From 3.05 Bedtime Stories, SAM fires the Colt, killing the CROSSROADS DEMON.

Figure 13.1

Approximately half of transcribed "THEN" (recap) segment from *Supernatural* episode 5.06, "I Believe the Children Are Our Future." Source: Supernatural Wiki, "5.06 I Believe the Children Are Our Future (Transcript)," Then section, accessed August 5, 2014. www. supernaturalwiki.com/index.php?title=5.06_I_Believe_the_Children_Are_Our_Future_ (transcript).

Likewise, I encountered some transcripts that interspersed the credits with the dialogue in Act 1. See figure 13.2.

ACT ONE [edit]

INT. WAREHOUSE – NIGHT

THE SONG REMAINS THE SAME

ANNA
I'm sorry but we have no choice. He's Lucifer's vessel.

Starring
JARED PADALECKI

CASTIEL
He's not the only one.

ANNA
What, that guy Nick?

JENSEN ACKLES

ANNA
He's burning away as we speak. No.

MISHA COLLINS

ANNA
Sam is the only vessel that matters. You know what that means? If Lu

Guest Starring
JULIE McNIVEN

ANNA
The Horsemen go back to their day jobs.

CASTIEL
Even if you could...kill Sam, Satan would just bring him back to life.

AMY GUMENICK

ANNA
Not after I scatter his cells across the universe.

Figure 13.2

Partial view of transcript of *Supernatural* episode 5.13, "The Song Remains the Same," with credits highlighted. Source: Supernatural Wiki, "5.13 The Song Remains the Same (Transcript)" Act One section, accessed August 5, 2014, www.supernaturalwiki.com/index.php?title=5.13_The_Song_Remains_the_Same_(transcript).

In the first instance, once I decided that I did not want to include any tables of contents or recaps in my mineable file, it was simple enough to select a block of text and delete it. In the case where screen credits were placed within the dialogue and action of the episode, I needed to pay more attention in order to remove that information. Transcribers also varied in the manner in which they formatted stage directions, voice-overs, gestures, and so on. Even though this was all information that I was removing, the differences in transcribing styles meant that I had to mind what I was doing to avoid accidentally removing dialogue or speakers. Figures 13.3, 13.4, and 13.5 show three different styles used by transcribers.

DEAN
'Night, Sam.

MARY leans over SAM as well.

MARY
Good night, love.

MARY brushes SAM's hair back and kisses his forehead.

MAN
Hey, Dean.

Figure 13.3

Portion of transcription of *Supernatural* episode 1.01, "Pilot." Source: Supernatural Wiki, "1.01 Pilot (Transcript)," Prologue section, accessed August 6, 2014, www. supernaturalwiki.com/index.php?title=1.01_Pilot_(transcript).

Further down the corridor DEAN sniggers.

SAM
(Throwing DEAN a dirty look) Yeah of course.

SAM
(Quickly flashing the ID, holding his thumb over part of it) Now could you direct me to the pediatrics ward please?

RECEPTIONIST
Okay well, just go down that hall, turn left and up the stairs.

Sam approaches a grinning DEAN, giving major bitchface.

Figure 13.4

Portion of transcription of *Supernatural* episode 1.18, "Something Wicked." Source: Supernatural Wiki, "1.18 Something Wicked (Transcript)," Act One section, accessed August 6, 2014, www.supernaturalwiki.com/index.php?title=1.18_Something_Wicked_ (transcript).

SAM Jody!

JODY Sam?

SAM Dean! We're here! We're gonna get you out!

Jody, I found it!

DEAN [hears SAM's voice and climbs the ladder to the trap door. He bangs in the door.] Sammy? Sammy! Sammy!

Figure 13.5

Portion of transcription of *Supernatural* episode 9.08, "Rock and a Hard Place." Source: Supernatural Wiki, "9.08 Rock and a Hard Place (Transcript)," Act Three section, accessed August 6, 2014, www.supernaturalwiki.com/index.php?title=9.08_Rock_and_a_Hard_ Place_(transcript).

In figure 13.3, the action is set off only with white space. In figure 13.4, action is set off by white space or with parentheses, depending upon whether it happens more or less simultaneously with the speaker's words. In figure 13.5, a character's name immediately precedes his speech, with no punctuation or line break to separate the speaker from the speech, and action is enclosed in square brackets.

Supernatural has an international viewership, and variant spellings were used by the transcribing fans. I noticed British spellings (*colour, realise*), and the way relaxed pronunciation was recorded varied as well. One person's "gonna" and "woulda" was another's "gunna" and "wudda." I briefly considered standardizing the spelling, but quickly discarded that idea. I decided that these variations were probably too minor to make a significant difference in the results, and that I could always go back and standardize spelling if it seemed necessary. I also did not spell-check the transcripts, even though I noticed the occasional typo. When I transcribed two episodes using subtitle files, I discovered only one error, so I concluded that most typos were likely in the fan-added description that I was removing.

I might have been able to create macros or use a search function in producing my raw data, (i.e., stripped-down transcripts), if formatting and content among episode transcripts were consistent. That was not the case, however, and I found no way to automate the process. Ultimately, it took me about twenty minutes to produce each file for mining. There are 195 episodes in the nine aired seasons, and it would have taken me approximately sixty-five hours to prepare them. Therefore, I modified my original intention to mine all of the series's episodes and selected three seasons instead, a total of sixty-seven episodes. The seasons I chose were the first, the ninth (the most recent complete season), and the fifth. This was not an entirely arbitrary decision. Though he continues in the role of executive consultant, Eric Kripke, *Supernatural*'s creator, stepped down as show runner after the fifth season. The main story arc begun in the pilot episode ended with the season 5 finale, which made for a natural dividing point.

To have the option of sorting by name to compare the speech patterns and habits of one character to another, I kept the speakers' names with the dialogue. An hour or so of experimentation would have determined whether it was easier to start with the subtitle files and add the speakers or to take the fan transcriptions and delete everything except the speakers and speeches. The lesson here is to get some basic information before delving in to a project; if you are gathering data, find out how it was created.

The Right Tool for the Job

The first question I had to answer in selecting potential tools for the task at hand was: What *is* the task at hand? What would I like to accomplish? Browsing a number of tools helped me to understand the various options for analyzing texts, as well as the range of skill required to use them. Given my absence of computational linguistic analysis knowledge, I decided on what seemed to be modest objectives. I wanted to

- be able to see a list of words in my *Supernatural* transcript files

- sort them by frequency

- find keywords and phrases in context

- search for words adjacent to or near other words

Every *Supernatural* fan knows, for example, that Dean overuses the word *awesome*, that Sam is fond of saying "get this," and that it is always significant when Dean calls his brother "Sammy." I wanted to be able to quantify and contextualize this verbal information.

There are a great many text-analysis tools to be found from a simple Google search, but I started with two gateways I had learned about in various DH workshops: Digital Research Tools, or DiRT (formerly Bamboo DiRT) and Text Analysis Portal for Research, or TAPoR.[13] DiRT organizes digital research tools by category and allows for limiting by platform, cost, and other factors. In addition to categories like data collection and image editing, some of the categorized tasks include authoring interactive works, brainstorming, mapping, and staying current, so the site has usefulness beyond digital humanities projects. TAPoR's organization is less hierarchal than DiRT's and more dependent upon tagging. A View Tools By section is a mix of function (e.g., visualization, programming language, statistical) and qualifiers (e.g., new, popular, reviewed). TAPoR can also be searched.

In addition to needing a tool that was easy to use, I also needed one that was free, worked with UTF-8 (.txt) formatted files, and was either Web-based or able to run on Mac OS 10.6. In DiRT, the category that best described what I needed was Analyze Text. After applying my limiters, I had fourteen tools that run on the Macintosh platform and twenty-eight Web-based tools from which to choose. On TAPoR's site, I searched "concording mac" ("concording" being one of the tool types listed) and "concording web based" and turned up fifteen and twenty-four tools, respectively.

The steepness of the learning curve I was facing in undertaking this project began to sink in while I was reading the descriptions of the tools I'd found through DiRT and TAPoR. For example, "Juxta [www.juxtasoft-ware.org] is an open-source cross-platform desktop tool for comparing and collating multiple witnesses to a single textual work."[14] *Witness*, as I learned, has a very specific meaning in textual analysis and did not apply to my project. "MorphAdorner [http://morphadorner.northwestern.edu] is a Java command-line program which acts as a pipeline manager for processes performing morphological adornment of words in a text."[15] This description scared me off on multiple counts: it seems to require some knowledge of Java, and what is "morphological adornment"? Other tools' descriptions were less mysterious to me, but I could see that the tools were not useful for what I was hoping to accomplish.

In addition to acting as a portal, TAPoR hosts its own Web-based suites of tools for use with XML, HTML, and plain text. TAPoR Text Analysis offers simple tools that would accomplish my objectives, but individually:[16] the List Words tool displays word frequency, the Concordance tool allows for searching a word or phrase and seeing the keywords in context, and the Collocates tool shows words in relation to one another. There was one big drawback for my project, however; with the exception of the Comparator tool, which allows for two texts to be compared, I could load only one file at a time.

Ultimately I selected a downloadable program called AntConc, whose description on DiRT was promisingly simple: "AntConc is free concordance software."[17] AntConc's website offers a number of different download options covering many versions of the Macintosh, Windows, and Linux operating systems. It also points to a series of eleven video tutorials made by the developer, Laurence Anthony, covering everything from downloading the software to using all of its tools.[18] Online help and a written manual are also available. After watching a few of the videos, I decided that AntConc would suit my needs, and I downloaded the latest version for my operating system.

Despite the guidance available to AntConc's users, it is assumed—wrongly, in my case—that the user has some basic knowledge of computational linguistics. Some terminology was unfamiliar to me, beginning with *corpus file*. The corpus file is the set of data being examined; each one of my modified transcripts is a corpus file, and taken together, they constitute the corpora. Because I saved each episode separately, I have the option of comparing them in different ways, for example, one season to another, by season premieres and finales, by screenwriter, and so on. *Lemma* was another stumper; it means the dictionary form of a word, for example, *eat*, not *ate* or *eating*. There were some terms and functions that, after a little investigation, I determined I probably do not need to know at this point. These include *regex* (short for regular expression) and *N-gram*, among others.

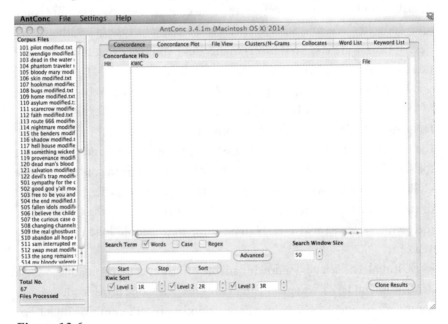

Figure 13.6

AntConc 3.4.1m screen, with corpora added.

Figure 13.6 shows the AntConc screen, populated with the text files of *Supernatural* transcripts that I had prepared. Inserting the files was a simple matter of using the File pull-down menu and then selecting the folder into which I'd placed all of my files. There is also the option to select and open individual files. One drawback of AntConc is that it is not possible to save work in progress once the program is closed, though it is possible to save results to a text file. This means that every time the program is opened, the corpus files need to be reloaded. Fortunately, this is a very fast process.

The Concordance tool is the default, but starting with Word List will generate a list of every word in the corpora, sortable in a number of ways, the default being frequency. Sorting alphabetically, I could easily see that *gunna* appeared twenty-seven times while *gonna* appeared 693 times. Further, clicking on *gunna* switched me to the Concordance tool, where I could see the word in context and which files it appeared in. In this case, *gunna* was used in five transcripts, so if I decide to standardize the spelling of relaxed pronunciation I can easily do so by going into those files and performing a search-and-replace. Or I can use a wildcard; "g?nna" will show both *gunna* and *gonna* in context. The asterisk can be used to stand for characters at the end of a word, so "chick*" showed results for *chick*, *chicks*, *chicken*, and *chickens*. Several other wildcards are available and can be found under the Settings > Global Settings pull-down menu.

Phrase searching is also possible in AntConc. A string of words is assumed to be a phrase. Boolean Or searches can be done using the advanced search and entering terms in a list. Figure 13.7 shows a search for all words in which *kill* is the root or all words in which *gank* (a slang synonym for *kill* used on *Supernatural*) is the root.

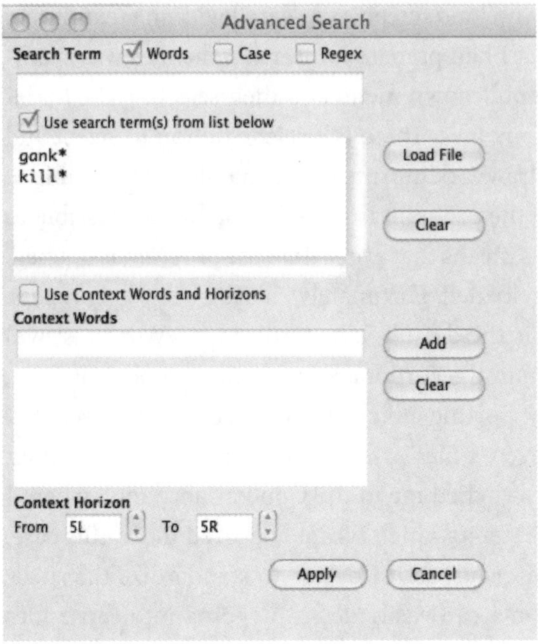

Figure 13.7
AntConc advanced search screen with terms listed to perform a Boolean Or search.

It was not too difficult for me to figure out how to create a stop list of words to exclude. The option to do so can be found in the preferences for the Word List tool. The same window lets the user specify words to include. There is a text file of English stop words on the AntConc site that can be used.

The option to recognize case allowed me to find, for example, every instance where Dean begins a sentence with the word *Sam* because transcribers uniformly used the convention of writing a speaker's name in all capital letters. Thus, by typing "DEAN Sam" in the basic search box in the Concordance tool and checking the Case option, I can see how many times Dean begins a sentence with his brother's name (sixty-two times in the first season alone, and in twenty of the twenty-two episodes). In the Concordance tool advanced search, I can set parameters to see how often the phrase *my brother* or *little brother* appear within six words to the right of the word *DEAN* by using the Context Horizon feature (see figure 13.7).

I had some display and stalling issues with AntConc 3.4.1m that were frustrating, but the biggest problem was that, after running a search in the Concordance tool, only some of the keywords in context were hot-linked. That meant that even though I could see the words to the right and left of my term, I couldn't click on it to see the file view. I reported the issues to Laurence Anthony, the developer, by e-mail. He responded quickly to tell me that the problems sound like ones that occur with a Mac operating system upgrade (version 10.9), but I have not done that upgrade. He is looking into the problems further and, in the meantime, pointed me to an earlier version of the software I could use.

Although I have by no means mastered AntConc, I was able to accomplish some simple tasks, including generating a word frequency list, creating a stop list, seeing a word or phrase used in context, and finding the AntConc equivalents of some Boolean functions. The thing I would most like to learn more about is using lemmas with the program.

There are some well-established resources that I did not test, but which I could see would be worth looking into, most notably, TextGrid Virtual Resource Environment for the Humanities.[19] TextGrid offers not only tools, but also storage of data and projects. It requires registration and verification that the user has scholarly credentials.

Learn from My Mistakes

For those considering taking on a digital humanities experiment such as mine, here are some tips:

- Define your goals. If you are unsure of your goals, examine different tools to see which tasks can be performed given your time and knowledge constraints.

- Understand the basics of working with your data, or partner with someone who does. Does your text need to be converted to a different format in order to be processed? Will preliminary steps such as applying tags or coding improve your results?

- Determine how to gather your data. It is possible that your raw data already exists, possibly in more than one format.

- Failure is an option. The path to success is seldom straight.

Next Steps and Conclusion

For the purposes of this chapter, the point of my *Supernatural* text-mining project was to experience the process. I expected to flounder, and I did. Having taken on this project alone with no computational analysis skills, I made many mistakes in the preparation of my data. I did not, for example, do any tagging or coding of my text files using XML or another markup language. Doing so would allow me to distinguish, among other things, when a name is identifying a speaker, or when someone is being addressed or referred to. But my goal was to learn, and I did learn quite a bit about preparing and using textual data.

I intend to follow up this experiment with a meaningful examination of *Supernatural* dialogue, which I hope will add to the scholarly discourse about the show. To that end, I have outlined my next steps. Clearly, my original plans were overly ambitious for one person to take on, so I will seek out one or two research partners who are both fans of *Supernatural* and familiar with computer-assisted textual analysis. The necessity for a research partner with computational analysis skills is obvious; the requirement that he or she be a fan of the show will assure that I am working with someone who understands and can help me refine my project. There are several methods by which I can solicit help, including posting to various e-mail lists aimed at librarians, DH practitioners, and aca-fans (academics who identify as fans), and by placing a request on the "Reference Desk" of Fanhackers, the blog of the Organization for Transformative Works.[20] OTW is a nonprofit organization that, among other things, hosts fanworks and publishes *Transformative Works and Cultures*, an open-access peer-reviewed journal. If it is feasible, I would like to analyze every episode in the first nine seasons; since I do not have a budget for the project, I might call upon my network of fellow fans to perform tasks such as marking up text. The *Supernatural* fandom is notoriously responsive to requests for help; to give just one example, on June 12, 2014, the Supernatural Wiki administrators began a fundraising campaign to pay for a new server. They reached their target in less than twelve hours, and by the end of the campaign on July 17, 2014, they had raised 194 percent of their goal.[21]

As to improving my knowledge of the digital humanities in order to be able to assist others, I feel I have accomplished that. There is value is finding out that something is more involved than it would initially appear. I am now equipped to point interested users to a set of tools for concordance building, to alert them to problems I experienced, and to give a sense of what to expect.

In my capacity as a fan, if this chapter has made anyone curious enough about *Supernatural* to watch the program, then, as we say in the fandom, my work here is done.

Notes

1. Ephim G. Fogel, "Electronic Computers and Elizabethan Texts," *Studies in Bibliography* 15 (1962): 15–31.
2. Louis Marder, "A Guide to 50 Computer Projects in Shakespeare," *Shakespeare Newsletter* 15, no. 85 (1965): 53.
3. Paul J. Thibault, "The Multimodal Transcription of a Television Advertisement: Theory and Practice," in *Multimodality and Multimediality in the Distance Learning Age: Papers in English Linguistics*, ed. Anthony P. Baldry, 311–83 (Campobasso, Italy: Palladino, 2000); Giuseppe Balirano, "De-Stereotyping Otherness: A Multimodal Script Analysis of Semiotically Expressed Humour," *Linguistic Insights: Studies in Language and Communication* 54 (2007): 487–505.
4. See, e.g., Catherine Tosenberger, "Love! Valor! 'Supernatural'!" *Transformative Works and Cultures* 4 (2010), doi:10.3983/twc.2010.0212"; Lynn S. Zubernis and Katherine Larsen, *Fandom at the Crossroads: Celebration, Shame and Fan/Producer Relationships* (Newcastle upon Tyne, UK: Cambridge Scholars Publishing, 2012); Katherine Larsen and Lynn S. Zubernis, *Fangasm: Supernatural Fangirls* (Iowa City: University of Iowa Press, 2013); Lynn S. Zubernis and Katherine Larsen, eds., *Supernatural,* Fan Phenomena Series (Bristol, UK: Intellect Books, 2014).
5. See, e.g., Erika Engstrom and Joseph M. Valenzano III, *Television, Religion, and* Supernatural: *Hunting Monsters, Finding Gods* (Lanham, MD: Lexington Books, 2014); Galen A. Foresman, ed., Supernatural *and Philosophy: Metaphysics and Monsters… for Idjits*, Blackwell Philosophy and Pop Culture Series (Hoboken, NJ: Wiley-Blackwell, 2013); Susan A. George and Regina M. Hansen, eds., Supernatural, *Humanity, and the Soul: On the Highway to Hell and Back* (New York: Palgrave Macmillan, 2014); Alyssa Silva, "Dean Winchester: An Existentialist Hero?/Dean Winchester: ¿Un héroe existencialista?" *Sesión no numerada: Revista de letras y ficción audiovisual,* no. 2 (2012): 67–83.

6. See, e.g., Melissa Bruce, "The Impala as Negotiator of Melodrama and Masculinity in 'Supernatural,'" in "Saving People, Hunting Things," ed. Catherine Tosenberger, special issue, *Transformative Works and Cultures* 4 (2010); Bronwen Calvert, "Angels, Demons, and Damsels in Distress: The Representation of Women in *Supernatural*," in *TV Goes to Hell: An Unofficial Road Map of* Supernatural, ed. Stacey Abott and David Lavery, 90–104 Toronto: ECW Press, 2011); Darren Elliott-Smith, "'Go Be Gay for That Poor, Dead Intern': Conversion Fantasies and Gay Anxieties in *Supernatural*," ibid., 105–18; Lorrie Palmer, "The Road to Lordsburg: Rural Masculinity in *Supernatural*," ibid., 77–89; Julia M. Wright, "Latchkey Hero: Masculinity, Class and the Gothic in Eric Kripke's *Supernatural*," *Genders*, no. 47 (2008), www.genders.org/g47/g47_wright.html.

7. See, e.g., Michael Fuchs, "'Play It Again, Sam... and Dean': Temporality and Meta-Textuality in *Supernatural*," in *Time in Television Narrative: Exploring Temporality in Twenty-First-Century Programming*, ed. Melissa Ames, 82–94 (Jackson: University Press of Mississippi, 2012); Dusty Lavoie, Dusty, "Marijuanatopia?—Placing Pot Media in the US Social Imaginary: Surveillance, Consumption and Pleasure" (PhD diss., University of Maine, 2011), DigitalCommons@UMaine, Electronic Theses and Dissertations, paper 1635, http://digitalcommons.library.umaine.edu/etd/1635.

8. Mike Hale, "Eternal Life, Thanks to Angels and Abs: Secrets to the Long Life of 'Supernatural,'" *New York Times*, April 18, 2014, www.nytimes.com/2014/04/20/arts/television/secrets-to-the-long-life-of-supernatural.html; Neda Ulaby, "The Few, The Fervent: Fans Of 'Supernatural' Redefine TV Success," *All Things Considered*, January 15, 2014. National Public Radio audio, 5:15, www.npr.org/2014/01/15/262092791/the-few-the-fervent-fans-of-supernatural-redefine-tv-success.

9. David Nutter, "Wendigo," *Supernatural*, season 1, episode 2, directed by David Nutter, aired September 20, 2005 (Burbank, CA: Warner Home Video, June 15, 2010), Blu-ray.

10. Eric Kripke, in Ben Edlund, Eric Kripke, and Robert Singer, "Commentary to 'The End,'" *Supernatural*, season 5, disc 1 (Burbank, CA: Warner Home Video, September 7, 2010), Blu-ray.

11. Supernatural Wiki website, accessed September 16, 2014, www.supernaturalwiki.com/index.php.

12. "Super-wiki: Portal," Supernatural Wiki website, accessed August 5, 2014, www.supernaturalwiki.com/index.php?title=Super-wiki:Portal.

13. DiRT: Digital Research Tools website, accessed August 16, 2014, http://dirtdirectory.org; TAPoRware website, accessed August 17, 2014, http://taporware.ualberta.ca/~taporware/textTools.

14. "Text Mining," DiRT website, accessed August 16, 2014, http://dirtdirectory.org/categories/text-mining.

15. Ibid.

16. "Plain Text Analysis Tools," TAPoRware website, accessed August 17, 2014, http://taporware.ualberta.ca/~taporware/textTools.

17. "Text Mining," DiRT website.

18. Lawrence Anthony, "AntConc 3.4.0 Tutorial 1: Getting Started," YouTube video, 5:57, posted February 3, 2014, www.youtube.com/watch?v=O3ukHC3fyuc&feature=youtube_gdata_player.

19. TextGrid website, accessed August 17, 2014, www.textgrid.de/en.
20. Organization for Transformative Works website, accessed September 16, 2014, http://transformativeworks.org.
21. "Supernatural Wiki," Indiegogo website, accessed September 16, 2014, https://www. indiegogo.com/projects/supernatural-wiki.

Bibliography

Anthony, Lawrence. "AntConc 3.4.0 Tutorial 1: Getting Started."
YouTube video, 5:57. Posted February 3, 2014. www.youtube.com/
watch?v=O3ukHC3fyuc&feature=youtube_gdata_player.

Balirano, Giuseppe. "De-Stereotyping Otherness: A Multimodal Script Analysis of Semiotically Expressed Humour." *Linguistic Insights: Studies in Language and Communication* 54 (2007): 487–505.

Bruce, Melissa. "The Impala as Negotiator of Melodrama and Masculinity in 'Supernatural.'" In "Saving People, Hunting Things," ed. Catherine Tosenberger. Special issue, *Transformative Works and Cultures* 4 (2010).

Calvert, Bronwen. "Angels, Demons, and Damsels in Distress: The Representation of Women in *Supernatural.*" In *TV Goes to Hell: An Unofficial Road Map of Supernatural*, ed. Stacey Abott and David Lavery, 90–104. Toronto: ECW Press, 2011.

Edlund, Ben, Kripke, Eric, and Robert Singer. "Commentary to 'The End.'" *Supernatural*, season 5. Disc 1. Burbank, CA: Warner Home Video, 2010. Blu-ray.

DiRT: Digital Research Tools website. Accessed August 16, 2014. http://dirtdirectory.org.

Elliott-Smith, Darren. "'Go Be Gay for That Poor, Dead Intern': Conversion Fantasies and Gay Anxieties in Supernatural," In *TV Goes to Hell: An Unofficial Road Map of* Supernatural, ed. Stacey Abott and David Lavery, 105–18. Toronto: ECW Press, 2011.

Engstrom, Erika, and Joseph M. Valenzano III. *Television, Religion, and* Supernatural: *Hunting Monsters, Finding Gods*. Lanham, MD: Lexington Books, 2014.

Fogel, Ephim G. "Electronic Computers and Elizabethan Texts." *Studies in Bibliography* 15 (1962): 15–31.

Foresman, Galen A., ed. Supernatural *and Philosophy: Metaphysics and Monsters… for Idjits*. Blackwell Philosophy and Pop Culture Series. Hoboken: Wiley-Blackwell, 2013.

Fuchs, Michael. "'Play It Again, Sam… and Dean': Temporality and Meta-Textuality in *Supernatural.*" In *Time in Television Narrative: Exploring Temporality in Twenty-First-Century Programming*, edited by Melissa Ames, 82–94. Jackson: University Press of Mississippi, 2012.

George, Susan A., and Regina M. Hansen, eds. Supernatural, *Humanity, and the Soul: On the Highway to Hell and Back*. New York: Palgrave Macmillan, 2014.

Hale, Mike. "Eternal Life, Thanks to Angels and Abs: Secrets to the Long Life of 'Supernatural.'" *New York Times*, April 18, 2014. www.nytimes.com/2014/04/20/ arts/television/secrets-to-the-long-life-of-supernatural.html.

Kripke, Eric. "Wendigo." *Supernatural*, season 1, episode 2. Directed by David Nutter. Aired September 20, 2005. Burbank, CA: Warner Home Video, 2010. Blu-ray.

Larsen, Katherine, and Lynn S. Zubernis. *Fangasm: Supernatural Fangirls.* Iowa City: University of Iowa Press, 2013.

Lavoie, Dusty. "Marijuanatopia?—Placing Pot Media in the US Social Imaginary: Surveillance, Consumption and Pleasure." PhD diss., University of Maine, 2011. DigitalCommons@UMaine, Electronic Theses and Dissertations, paper 1635. http://digitalcommons.library.umaine.edu/etd/1635.

Marder, Louis. "A Guide to 50 Computer Projects in Shakespeare." *Shakespeare Newsletter* 15, no. 85 (1965): 53.

Organization for Transformative Works website. Accessed September 16, 2014. http://transformativeworks.org.

Palmer, Lorrie. "The Road to Lordsburg: Rural Masculinity in *Supernatural.*" In *TV Goes to Hell: An Unofficial Road Map of* Supernatural, ed. Stacey Abott and David Lavery, 77–89. Toronto: ECW Press, 2011.

Silva, Alyssa. "Dean Winchester: An Existentialist Hero?/Dean Winchester: ¿Un héroe existencialista?" *Sesión no numerada: Revista de letras y ficción audiovisual*, no. 2 (2012): 67–83.

Supernatural Wiki website. Accessed September 16, 2014. www.supernaturalwiki.com/index.php.

"Supernatural Wiki." Indiegogo website. Accessed September 16, 2014. https://www.indiegogo.com/projects/supernatural-wiki.

"Super-wiki: Portal." Supernatural Wiki website. Accessed August 5, 2014. www.supernaturalwiki.com/index.php?title=Super-wiki:Portal.

TAPoR. "Plain Text Analysis Tools." TAPoRware website. Accessed August 17, 2014. http://taporware.ualberta.ca/~taporware/textTools.

TAPoR website. 2014. www.tapor.ca.

TextGrid website. Accessed August 17, 2014. www.textgrid.de/en.

Thibault, Paul J. "The Multimodal Transcription of a Television Advertisement: Theory and Practice." In *Multimodality and Multimediality in the Distance Learning Age : Papers in English Linguistics*, edited by Anthony P. Baldry, 311–83. Campobasso, Italy: Palladino, 2000.

Tosenberger, Catherine. "Love! Valor! 'Supernatural'!" *Transformative Works and Cultures* 4 (2010). doi:10.3983/twc.2010.0212.

Ulaby, Neda. "The Few, The Fervent: Fans Of 'Supernatural' Redefine TV Success." *All Things Considered*, January 15, 2014. National Public Radio audio, 5:15. www.npr.org/2014/01/15/262092791/the-few-the-fervent-fans-of-supernatural-redefine-tv-success.

Wright, Julia M. "Latchkey Hero: Masculinity, Class and the Gothic in Eric Kripke's *Supernatural.*" *Genders*, no. 47 (2008). www.genders.org/g47/g47_wright.html.

Zubernis, Lynn S., and Katherine Larsen. *Fandom at the Crossroads: Celebration, Shame and Fan/Producer Relationships.* Newcastle upon Tyne, UK: Cambridge Scholars Publishing, 2012.

———, eds. *Supernatural.* Fan Phenomena Series. Bristol, UK: Intellect Books, 2014.

CHAPTER FOURTEEN

Second Time Around; or, The Long Life of the Victorian Women Writers Project
Sustainability through Outreach

Angela Courtney and Michael Courtney

Introduction

This chapter describes and reflects on the involvement and impact of subject librarians in one specific digital humanities (DH) project over the course of its conception, development, respite, and reawakening. With a dual charge of maintaining a level of sustainability needed for an ongoing endeavor while overcoming the difficulties surrounding the quest to revive this once-languishing DH text collection, the Victorian Women Writers Project (VWWP) has become a feisty creature, kept afloat by two teams: eager and energetic graduate students, originally hired to encode, but who now also train, lead, and innovate; and dedicated editors who constantly battle to make time for the VWWP on top of their other full-time job responsibilities.

Keeping with the theme of this book, this chapter will explore the potential roles of subject librarians in DH, coming from the point of view of a subject librarian willingly let loose to help restart a project and now working to maintain and grow the project after it has been reintroduced as an online, freely available resource to students, scholars, and the general public. This is a case study of subject librarian involvement in DH. It is not meant to be prescriptive, but we hope it will encourage other subject librarians who want to become involved in DH. Much important work with the VWWP has not been technical, but rather has involved person-to-person contact. This case study chapter will investigate and illustrate the potential roles of subject librarians not only in project development, but also in the difficult and imperative area of the sustainability of a DH project.

Integral to much of the ongoing work discussed throughout this chapter is the need for librarians and collaborators to create a sharing culture in open environments, one whose very structure is designed to reach beyond the local community. As digital humanities scholarship reaches beyond its own inherent disciplinary boundaries, the focus on digital humanities work itself encompasses efforts with very real public value, beyond even its own scholarly origins (for examples of digital public humanities see the University of Iowa's Public Humanities in a Digital World at http://www.uiowa.edu/~phdw/ and the NEH Digital Projects for the Public grant program at http://www.neh.gov/grants/public/digital-projects-the-public). Considering new forms of knowledge mobilization (and management) and outreach, then, reinforces the more classical skills of the subject librarian while advancements in technology enable seemingly limitless opportunities. While ideally a humanities subject librarian would have an interest in the technical side of DH work, such as text encoding, visualization, and so on, there are many projects that would benefit from the abilities of a *traditional* subject librarian who is open to expanding his or her involvement. A goal of this chapter is to depict DH projects in a large and complex ecosystem that depends on much more than technical capacity. The skills, talents, and carefully forged relationships of a subject librarian are invaluable to a DH project.

History of the VWWP

In 1995, the VWWP was planned, developed, and unveiled by Perry Willett, a subject librarian whose work as the liaison to the English department placed him in the position to become an early example of a librarian actively involved in DH work. He acknowledges a sentiment that still holds true today, that librarians "are not generally looking for major new job responsibilities," and he already had taken on the duties of Head, Library Electronic Text Resource Service (LETRS) when he began to explore the potential of the VWWP.[1] He was, however, an attentive and responsive literature librarian and saw an opportunity when in the spring semester of 1995, he received an enquiry from a student who was dissatisfied with vendor-provided online full-text databases. The series of events that begat the VWWP is an interesting one, and one that could have completely derailed at many times. Looking back at the project's beginnings, Willett admits, "Fortunately, none of us knew what we were in for."[2]

Willett was approached by undergraduate Felix Jung who inquired about the possibility of adding more texts to the then-Chadwyck-Healey (now ProQuest) product The English Poetry Full-Text Database (now English Poetry in its newest and updated iteration). A robust database, based on *The New Cambridge Bibliography of English Literature (NCBEL)*, published in 1969 (itself heavily based on the *Cambridge Bibliography of English Literature*), The English Poetry Full-Text Database of the mid-1990s reflected an era that, among other issues, was not particularly comprehensive in its inclusion of women authors. After Willett explained to Jung that the library was not the creator of the database and did not have the ability to add to the contents, the apparently eager and determined student, characterized by Willett as the "right mix of enthusiasm, savvy and naïveté for such an undertaking," still wanted to make more Victorian poetry available online.[3] Willett realized this was a logical time for LETRS to take a leadership role in developing digital versions of hard-to-find literature. Working with Professor Donald Gray from Indiana University's English department, the small team compiled a list of authors who were important or otherwise noteworthy for potential inclusion. The authors were mainly women, and thus the Victorian Women Writers Project developed out of a perceived major shortcoming in The English Poetry Full-Text Database.

Willett decided on using the Text Encoding Initiative Standards for marking up the works to be included in the collection.[4] Over the course of a few months, Willett and Jung encoded nine texts and unveiled the project in October 1995. As the project continued, the purpose evolved from creating a needed correction to omissions in the NCBEL and The English Poetry Full-Text Database to a grander and more important objective. Literary scholarship had omitted a broad swath of literary and cultural history from the canon by marginalizing countless women writers who worked in many genres beyond poetry. The scope of the VWWP grew to include women from English-speaking countries writing in all genres.

The Fall and Rise

As Willett's responsibilities increased and he eventually left Indiana University, the VWWP was left without staff, volunteers, or, most important, a leader. With nearly 200 texts, the VWWP was a known resource for librarians as well as scholars and students. While the Indiana University Libraries were able to maintain the project as it was when Willett left IU, the VWWP was (like many of its authors) trapped in time. It remained accessible to users, but it had not advanced with other similar online text resources. Functionality and look made it appear aged, as if it had outlived its usefulness and was no longer needed by the academic community or anyone else. This perception based on appearance was, however, vastly incorrect. Leaders of other DH projects inquired about the state of the VWWP and even offered to absorb the texts into other initiatives.

In 2007, Michelle Dalmau, then Digital Projects Librarian at IU, was approached by colleagues at other institutions about the viability of the VWWP. The possibility of it being subsumed into other initiatives became a very real one. At the same time, in a situation very similar to the request that started the VWWP a dozen years earlier, the English Literature Librarian, Angela Courtney, was contacted by graduate students who were frustrated at their inability to find enough usable copies of texts for classes they were teaching at the undergraduate level.

This time it was possible to fulfill the graduate students' request. It was unquestionably possible to begin adding to the collection again. The confluence of two eager librarians with completely different jobs and skill sets, each hoping to revitalize this project, set in place the resurrection of the VWWP. The librarian team realized quickly that in order to position the VWWP for immediate viability, there needed to be a direct connection to IU's English department, and particularly to the graduate students. The VWWP needed a environment of support, participation, use, and interest in order to create a sustainable setting as it started on its new path.

Moving forward, Dalmau and Courtney, as the two new project editors, each drew on their individual strengths and professional connections. While working closely together, the editors by necessity took different and complementary roles. Dalmau was the project manager, coordinating the project upgrade, editing the encoding guidelines, and keeping the project on schedule. Courtney directed efforts at leveraging her connection to the English department, recruiting TEI-proficient student encoders (who also helped create the new encoding guidelines), and generally working to develop a broad and far-reaching community of support for the project. These efforts at sustainability relied on the subject librarian's connections to involve parties within the university as well as elsewhere. As a general observation, the more people who use and contribute to a DH project, the greater the chances are that it will thrive.

The Trouble with "Ongoing"

The very notion of DH project sustainability is intrinsically tied to digital preservation. On first thought, one might consider preserving the look and feel of a project over time, enabling new users to experience the project exactly as it was first presented. Given the nature of almost constant change in the online environment, this approach proves quite likely to be impossible and unappealing. Alternatively, the content itself could be preserved and its original shell ignored. The latter approach could prove unpopular, particularly if the project's end users had become used to its original look and feel, and doubly so if way the user interface worked was altered substantially. These issues need to be resolved when a digital project's home is transferred to a new institutional host. Decisions about what will be preserved and how it will be presented can change considerably when a new host's vision is in stark contrast to the project's originator. Leslie Johnston suggests that sustainability and preservation for DH projects "depend of active management of a project" and must "start at the beginning of the life cycle."[5] Active management implies careful consideration of technology support over time and requires project managers to "continually review and revise the underlying technology and content formats over time."[6] Similarly, project managers should place careful thought and attention into even the very earliest planning stages on how a project will address the problem of keeping up with changes in technology and ensuring that content can still be delivered as those changes occur. Considering open-source technologies and widely accepted, used, and supported standards as well as thoughtful planning for structural and content updating for a digital project are paramount to long-term sustainability.

An undertaking such as the VWWP, then, can be problematic because there is no clear logical end. Once a project is announced as a live resource for students and scholars, it is often considered to be in a comfortable position, with a certain sense of security in its longevity. This status as a project that is ready for use implies a completeness that is deceptive. This new status brings with it a new demand for ongoing care. Efforts to upgrade and add new texts, for example, were not strong candidates for grant funding because it is hard to make a case for an old project being new or innovative, and the editors decided not to pursue grant funding. As a result, in addition to the many considerations of active management of the technological infrastructure, the VWWP currently relies on a variety of ad hoc and often opportunistic outreach efforts that are underway. These efforts serve to increase the project's name recognition, widen the national network of volunteers, and buttress the project by working to create a community of public users who expect continued free availability of this text collection.

Building a Community of Outreach

The concept of outreach, as both a discourse and an end objective as it pertains to libraries, is rather difficult to quantify in an historical sense. Examples of library extension services persist throughout the literature, dating back hundreds of years. Outreach as currently defined, particularly in academic libraries, is a contemporary construct, one that has evolved over the past half century to incorporate new modes of information delivery that radically transform how users engage with multimodal content. From early innovations such as the telegraph and telephone to the more developed twentieth-century technologies of radio, television, and film, electronic media in particular has had a dramatic impact on the dissemination of information. As digital humanists reach beyond the physical boundaries of the traditional library model, so too do they reach beyond implicit disciplinary boundaries when engaging the public in new environments. In fact, the very public nature of DH suggests open accessibility and a culture of sharing (in turn creating a sense of community in and of itself—all concepts inherent to outreach). The digital humanist, then, must focus not simply on sustainability and preservation of digital projects, but also on creating a community (and culture) that fosters collaboration and sharing as well as shifting the focus to creating projects that have a much broader public appeal (and not simply focusing on the scholarly aspect of DH work).

The VWWP's outreach efforts began in earnest well before the new editors realized they were actively developing outreach initiatives. Vital to a successful relaunch of the VWWP was a partnership between the library and the English department's graduate program, one that features a strong and nationally recognized Victorian studies program. Courtney, the English literature librarian, met with the head of the department about the possibility of involving the VWWP in the graduate curriculum. That meeting was followed by a meeting with the Victorian faculty, with a goal of integrating digital competencies into a graduate class. The result was the faculty suggesting and supporting an entire class that focused of incorporating DH in the professional lives of students who would soon need such skills on the job market.

The class was developed and taught through a collaborative effort among the VWWP's editors, Courtney and Dalmau, a member of the Victorianist faculty, Professor Joss Marsh, and graduate assistant Adrianne Wadewitz. To initiate this daunting task, the four aforementioned instructors put together a working syllabus, supported by a variety of guest speakers from across the university to introduce the students to DH work. The VWWP and its editors took a central role, and working on the project (encoding and editing) was the expressed reason several of the students enrolled. Within the context of an overview of DH, each student chose and encoded a text from a broad range of titles that were digitized specifically for these students in the hope of providing an assortment from which all participants—Medievalists, Renaissance experts, Victorianists, and so on—could find something of interest for the duration of the semester.

The syllabus included several days in which the students would receive an introduction to encoding based on the TEI standards as adapted by the VWWP, and the editors held weekly office hours in a computer lab for students who needed extra assistance with particular problems they encountered as they worked on their chosen texts. As the course progressed, the students wanted to be able to do more with the text encoding, such as creating personographies that delineate the characters and relationships in any text. These students' ideas pushed the editors to advance the capacity of the encoding guidelines. The syllabus also included days for students to explore the concept of critical editing (particularly the additions of footnotes that explain potentially unfamiliar contexts or that correct erroneous information or incorrect citations, and translations of foreign language passages) with Marsh, an important addition to the revitalized project. Students also were responsible for creating contextualizing content in the form of author biographies and scholarly introductions to the texts, a new feature of the second iteration of the project. The group of dedicated encoders undertook the difficult task of translating foreign language passages, again working closely with Marsh. The class always had access to their subject librarian, and that connection helped them to develop footnotes, often quite extensive, that either explained unfamiliar concepts or corrected factual errors by the authors. For many, biographical and historical research was quite different from their traditional literary research, and this expansion of scope broadened their approach to research. Marsh summed up the class: "The result is that we now have seven texts encoded, seven sets of footnotes ready for embedding, and seven introductions ready for web publication—all of them first-class professional pieces of writing, all fine models for future work, and all items of record for each class participant."[7]

Unexpectedly, after the class ended, some of these busy graduate students wanted to continue working on the project. Mara Inglezakis, a member of the class who continues to work with the project, now extends her efforts to selecting texts to add to the collection. Going forward, the texts selected are added in part based on topics of current or developing interest in the academic realm, and her awareness helps guide the growth of the VWWP. Reflecting on the impact of the project on her scholarship, Inglezakis explains that the "Digital Humanities class taught us to produce scholarly editions of texts that ranged from literary to political to scientific." A student with broad-ranging research interests, she appreciated being part of a class that "allowed us to do interdisciplinary work that included information modeling and metadata production."[8] She actively recruits her classmates to participate, and she has also become an expert trainer for new encoders.

Mary Borgo, one of the students who has remained dedicated to the VWWP, and who has taken an active role in recruiting participants, appreciates the "professional experience that would have been difficult to acquire if I had been pursuing more traditional forms of scholarly work." She explains further that for her, "Learning TEI has given me the vocabulary and technical skills needed to engage digital humanities scholarship in meaningful and intellectually generative ways."[9] Since the class, she has presented a DH-focused paper at an international conference, and she has been selected to attend an NEH-funded advanced TEI workshop. Her outreach efforts have been earnest and ongoing, at conferences, during workshops, in the classroom, and so on, and always the result of her belief in the importance of the VWWP as a resource, learning tool, and academic endeavor.

These graduate students also recruited and trained others, near and remote. A simple message posted by Borgo to the English graduate student e-mail list offering to train volunteer encoders was rewarded not only by a handful of new young scholars willing and eager to participate in the project, but also a request to work with undergraduates. Chris Hokanson, a graduate of the Indiana University English PhD program, was the head of the English department at Judson College, a small Baptist school in Alabama. He responded to the e-mail, curious to know if there was a way that the VWWP could be an appropriate part of the curriculum for his undergraduates. The authors and texts initially included in the project did not have biographies or critical introductions, and this inquiry offered an opportunity for students to see their work have impact outside of the classroom. By working with database providers, including Gale, ProQuest, and Readex, the VWWP arranged for our new undergraduate partners to have access to several historical and literary resources that would have otherwise been unavailable at their institution. Armed with the necessary research tools, the students at Judson were able to develop solid biographies for VWWP authors. With several levels of editorial oversight, the project added ten new biographies to the original database contents.

Each of these activities has an impact on the success and perception of the project, but when considered together, the overall impact has been instrumental in keeping the project active and maintaining forward momentum. Due in large part to the increased vitality, more opportunities are now being presented to the VWWP. In recent months, the project has been approached to encode a digitized version of the first London edition of Mary Shelley's 1830 novel, *Perkin Warbeck*. This should be unveiled concurrently with the publication of a new scholarly edition of the text in print in late 2014. Another unsolicited opportunity came when the VWWP was invited to participate along with several long-running and esteemed text projects in a grant application for study on the use of such projects. These opportunities are possible only because of the organized and nimble outreach that now surrounds the VWWP.

Efforts at reaching out to a broad potential audience of users and collaborators are continuing. The VWWP has entered into the world of social media, slowly and with caution. With a Twitter feed (http://twitter.com/ VWWP_IU) and a more recent foray into Tumblr (http://vwwp.tumblr. com), the project approaches this realm with the hopes of increasing its user population. Going forward, the project is expanding outreach efforts to *Wikipedia*. By adding links to the bibliographies for articles in *Wikipedia*, the VWWP will increase its potential user base exponentially. A quick click in *Wikipedia* can take users to the full text of works by Victorian women. In this manner, it will be developing a new potential group of contributors to the project in the *Wikipedia* contributor population.

Risk, Reflection, Opportunity

Looking back, Willett's recollection of the VWWP's creation illustrates a classic example of a librarian who saw an opportunity, assessed the situation, and took a risk. He was able to take advantage of a confluence of diverse factors: "Victorianism, so important at IU,… a great collection both in the main collection and the Lilly Library," coupled with a situation in which "people were just beginning to re-examine the importance of women writers of the period, but were hindered by the lack of access to their works."[10] With the added luxury of working within a literary era that was free of copyright restrictions and a belief that this was an undertaking that a library could do without the support of a commercial publisher, the VWWP was created to fill a gap that limited the availability of a large body of nineteenth-century writing by a traditionally underrepresented group.

It is difficult to ignore the vast impact that competing technologies over time have had on library outreach. While some technologies proved relatively meritless (the telegraph, for example, was revolutionary in using electricity to transmit information over great distances throughout much of the nineteenth century, yet proved fruitless in library adoption perhaps due to the amount of specialized training and practice required), others proved quite revolutionary. The telephone is often considered the principal technology that single-handedly transformed library outreach. In a case of "build it and they will come," John W. Fritch offered, "Telephone use [in libraries] was so heavy in the 1920s and 1930s that articles warned against advertising too much for fear that librarians would be unable to handle the deluge of questions."[11] Certainly, library outreach concerns in the twenty-first century have moved beyond such a "fear of deluge," yet the very rapid growth of technological innovation has sparked new approaches to delivering information to the general public anytime, anywhere. Perhaps we're no longer fearful of a large public competing for our services; rather, viewing the public as not simply our audience but, instead, our community, places DH outreach in a new and exciting framework. The communities that are created around digital projects not only add value to information dissemination, but also present opportunities and possibilities for content creation and vision.

Notes

1. Perry Willett, "The Victorian Women Writers Project: The Library as a Creator and Publisher of Electronic Texts," *Public Access-Computer Systems Review* 7, no. 6 (1996): (5), https://journals.tdl.org/pacsr/index.php/pacsr/article/view/6009.
2. Willett, Perry. "VWWP." Email to Angela Courtney. August 4.
3. Ibid.
4. See TEI: Text Encoding Initiative website, last updated March 12, 2013, www.tei-c.org/index.xml.
5. Leslie Johnston, "Digital Humanities and Digital Preservation," *The Signal: Digital Preservation* (blog), Library of Congress, April 12, 2013, http://blogs.loc.gov/digitalpreservation/2013/04/digital-humanities-and-digital-preservation.
6. Ibid.
7. Marsh, Joss. 2010. L501 Final Report 2010. (internal report, Department of English,) Indiana University, 2010.
8. Inglezakis, Mara. "VWWP." Email to Angela Courtney. August 4.
9. Borgo, Mary. 2014. "VWWP." Email to Angela Courtney July 30.
10. Willett, "VWWP."
11. John W. Fritch, "Electronic Outreach in America: From Telegraph to Television," in *Libraries to the People: Histories of Outreach*, ed. Robert S. Freeman and David M. Hovde (Jefferson, NC: MacFarland & Company, 2003), 167.

Bibliography

Borgo, Mary. 2014. "VWWP. Email to Angela Courtney July 30.

Freeman, Robert S., and David M. Hovde. *Libraries to the People: Histories of Outreach.* McFarland, 2003.

Fritch, John W. "Electronic Outreach in America: From Telegraph to Television." In Freeman and Hovde, *Libraries to the People*, 165–80.

Inglezakis, Mara. 2014. "VWWP." Email to Angela Courtney. August 4.

Johnston, Leslie. "Digital Humanities and Digital Preservation." *The Signal: Digital Preservation* (blog), Library of Congress, April 12, 2013.

Marsh, Joss. 2010. *L501 Final Report 2010.* (internal report, Department of English,) Indiana University, 2010.

TEI: Text Encoding Initiative website. Last updated March 12, 2013. www.tei-c.org/index. xml.

Willett, Perry. "The Victorian Women Writers Project: The Library as a Creator and Publisher of Electronic Texts." *Public Access-Computer Systems Review* 7, no. 6 (1996). https://journals.tdl.org/pacsr/index.php/pacsr/article/view/6009.

———. 2014. "VWWP." Email to Angela Courtney. August 4.

Appendix
Tools and Resources Referenced in this Book[*]

Tools

Adobe Creative Cloud (https://www.adobe.com/creativecloud.html). Commercial cloud-based host of Adobe products such as Photoshop, Illustrator, and InDesign.

AntConc (http://www.laurenceanthony.net/software/antconc/). Freeware corpus analysis toolkit for concordancing and text analysis.

Apache OpenOffice (http://openoffice.apache.org/index.html). Free and open productivity suite.

Bookworm (http://bookworm.culturomics.org/). A simple and powerful way to visualize trends in repositories of digitized texts.

CanvasX (http://www.canvasx.com/en/products/canvasx-pro-16). Commercial tool for creating, enhancing, and sharing technical illustration.

Cascading Style Sheets (CSS) (http://www.w3.org/Style/CSS/Overview.en.html). A simple mechanism for adding styles (e.g., fonts, colors, spacing) to Web documents.

Celtx (https://www.celtx.com/index.html). Software for creating storyboards, scripts, and other film-production related uses.

Corpus.byu.edu (http://corpus.byu.edu/). A set of corpora with many uses for the the study of linguistics and language use.

Digital Research Tools (DiRT) (http://dirtdirectory.org/). Registry of digital research tools for scholarly use.

Dublin Core (http://dublincore.org/documents/dcmi-terms/). A set of standardized metadata terms maintained by the Dublin Core Metadata Initiative (http://dublincore.org/).

---

[*]   Descriptions for resources were taken from the resource's official online presence.

Final Cut Pro (https://www.apple.com/final-cut-pro/). Commercial Apple software for video editing.

iMovie (http://www.apple.com/ios/imovie/). Commercial Apple software for browsing and sharing HD video shot using an iOS device.

Jing (http://www.techsmith.com/jing.html). Computer service that lets you capture basic video, animation, and still images, and share them on the web.

Juxta (http://www.juxtasoftware.org/). Open-source tool for comparing and collating multiple witnesses to a single textual work.

Lexos (http://wheatoncollege.edu/lexomics/tools/). An integrated lexomics workflow. Scrub tags, remove stop words, apply lemma list, cut texts into segments, make dendrograms and other analyses.

Named Entity Recognizer (http://nlp.stanford.edu/software/CRF-NER.shtml). Labels sequences of words in a text which are the names of things, such as person and company names, or gene and protein names.

Microsoft Office (https://products.office.com/en-US/). Suite of applications for creating documents, spreadsheets, slideshows, databases, etc. Commercial product.

MorphAdorner (http://morphadorner.northwestern.edu). Java command-line program which acts as a pipeline manager for processes performing morphological adornment of words in a text.

MySQL (http://www.mysql.com/). Open source relational database management system.

Omeka (http://omeka.org/). Free, flexible, and open source web-publishing platform for the display of library, museum, archives, and scholarly collections and exhibitions.

Paper Machines (http://papermachines.org/). Open-source extension for the Zotero bibliographic management software. Allows individual researchers to generate analyses and visualizations of user-provided corpora, without requiring extensive computational resources or technical knowledge.

Photoshop (http://www.photoshop.com/). Commercial software from Adobe for creating and editing digital images.

PHP (http://php.net/). Popular general-purpose scripting language that is especially suited to web development.

Poem Viewer (http://ovii.oerc.ox.ac.uk/PoemVis/). Web-based tool for visualizing poems in support of close reading.

Premiere Pro (http://www.adobe.com/products/premiere.html). Commercial video editing software from Adobe.

Python (https://www.python.org/). Open source programming language for beginner and experienced programmers.

Semantic Web (http://www.w3.org/standards/semanticweb/). A web of data such as would be found in databases. A project of the World Wide Web Consortium (W3C) (http://www.w3.org/Consortium/).

Squarespace (http://www.squarespace.com/). Web hosting site.

SU Time (http://nlp.stanford.edu/software/sutime.shtml). A library for recognizing and normalizing time expressions.

TAPoR Text Analysis Portal (http://www.tapor.ca/). A gateway to the tools used in sophisticated text analysis and retrieval.

TextGrid (https://www.textgrid.de/en/ueber-textgrid/projekt/). Offers humanist researchers sustainable editing, storing, and publishing of their data in a thoroughly tested and safe environment.

VoiceThread (http://voicethread.com/). Cloud-based application for uploading, sharing, and discussing documents, presentations, images, audio files and videos.

Voyant (http://voyant-tools.org/). Web-based reading and analysis environment for digital texts.

Windows Movie Maker (http://windows.microsoft.com/en-us/windows-live/movie-maker). Commercial software for video editing.

Wordle (http://www.wordle.net/). Toy for generating "word clouds" from text that you provide.

WordPress (https://wordpress.com/). Free hosting platform for websites and blogs.

Zotero (https://www.zotero.org/). Free, easy-to-use tool to help you collect, organize, cite, and share your research sources.

Tutorials and Online Courses

Code (http://code.org/). Online tutorials teaching coding, and gateway to commercial online learning sites. Aimed at K-8.

Code School (https://www.codeschool.com/). Teaches web technologies using video lessons, coding challenges, and screencasts. Fee-based.

Glogster (http://edu.glogster.com/). Commercial site for learning multimedia web applications.

Scratch (http://scratch.mit.edu/). Creative learning community teaching coding through creation of stories, games, and animations. Designed for ages 8-16, but used by people of all ages. Scratch is a project of the Lifelong Kindergarten Group at the MIT Media Lab.

Communities and Professional Organizations

Alliance of Digital Humanities Organizations (http://adho.org/). Promotes and supports digital research and teaching across all arts and humanities disciplines, acting as a community-based advisory force, and supporting excellence in research, publication, collaboration and training. Also see its discussion group, Humanist (http://dhhumanist.org/).

Association for Computers and the Humanities—Digital Humanities Questions and Answers (http://digitalhumanities.org/answers/) and its Twitter feed (@ DHanswers). Community-run Q&A board for digital humanities questions.

Boston Digital Humanities Consortium (http://bostondh.org/). Informal association of educational and cultural institutions in New England committed to the collaborative development of teaching, learning, and scholarship in the digital humanities and computational social sciences. Also on Twitter (@Boston_DH).

dh + lib (@DHandLib). Where the digital humanities and librarianship meet. A project of the ACRL DH Interest Group. Also see its email list (http://lists.ala.org/wws/info/acrldigitalhumanitiesig).

DH Commons (http://dhcommons.org/). A hub for people and organizations to find projects to work with, and for projects to find collaborators. Also onTwitter (@ DHCommons).

DigitalHumanitiesNow (@dhnow). Showcases digital humanities scholarship and news of interest to the DH community. Twitter feed for the online publication *Digital Humanities Now* (http://digitalhumanitiesnow.org/).

Digital Library Federation (http://www.diglib.org/). A robust and diverse community of practitioners who advance research, teaching, and learning through the application of digital library research, technology, and services.

Humanities, Arts, Science, and Technology Alliance and Collaboratory (HASTAC) (http://www.hastac.org/). An alliance of more than 13,000 humanists, artists, social scientists, scientists and technologists working together to transform the future of learning.

National Institute for Technology in Liberal Education (NITLE) (http://www.nitle.org/). Organization for small colleges that want to use available tools and resources strategically and sustainably to collaborate, engage students, and advance liberal education.

NYC Digital Humanities (http://nycdh.org/). An an open community site dedicated to the digital humanities in New York City. Also on Twitter (@nycdh).

Text Encoding Initiative (http://www.tei-c.org/index.xml). A consortium which collectively develops and maintains a standard for the representation of texts in digital form.

THATCamp (The Humanities and Technology Camp) (http://thatcamp.org/). Inexpensive meetings where humanists and technologists of all skill levels learn and build together in sessions proposed on the spot.

Zotero's Digital Humanities Group (https://www.zotero.org/groups/digital_humanities). A place for all of those interested in how digital media and technology are changing the humanities to discuss and create the future together.

Contributors

Tami Albin is an Associate Librarian in the Center for Faculty/Staff Initiatives and Engagement at the University of Kansas. Her areas of expertise and research include oral history, information literacy, LGBTQ studies, and digital humanities.

Sean Atkins, PhD, is a sessional instructor in the Department of Humanities at Grant MacEwan University and the Faculty of Native Studies at the University of Alberta where he teaches Canadian history. His publications include *Native Studies Review* and *Found in Alberta: Environmental Themes for the Anthropocene.*

Christina Bell is the Humanities Librarian at Bates College. In addition to liaison duties, she co-chairs the Bates Digital Initiatives working group and serves on a number of committees related to digital scholarship, pedagogy, and the college writing curriculum. Her research interests focus on critical pedagogy and instruction, feminism and gender studies, digital humanities, and the intersections of these topics within librarianship.

Zoe Borovsky, PhD Scandinavian Studies, is the Librarian for Digital Research and Scholarship at the Charles E. Young Research Library at UCLA and subject specialist for digital humanities, anthropology, and archaeology. Before joining the library in 2010, Borovsky worked for the

UCLA Center for Digital Humanities as a project manager and liaison for research digital humanities projects.

Laura R. Braunstein is the Digital Humanities and English Librarian at Dartmouth College. She has a doctorate in English from Northwestern University, where she taught writing and literature classes. She has worked as an index editor for the MLA International Bibliography, and serves as a consultant for the Schulz Library at the Center for Cartoon Studies in Vermont. Her research interests include collaborative learning, using archival materials in teaching, and the impact of the digital humanities on teaching and learning.

Peter Carini is the College Archivist at Dartmouth College, and has worked on numerous digital humanities projects over the past twenty years.

Angela Courtney is the Head of the Arts & Humanities Department and the Reference Services Department at the Indiana University Bloomington Libraries. She is also the Librarian for English Literature and Theatre. She is Co-Editor of the *Victorian Women Writers Project,* the author of *Literary Research and the Era of American Nationalism and Romanticism*, and co-author of *Literary Research and the Literatures of Australia and New Zealand* and *Literary Research and Postcolonial Literatures in English* in the Scarecrow Press series: *Literary Research: Strategies and Sources.* She edited the *Dictionary of Literary Biography: 19th-Century British Dramatists* volume.

Michael Courtney is Outreach and Engagement Librarian at Indiana University Bloomington where he is also the Librarian for Online Learning. As a member of the Department of Teaching and Learning in the IUB Libraries, he has served as the liaison to the International Studies Program and the Global Village Living Learning Center. In addition, Michael is an adjunct faculty member in the School of Library and Information Science (IUB), where he teaches the core Reference course. Prior to coming to IUB, he has worked in many facets of librarianship, in both public and technical service positions within public and academic libraries over the past 19 years.

Frances Devlin is a Librarian in the Center for Faculty/Staff Initiatives and Engagement at the University of Kansas Libraries. Her areas of expertise and research include information literacy, assessment of reference services, digital humanities, and teaching research methods for French literature.

Hazel-Dawn Dumpert is the Occom Circle Project Manager at Dartmouth College. She is also a writer and editor with extensive experience in shepherding various projects from conception to completion.

Brian Wade Garrison is an Assistant Librarian in the Center for Faculty/Staff Initiatives and Engagement at the University of Kansas and project manager of an NEH grant to make available the illustrations of nineteenth-century ornithologist John Gould. His areas of expertise and research include audio and video digital collections, humanities data, and support for faculty digital projects.

Katie Gibson is a Humanities Librarian and liaison to the departments of Spanish and Portuguese, French and Italian, comparative religion, and philosophy, as well as the German and Latin American studies programs at Miami University of Ohio. She also serves as a member of the Libraries' Digital Humanities Working Group and is currently working on developing a digital humanities project involving documents from the Rodolfo Usigli Collection in the Walter Havighurst Special Collections.

Liorah Golomb is the Humanities Librarian at the University of Oklahoma. She holds a doctorate in Drama from the University of Toronto and earned her MLIS at Pratt Institute. She has published several articles and chapters both within and outside of the field of librarianship, and is a co-author of Literary Research and Postcolonial Literatures in English: Sources and Strategies (Scarecrow Press, 2012).

Arianne Hartsell-Gundy is the Head, Humanities Section and Librarian for Literature and Theater Studies at Duke University. She has a Master of Arts degree in Comparative Literature and a Master of Library Science from Indiana University. Her research interests include information literacy, graduate student pedagogy, collection analysis, and digital humanities, and she is the co-author of the forthcoming Literary Research and British Postmodernism: Strategies and Sources.

Kathleen A. Johnson, Professor of Libraries, has been the subject librarian for English at University Libraries, University of Nebraska-Lincoln, since the beginning of digital scholarship at UNL. She participated in early planning and development of electronic scholarship at UNL and has continued to engage with digital humanities both as the English subject librarian and with her own projects.

Marcus Ladd is the Special Collections Digital Librarian and liaison to the Center for Digital Scholarship at Miami University, where he has worked since completing his MLIS degree at the Catholic University of America in January 2013. His current project is the Bowden Postcard Collection Online, a constantly-growing digital collection developed out of the roughly half a million postcards held in the Walter Havighurst Special Collections. Other recent digitization projects include Miami Tribe historical documents, Freedom Summer oral histories, and Miami University student-produced television and radio programs. He also serves on the Digital Humanities Working Group.

Kathleen A. Langan, Humanities Librarian at Western Michigan University, has facilitated various DH-related workshops and events for the WMU community. Other professional interests include assessment and information literacy, the learning and work habits of Millennials, and the use of social media and technology for teaching librarians.

Joan K. Lippincott is Associate Executive Director of the Coalition for Networked Information, a joint project of EDUCAUSE and the Association of Research Libraries. Since joining CNI in 1990, she has provided leadership for programs in teaching and learning, assessment, learning spaces, and collaboration among professional groups. She is a widely published author and frequent conference speaker. She is on the boards of portal and the Networked Digital Library of Theses and Dissertations (NDLTD). Joan has a Ph.D. in higher education from University of Maryland.

Elizabeth Lorang, Ph.D., is a senior associate editor of the Walt Whitman Archive, project co-director of Civil War Washington, and principal investigator of "Image Analysis for Archival Discovery: Poetic Content in Historic Newspapers." In her current position as Research Assistant Professor of Libraries at the University of Nebraska-Lincoln, she assists students and faculty in developing their digital humanities projects.

Elizabeth McAulay, MA English, is the Librarian for Digital Collection Development in the UCLA Digital Library Program and a Lecturer for San Jose State University's School of Library and Information Science. McAulay has extensive experience implementing digital humanities projects within a research library context.

Valla McLean is the University Archivist and Humanities Librarian at Grant MacEwan University in Edmonton, Alberta. Her academic interests include digital humanities in the undergraduate curriculum and digital preservation.

David D. Oberhelman is the W. P. Wood Professor of Library Service at the Oklahoma State University Library. He holds a PhD in English with an Emphasis in Critical Theory from the University of California, Irvine, and a MLIS degree from the University of Pittsburgh. He is the subject specialist for the humanities and performing arts, and he has published and presented on topics ranging from Anglo-American fantasy and science fiction, digital humanities in pedagogy, and changes in scholarly communications in the humanities.

Caro Pinto is a Librarian & Instructional Technology Liaison at Mount Holyoke College where she practices at the intersections of special collections, librarianship, and instructional technology. Her work has also appeared in the The Chronicle of Higher Education, Archive Journal and In the Library with the Lead Pipe. She is also a reviews editor for dh+lib.

Dot Porter is Curator of Digital Research Services in the Schoenberg Institute for Manuscript Studies at Penn Libraries. She works with Penn scholars in exploring new methods of research in the humanities, particularly the application of digital technologies to textual analysis and the electronic dissemination of humanities research. She has worked on a variety of digital humanities projects over a decade-long career, focusing on materials as diverse as ancient texts and Russian religious folklore, providing both technical support and scholarly expertise. She holds Master's degrees in Medieval Studies and Library Science and started her career working on image-based digital editions of medieval manuscripts.

Jenny Presnell is Humanities/Social Sciences Librarian at Miami University of Ohio with over twenty-nine years of liaison and collection development experience in the humanities, including history, American studies, and women's studies. She is a member of the libraries' Digital Humanities Working Group. She has published a book, *The Information-Literate Historian* (2nd ed., Oxford, 2013) to help history undergraduate students learn to do advanced research using both traditional and digital methodologies.

Brian Rosenblum is the Head of the Center for Faculty/Staff Initiatives and Engagement and CoDirector of the Institute for Digital Research in the Humanities at the University of Kansas. He has worked on numerous librarybased digital publishing projects and currently has administrative, production, and outreach responsibilities in support of a variety of digital initiatives and publishing services.

Ilse Schweitzer VanDonkelaar received her Ph.D. in English from Western Michigan University in December 2013. As a graduate student, she worked on digital projects including the Online Old English Paradigm Project and WMU's Literary Worlds site and contributed to a chapter about that project in Allen Webb's essay collection, *Teaching Literature in Literary Worlds: Immersive Learning in English Studies* (Routledge, 2011). As Social Media Specialist for the WMU Graduate College, Ilse was instrumental in spearheading workshops and presentations geared toward educating graduate students in the possibilities of DH research. Currently, she teaches at Grand Valley State University in Michigan and commissions titles related to environmental humanities and medieval studies for Amsterdam University Press and the Arc-Medieval Press.

Anu Vedantham is Director of the Weigle Information Commons at the Penn Libraries and manages the Education Commons. She supports faculty and student exploration of new technologies for teaching and learning. She has authored several articles and book chapters in the areas of library space design, media literacy studies, global warming models and federal funding for non-profit technology use. She holds her doctorate in Higher Education Management from Penn's Graduate School of Education, her New Jersey Principal Certificate, her Masters in Public Affairs from the Woodrow Wilson School at Princeton University and her Bachelors and Masters in Electrical Engineering and Computer Science from the Massachusetts Institute of Technology (MIT).

Judy Walker was the 2013 ACRL EBSS Distinguished Education and Behavior Sciences Librarian. With a strong background in education and instructional technology, Ms. Walker incorporates a wide variety of technologies into her library instruction. She has presented numerous workshops on how to use and incorporate a variety of digital humanity tools into the classroom and/or projects. Ms. Walker also assists students and faculty in developing their own digital projects.